THE WORLD
ECONOMIC CRISIS

THE
WORLD
ECONOMIC
CRISIS

Edited with an Introduction by
WILLIAM P. BUNDY

A *Foreign Affairs* Book

W. W. Norton & Company, Inc., 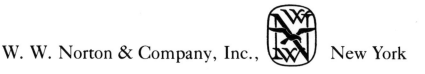 New York

Library of Congress Cataloging in Publication Data

Bundy, William P   1917-   comp.
  The world economic crisis.

  "A Foreign affairs book."
  Articles previously published in Foreign affairs, 1973-74.
  1. Petroleum industry and trade—Addresses, essays,
lectures. 2. Energy policy—Addresses, essays,
lectures. 3. International economic relations—Addresses,
essays, lectures. I. Foreign affairs (New York)
II. Title.
HD9560.5.B84 1975   382'.42'282   74-32279
ISBN 0-393-05545-0

Printed in the United States of America
1   2   3   4   5   6   7   8   9   0

CONTENTS

AUTHORS

JAMES E. AKINS, Foreign Service Officer, Ambassador to Saudi Arabia since late 1973; at the time of writing the article, Director of the Office of Fuels and Energy, Department of State, on detail to the White House.

CARROLL L. WILSON, Professor of Management, Sloan School of Management, Massachusetts Institute of Technology; General Manager, Atomic Energy Commission, 1947-51; mining executive, 1951-59.

JAHANGIR AMUZEGAR, Ambassador-at-Large and Chief of the Iranian Economic Mission, Washington, D.C.; Minister of Commerce (1961-62) and Minister of Finance (1962) of Iran; author of *Technical Assistance in Theory and Practice: The Case of Iran* and other works.

NADAV SAFRAN, Professor of Government and member of the staff of the Middle East Center and of the Center for International Affairs, Harvard; author of *From War to War: The Arab-Israeli Confrontation, 1948-1967* and other works.

HELMUT SCHMIDT, Chancellor of the Federal Republic of Germany since May 1974; at the time of writing the article, Minister of Finance and Vice-Chairman of the Social Democratic Party; author of *Balance of Power, Defense or Retaliation* and other works.

GERALD A. POLLACK, a Senior Economic Advisor at Exxon Corporation; formerly International Economist for the Joint Economic Committee of the Congress, 1963-65; Deputy Assistant Secretary of Commerce for Economic Affairs, 1965-68.

WILLIAM DIEBOLD, JR., Senior Research Fellow, Council on Foreign Relations; author of *The United States and the Industrial World: American Foreign Economic Policy in the 1970s* and other works.

BENSION VARON and KENJI TAKEUCHI, economists on the Development Policy Staff of the World Bank, Washington, D.C.

LYLE P. SCHERTZ, Deputy Administrator, Economic Research Service, U.S. Department of Agriculture; author of *Economics of Protein Improvement Programs* (USDA) and other works.

WALTER J. LEVY, oil consultant to industry and governments.

WALTER F. MONDALE, Senator from Minnesota since 1964; member of the Senate Committee on Finance.

INTRODUCTION

For years, economists, wise observers and a few statesmen have been saying that the world economy is in a new condition of interdependence, that what happens in industrialized or "advanced" nations like the United States is not only sharply affected by what happens in other industrialized nations, but also by the actions of the so-called developing nations. In short, any major change in status or policy within either group can have a drastic impact on the whole world.

In the fall and winter of 1973-74, the truth of this view was brought home to us all. The triggering event was, of course, the Yom Kippur War, in which the Arab oil-producing nations invoked the weapon of an oil embargo against the United States and others regarded as too partial to the cause of Israel. But what followed thereafter, in the form of a fourfold price rise for oil to all customers, reflected both wider causes and deeper underlying changes. Over a period of years, the oil-producing countries had acquired a new bargaining power and leverage. This they now set out to use to the full, pitchforking their "advanced" customers into wholly new balance-of-payments problems, greatly worsening an already serious worldwide inflationary situation, and threatening the developing nations that lacked oil or other natural resources with bankruptcy and a grinding halt in their laborious struggle toward economic progress. All over the world, a general picture of economic growth (if often unsteady and unevenly distributed in its benefits) was suddenly called in question. To those with a sense of history it seemed that the world was in a situation akin in many ways to 1930—when a failure to find the handle led on to vast depression and eventually to world war.

Such was and is the world economic crisis that gives this book its title. Made dramatic by developments in oil supply and price, it is in fact far wider. Into it flowed a brewing crisis in the price and availability of food that dated back at least to the massive 1972 wheat deal between the United States and the Soviet Union. With both the oil and food crises came a new pinch in crucial fertilizer supplies. And with the combined developments in all three it was widely surmised that producers of other raw materials might be able to raise their already rocketing prices as rapidly and unanswerably as the oil producers had done. By the spring of 1974 a whole new range of issues was being aired at a special session of the United Nations General Assembly: How could fairness and balance be achieved for all key raw materials? Must not the "advanced" nations act to curtail their often wasteful use of such materials, especially oil, and to bring the inflated prices of their own exports to the developing world under control? How could the needy developing nations be kept from outright ruin? These and other questions reverberated, unanswered for the time being, but hardly to be put off for long.

Obviously, it would take a treatise to do justice to the factors that have brought about the present situation, and to the lines of attack that may help to get out of it. But while Americans wait for such comprehensive treatment they have to think responsibly, to understand enough of the nature of the crisis to see how it may affect their own lives—as it plainly does already—and to put the weight of their opinion behind new and imaginative efforts that might be made by their government and others. In its fifty-two years of existence, the central aim of the quarterly magazine, _Foreign Affairs_, has been to play a part in just this task of forming a more thoughtful and enlightened public opinion. Its editors have sought to catch emerging issues "on the rise," before they become acute, and to grasp and present their implications for specific policy and action. Authors who can do these things may and should differ with each other and with the private views of the editors. The point is to advance discussion, not by avoiding heat but by as high a ratio of light as possible.

In the case of the present economic crisis, we think the magazine achieved this aim. The idea of collecting the relevant articles to make a separate book came originally from a professor of international economics who thought that they would help his students greatly. When the editors sat down to go over the material, dating back now nearly a year and a half, we concluded that it did stand the test of time extraordinarily well, and that it could and should be understood by a wider audience as well. Thus we were emboldened to attempt, for we believe the first time in our history, a compilation of this sort.

The articles have been assembled exactly as they originally appeared. In keeping with the nature of an American journal, eight of the eleven authors are Americans—one, Jahangir Amuzegar, is Iranian; another, Helmut Schmidt, a West German who has since become his country's Chancellor; and a third "author" is in fact Siamese twins from the World Bank, except that one is Turkish and the other Japanese. The focus of the articles is generally wider than simply American policy, which is, we believe, true to the nature of the crisis, as well as in the tradition of the magazine.

Let us briefly introduce the collection in order, with an explanatory word on each article.

In the fall of 1972, the editors of *Foreign Affairs* were, of course, far from alone in sensing the gravity of the emerging oil situation. Already a great deal had appeared on it, including an article in 1971 by Walter J. Levy in *Foreign Affairs* itself, in which he foresaw the new bargaining power of the oil producers.[1] One could pick up bits and pieces of the story in many quarters, but there was no single coherent account of what had happened since 1970, what had caused it, and what it might now portend.

For this purpose the editors turned to James E. Akins, who as he undertook the article was in the process of moving from his post as "Mr. Oil" in the State Department to the rigors of a White House assignment to participate in the framing of a new American energy policy. A Foreign Service officer and Arabist by training, Akins had become an oil expert only recently, and

---

[1] "Oil Power," July 1971.

perhaps this very detachment made him able to perceive and articulate trends better than some with longer experience. His article, published in April of 1973, defies a short summary; its combination of history, economics and policy prescription attracted wide attention. Akins' analysis of the oil market remains basic, while his prophecy of drastic political action by the Arabs was confirmed sooner than perhaps even its author expected. Incidentally, in late 1973 he became Ambassador to Saudi Arabia, and remains at this writing in the thick of the action.

Immediately thereafter, the Nixon Administration announced a domestic energy policy that seemed to many far too bland. One of these, Carroll Wilson of M.I.T., came forward to propose a far more drastic program of action, presented in the July 1973 *Foreign Affairs* as "A Plan for Energy Independence." One-time General Manager of the Atomic Energy Commission, later a mining executive, more recently a scientific mainstay of the Stockholm Environment Conference, Wilson brings to bear a variety of experience and careful research on specific energy sources. His article broadens the question from oil to energy as a whole; it pulls together a host of ideas that, it is fair to say, continue to compose the agenda of the unfinished energy programs that have been kicking around since, at far too leisurely a pace by his lights, between the executive and the Congress.

In the same issue, a representative of one of the key oil-producing countries had his say. Jahangir Amuzegar is Iran's Economic Ambassador in Washington; his brother was Iran's Finance Minister until very recently. His article put a case and expressed a sense of grievance that up to that time not many Americans had heard or understood. The author's arguments continue to echo in private negotiations and in the halls of the United Nations, and his most specific forecast—that the price of oil would be increased to a level determined largely by the cost of competing energy sources—proved accurate only six months later. In this respect, we had been warned.

But few had foreseen the outbreak of war in the Middle East in October 1973, although *Foreign Affairs* had not neglected that conflict and its dangerous state since 1967.[2] Once war did come as Akins had specifically (and almost uniquely) foreseen, the Arab embargo was highly selective in its targets, with the United States in the forefront. How the war came about, how it evolved, and why the Arabs used the oil weapon in this new way—all these aspects are developed in Nadav Safran's "The War and the Future of the Arab-Israeli Conflict" in January 1974. Now a Professor at Harvard (and like other Harvard professors keeping informal ties to other Cambridge alumni in government), Safran grew up in Cairo, later moved to Israel and became an Israeli citizen, and then came to America where he has been a U.S. citizen for many years. His book on the earlier Arab-Israeli wars had established a reputation for scholarship, clear analysis, and as near to objectivity as one can hope to get in this emotional area; the same qualities, we believe, are reflected in his article, written just after the firing stopped in late October. It is included here both because of its strong merits, and because the war was, as already noted, the triggering event for the really grave stage of the economic crisis that became clear in the winter of 1973-74.

The April 1974 issue of *Foreign Affairs* devoted to its various aspects no less than five articles, under the heading "The Year of Economics." The first of these was by Helmut Schmidt, then Finance Minister of the Federal Republic of Germany. "The Struggle for the World Product" pulls together questions of money, trade and finance, the new distribution of economic power that has arisen and its implications, and in the end the questions of morality and ethics that must lie at the root of new

---

[2]Going back to 1968, articles in *Foreign Affairs* on the Arab-Israeli conflict have included: a series of three articles in January 1968 on the 1967 War, comprising "How It Began," by Charles W. Yost, "The Consequences of Defeat," by Bernard Lewis, and "Israel's Administration and Arab Refugees," by Don Peretz; in January 1969, "Russia Enters the Middle East," by Walter Laqueur; in January 1970, "Arab Palestine: Phoenix or Phantom," by Don Peretz; in April 1970, "The Future of Israel," by Nahum Goldmann; in October 1970, "The Arab-Israeli Conflict: An American Policy," by John C. Campbell; in October 1972, "Where Egypt Stands," by Anwar el-Sadat; and in April 1973, "Israel in Search of Lasting Peace," by Golda Meir, and "The Depth of Arab Radicalism," by Arnold Hottinger.

solutions. "What is needed is a fundamental change in patterns of behavior both among individuals and among nations"—with specifics to match.

Next, under a title deliberately cribbed from Lord Keynes, Gerald A. Pollack describes "The Economic Consequences of the Energy Crisis." A former Deputy Assistant Secretary of Commerce who is now an economist with the Exxon Corporation—though writing, of course, on a personal basis—Pollack's essay is a full and dispassionate picture of the upheaval on the international financial scene including the prospects for inflation and the impact on the Third World. "The long and short of it is that no one can be sure that the financial side of the oil crisis is manageable. Perhaps the best that could be said is that, if the consuming and producing countries can coöperate in working out solutions, there is nothing about the institutional structure that would preclude a happy ending."

Whether nations would act selfishly or take account of the common interest was also the theme of William Diebold, Jr. Dealing with the prospect for trade negotiations in the new situation, Diebold—who is Senior Research Fellow at the Council on Foreign Relations—argues that trade policy must now embrace the question of fair access to raw materials, and that the United States is in a special position to lead. Because it is less vulnerable than Europe or Japan for oil, "this disparity in strength confers both bargaining power and responsibility. As a leading industrial power, the United States can speak as a consumer. As a major producer and exporter of raw materials and foodstuffs, it can see the other point of view. For its own welfare it needs to broaden its concept of trade policy. . . ."

Can the oil experience be duplicated in the case of other minerals not used for fuel? With the oil crisis this question became the subject of intense speculation and some emotional statements. *Foreign Affairs* turned to two economists at the World Bank, Bension Varon and Kenji Takeuchi, for an objective analysis by men whose institution must be concerned equally for the welfare of the developing countries that mainly produce raw materials and for the industrialized nations that mainly consume them. Their answer is tilted in the negative direction—that on the whole the markets in non-fuel minerals, as well as the political and economic factors bearing on possible cartels, do not lend themselves to "another OPEC" comparable to that association of oil producers. Bauxite is cited as a partial possible exception—borne out by more recent events in Jamaica—and the authors predict some upward pressure on prices. More tightly argued and with more professional economics than other articles in the series, the Varon/Takeuchi piece has been extensively cited as perhaps the most authoritative short summary of the subject.

Alongside oil and other key raw materials, the subject of food had to be dealt with. It might have been approached from the standpoint of immediate famine situations or from that of long-term adequacy, weather change, technological possibility, and the like, each a crucially important subject in itself. Rather, while drawing somewhat on all of these elements, Lyle P. Schertz, a career man in the U.S. Department of Agriculture, focuses on the medium-term problem of getting adequate food to the needy countries of the world at fair prices. He emphasizes the dominant role of the United States in world food trade, and the drastic effect of Soviet (and Chinese) food purchases, along with little-noticed American legislation, in virtually eliminating U.S. food stocks and thus pulling out—just at a time of increasing price volatility—the cushion that had previously kept world food markets reasonably stable. The solution? He sees no panacea, but leaves the door open for action in which the United States might join with others, notably to re-create food reserves. By strong implication, too, he suggests that U.S. dietary habits, with those of other rich countries, need to be looked at anew, that our high consumption of meat and similar resource-costly converted protein has a lot of bearing on whether the world will have enough basic grain to go round.

In short, the five articles from the April issue cover almost every aspect of the crisis in some depth. They require careful reading, for the issues do not lend themselves to pat description or prescription. But the quintet remains uniquely comprehensive and clear, not only summing up how intelligent men looked at the crisis in the spring of 1974, but laying out an agenda that may well occupy the world's statesmen for several years to come.

The most immediate and decisive problem remains that of oil. Can prices be brought down? Will supply again be threatened? How can a long-term arrangement be achieved that is fair to both producers and consumers, and at the same time provides relief for the needy countries who are hardest hit of all? Speaking partly from an American but more from a global viewpoint, Walter J. Levy—the "dean of American experts on oil," in the words of *Newsweek*—addressed these questions in July 1974 in "World Oil Coöperation or International Chaos." Like other writers in this series, his answers are not of the "instant" variety. Disposing first of the oil companies, which he finds essentially powerless today to affect price and supply, Levy calls for a far higher degree of coöperation among the consuming countries than has yet been officially proposed, let alone achieved. Second, while the consumers must understand the position and arguments of the producers, the converse is equally important—that producers "ask themselves whether they could expect to remain islands of prosperity in a worldwide depression, or of political stability when the will and ability of strategically powerful nations to support them had been eroded." Last, and most biting, the author argues that any satisfactory long-term arrangement requires "genuine austerity" in the use of energy by all the consuming countries—that is, truly sharp belt-tightening that goes way beyond anything now being discussed by any government leader. Levy ends on an almost apocalyptic note: "Today, governments are watching an erosion of the world's oil supply and financial systems, comparable in its potential for economic and political disaster to the Great Depression of the 1930s, as if they were hypnotized into inaction. The time is late, the need for action overwhelming."

The sense of possible economic disaster is shared by the last writer in the series, Senator Walter F. Mondale of Minnesota, who has been a member of the Finance and Banking Committees of the Senate (and was for a time a declared candidate for the Democratic nomination for President in 1976). Senator Mondale warns that unless the world economy can be brought back under control, the consequences could play havoc with détente itself; with security matters less pressing, the international economy can and must have first priority in American foreign policy. His article prescribes many specific actions to deal on an international basis with inflation and the problems of oil, other raw materials and food. In a closing section he proposes that the Soviet Union be brought much more into the picture, even that its coöperation be made a principal test of détente. In one way or another, Senator Mondale's article pulls together themes from all the others in the series, with recommendations that are wide-ranging, clearly stated, personal—and, as it happens, bipartisan in tone.

The world economic crisis goes on, and is affecting the outlook and pocketbook of every American. The editors of *Foreign Affairs* believe that this series of articles can help thoughtful readers, abroad as well as in the United States, to grasp the issues and make up their minds about what should be done, by governments and private interests both. This is, to repeat, no quickie "how to do it" kit; it is an aid to understanding and an action guide for the complex measures (and possibly sacrifices) that may be needed to get the world onto a better footing.

In addition to my normal debt to James Chace and Jennifer Whitaker, my editorial colleagues, special thanks are due to Eric Swenson and Grace Darling for carrying through the arrangements for this publication on behalf of W. W. Norton and *Foreign Affairs* respectively. The real makers of the book are, of course, the individual authors.

William P. Bundy
Editor,
Foreign Affairs

THE WORLD ECONOMIC CRISIS

THE OIL CRISIS:
THIS TIME THE WOLF IS HERE

By James E. Akins

OIL experts, economists and government officials who have attempted in recent years to predict future demand and prices for oil have had only marginally better success than those who foretell the advent of earthquakes or the second coming of the Messiah. The recent records of those who have told us we were running out of petroleum and gas are an example. Oil shortages were predicted in the 1920s, again in the late thirties, and after the Second World War. None occurred, and supply forecasters went to the other extreme: past predictions of shortages had been wrong, they reasoned, therefore all such future predictions must be wrong and we could count on an ample supply of oil for as long as we would need it.

It was the popular, almost universal theory of the 1960s—still vigorously defended today by a few of its early proponents—that this abundant supply of oil, whose cost of production was very low, and which was found in all corners of the earth, would soon be sold at its "proper" economic price—apparently $1.00 per barrel or less—and for some time it was confidently predicted that this price would prevail in the Persian Gulf by 1970.

As late as February 1970, President Nixon's Task Force on Oil Imports assumed that world price rises would be modest and that the United States could remain essentially self-sufficient in oil. It projected a demand in the United States in 1980 of around 18.5 million barrels per day of oil; of this only five million barrels per day would need to be imported, and most of this could come from the Western Hemisphere. The Task Force did not favor a complete freeing of imports, but thought that the quota system for imports was inefficient and should be replaced by tariffs (a recommendation eventually rejected by the President). Most important, recognizing the danger of importing large quantities of oil from outside the Western Hemisphere, the Task Force recommended that imports from the Eastern Hemisphere should be limited to ten percent of total national oil consumption. If this level should be approached—and the Task Force thought it would not be before the mid-1980s—then barriers should be raised. In fact, as soon as the level of Eastern Hemisphere imports reached *five* percent of total consumption, "the volumetric limits on imports from the Western Hemisphere should be expanded proportionately to forestall such excess imports," i.e. Canadian and Venezuelan oil could largely take the place of Middle East oil above five percent of U.S. consumption.

These projections were spectacularly wrong. Total imports this very year, 1973, will be well over six million barrels per day—substantially above the level the Task Force predicted for 1980. Imports from the Eastern Hemisphere constituted 15 percent of consumption in 1972, and are expected to rise in 1973 to 20 percent of a total consumption that will already be around 17 million barrels.

The errors of the Task Force were not those of isolated academics, as its critics were (and still are) wont to charge. The staff based its projections on information provided by the major oil companies, by the National Petroleum Council and by the Department of the Interior. There were two main reasons for their errors. Perhaps both should have been avoided, but as always, hindsight is clear and uncluttered. The first error was an uncritical acceptance of oil company and well owners' estimates of the capacity of their own domestic producing wells. These were almost always exaggerated. The second was the ignoring, or at least the deëmphasis, of the decline in natural gas supplies and its effect on oil demand. We were, by 1970, already consuming far more gas than we were finding, and demand for gas continued to grow unabated, while domestic gas production leveled off (1973 production will actually be below that of 1972). The unsatisfied demand for gas was, of course, a real demand for energy. It could be covered only by oil—in fact, only by imported oil.

During 1970 the effect of drawing down natural gas reserves became fully apparent, at least to the State Department, which converted the shortfall to oil equivalents and added it to projected oil demand. The resulting estimate was that by 1980 the United States would consume 24 million barrels of oil a day, that domestic production would cover only half of this, and that two-thirds or more of the imports (or about 35 percent of total consumption) would, of necessity, come from the Eastern Hemisphere.

These figures were not immediately accepted as a new insight; they were, in fact, attacked as alarmist or provocative when first made public. And the Department's sins were compounded by its making public, during 1970, an estimate that oil prices in the Persian Gulf (then somewhat less than $2.00 per barrel) would rise by 1980 to a level equal to the cost of alternate sources of energy, i.e. to $4.50 in the Persian Gulf or an even $5.00 landed in the U.S. Gulf of Mexico.[1] These figures were used in testimony in the House and Senate and in various public speeches, both because they were honestly believed to be reasonable judgments and because it seemed essential to alert the Congress and the public to the impending dimensions of the problem. They were (and still are by some) considered even more provocative than the supply-demand projections.

It is not my main purpose to defend these and other actions by the Department of State. They can be best judged in a context badly needed for its own sake, that of the best possible assessment of the basic facts of the world oil situation as it affects the United States. Have the startling changes in prediction and experience in the last three years been an aberration? Have the Department and others been crying wolf unnecessarily, or is the "oil crisis" a reality? If it is, what can the United States and other countries do to live bearably with it?

II

The place to start is with world oil reserves, those that are "proven" or sure, those that appear "probable" of early discovery and development at reasonable cost, and those that might be called "secondary"—conceivable or involving special cost or technology.

Figures on proven reserves of oil would be more useful if the companies involved did not generally understate them, usually for tax purposes, and if governments did not use them for political purposes. Those governments with large reserves tend to understate them in order to reduce the envy of their neighbors; those with smaller reserves and large populations tend to greet every new discovery as the cure for all present and future economic ills. Nonetheless, there are a few figures which it is probably safe to accept.

Proven reserves in the non-Communist world today amount

[1] In terms of currency value, all price and tax figures used in this article are in "current dollars," i.e. dollars at their value in the given year. Dollar values after 1972 are projected at an assumed inflation rate of 3.5 percent per year.

roughly to 500 billion barrels.[2] On present trends, world demand (exclusive of the Soviet Union and China) will rise by 1980 to 85 million barrels per day—compared to an actual 39 million barrels per day in 1970.[3] Consumption between now and 1980 would then total 200 billion barrels, and even if no more oil were found—a most unlikely eventuality—the remaining 300 billion barrels would be ten years' supply at the 1980 consumption level, about the ratio of reserves to production that has historically applied to U.S. domestic oil.

Those who feel no concern about oil availability cite this comparison. And indeed it is agreed on all sides that there is no question of a physical shortage of fuel in the world, up to 1980 or 1985, at costs of production comparable to today's. But to sustain the view that physical supply and cost are decisive, one must assume that the world's oil is distributed, if not uniformly, at least so that adequate amounts will always be available to all users, in all circumstances and at reasonable prices. This is an assumption that has never been well founded. To begin with, at least 300 billion of these proven 500 billion barrels are in the Arab countries of the Middle East and North Africa.

Far more important is that the world's probable reserves, those which must still be found to make up for the consumption of the coming decades, will also be in the Middle East on any presently realistic prediction. This is not for want of effort by the major oil companies to find new sources of supply. In fact, 95 percent of their exploration activities (as opposed to development of discoveries already proven) are now outside the Middle East. Bluntly, the companies have little incentive to explore in the Middle East, for they already have all the reserves they can use before the dates presently set for the expiration of their concessions. Instead they are active on a large scale in Indonesia, in Australia, in the Canadian and American Arctic, in the North Sea—wherever there are sedimentary basins. The results have not been encouraging.

---

[2] Calculations here and throughout this article omit the U.S.S.R. and China, which appear likely to be roughly self-sufficient at least in this time-frame. Other Communist countries will probably be importing most if not all of their oil from non-Communist sources by the end of this decade.

[3] This estimate of 1980 world demand is that of the Department of State. Its principal components are: United States, 24 million barrels per day; Western Europe, 28 million; Japan, 14 million; others, 19 million. Compare the 1971 estimates of Walter J. Levy, "Oil Power," *Foreign Affairs*, July 1971. Mr. Levy estimated world demand at 67 million barrels per day in 1980, with the United States taking 21, Western Europe 23, and Japan 10.

In the first flush of activity in Indonesia, the State Department projected, in its internal working papers, a production of five million barrels per day in 1980 in that country. When oil was found in Prudhoe Bay, in the Arctic, one famed economist stated that the world's oil center had shifted permanently from the Persian Gulf to the north coast of the North American continent. Another economist, in a meeting of oil experts and oil company executives, said in 1970 that the North Sea discoveries would free Europe forever from dependence on the Middle East. All of this was wishful thinking. It would certainly make us more comfortable if true, but alas, all these "facts" have had to be revised. Indonesia, we now hope, will produce two or three million barrels per day by 1980; Alaska, if we are lucky (and if the courts approve the pipeline), will only enable the United States to keep national production levels at those of 1972 (12 million barrels per day). And the North Sea, important as it is, will produce no more than 15 percent of Europe's requirements in 1980; phrased differently, if North Sea production then reaches three million barrels per day this amount will cover two years of Europe's intervening *growth* in demand—leaving Europe still dependent on the Middle East not only for its basic demand but for future growth.

The world's oil reserve picture is even more startling when looked at in detail, for the oil is not distributed uniformly even through the Arab world. Jordan, Lebanon, Tunisia, Morocco and Yemen have virtually none; Egypt has little, Algeria and Libya somewhat more; but the giant reserves are concentrated in the countries of the Persian Gulf: the Federation of Arab Amirates, Kuwait, Iran, Iraq and, by far the most important, Saudi Arabia. The proven reserves of Saudi Arabia are frequently listed as 150 billion barrels, but this is almost certainly too low. One company with extensive experience in that country believes that the present proven reserves are over twice that figure. And the probable reserves could double the figure again.

True, the above picture takes no account of the enormous quantities of shale or coal in the United States, the tar sands of Canada or the heavy oils of Venezuela. The proven and probable reserve figures used above are only those which can be recovered easily by present technology and at costs near today's world prices. Let us come back later to what might be called the "secondary reserves" of shale and heavy oils.

III

That most of the world's proven oil reserves are in Arab hands is now known to the dullest observer. That the probable reserves are concentrated even more heavily in the Middle East must also be the judgment of anyone who is willing to look at the evidence. And that relations between the United States and the Arab countries are not generally cordial should be clear to any newspaper reader. Even King Faisal of Saudi Arabia, who has said repeatedly that he wishes to be a friend of the United States and who believes that communism is a mortal danger to the Arabs, insists to every visitor that U.S. policy in the Middle East, which he characterizes as pro-Israeli, will ultimately drive all Arabs into the Communist camp, and that this policy will bring disaster on all America's remaining Arab friends, as earlier Anglo-American policies did to Nuri Said of Iraq. Others in the Middle East frame their predictions in a different but almost equally menacing vein, in terms of a growth of radical anti-Americanism, manifesting itself in behavior that may at times be irrational.

King Faisal has also said repeatedly that the Arabs should not, and that he himself would not, allow oil to be used as a political weapon. But on this issue it seems all too likely that his is an isolated voice. In 1972, other Arabs in responsible or influential positions made no less than 15 different threats to use oil as a weapon against their "enemies." Almost all of them singled out the United States as the prime enemy.

These threats have been well publicized; the common response among Americans has been: "They need us as much as we need them"; or "They can't drink the oil"; or "Boycotts never work." But before we accept these facile responses, let us examine the facts more carefully. First of all, let us dispose of the straw man of a total cut-off of all oil supplies, which some Arab governments, at least, could not survive. Apart from threats made during the negotiations of December 1970, no Arab has ever taken such a position, and Arab representatives took it at that time, in concert with other governments, for economic bargaining purposes, not for political reasons.

Rather, the usual Arab political threat is to deny oil to the Arabs' enemies, while supplies would continue to their friends. In such a case, the producing countries would still have a considerable income under almost any assumption—unless we could assume complete Western and Japanese solidarity, including a complete blocking of Arab bank accounts and an effective blocking of deliveries of essential supplies to the Arabs by the Communist countries—in other words, something close to a war embargo. We must recognize that most of the threats are directed against Americans alone. Many of our allies and all others would be allowed to import Arab oil.

In the 1967 Six Day War a boycott was imposed against the United States on the basis of the false accusation that it had participated with Israeli planes in the attack on Cairo. The charge was quickly disproven, although the boycott lasted for over a month. It was then lifted through the efforts of Saudi Arabia, and its effects never became bothersome. We were then importing considerably less than a half-million barrels per day of oil from the Arab countries, and this was easily made up from other sources.

Today the situation would be wholly different, and tomorrow worse still. By 1980 the United States could be importing as much as eight million barrels of oil a day from the Middle East; some oil companies think it will be close to 11 million. Suppose that for some reason, political or economic, a boycott is then imposed —which, if the Middle East problem is not solved by that time, cannot be called a frivolous or unlikely hypothesis. The question we must face now, before we allow ourselves to get into such a position, is what would be our response? The choices would be difficult and limited: we could try to break the boycott through military means, i.e. war; we could accede to the wishes of the oil suppliers; or we could accept what would surely be severe damage to our economy, possibly amounting to collapse. Europe and Japan might conceivably face, or be asked by us to face, the same problems at the same time. Would their responses be in line with ours?

Moreover, a collective Arab boycott is not the only conceivable political threat. Until now the world has enjoyed the luxury of considerable surplus production capacity, relative to total demand. Now that has changed. The United States now has no spare capacity and within the next few years, assuming other producer governments and companies do not invest in huge added capacity, the production of *any one* of seven countries—Saudi Arabia, Iran, Iraq, the Federation of Arab Amirates, Kuwait, Libya or Venezuela—will be larger than the combined spare capacity of the rest of the world. In other words, the loss of the production of any one of these countries could cause a temporary but significant world oil shortage; the loss of any two could cause a crisis and quite possibly a panic among the consumers.

No, the threat to use oil as a political weapon must be taken seriously. The vulnerability of the advanced countries is too great and too plainly evident—and is about to extend to the United States.

IV

So much for political nightmares. Closer to immediate reality, indeed already upon us, is the question of the economic leverage of the oil-producing countries, 90 percent of whose reserves are now represented in the 11-nation Organization of Petroleum Exporting Countries (OPEC).[4] Even if there should be no overtly political interference with the flow of oil, the OPEC group now has formidable economic power and has shown itself willing to use it to the full. Will OPEC hold together, to raise prices and conceivably to limit output? Or will it break apart, as producer cartels have historically done where the product is substantially the same from one member and place to another?

The answers require, first, a review of the history of OPEC. In 1958 and 1959, the international oil companies reduced their posted prices and tax payments because of a world surplus of oil. In reaction, Venezuela, Iran and Saudi Arabia took the lead in forming OPEC in 1960 with the avowed purpose of restoring the 1958 price level. They did not succeed, as the world surplus of oil continued and the OPEC countries were unable to agree on a formula for prorationing to limit output. Venezuela, then the largest producer, thought that historical levels of production should be used as the base, Iran favored national population, and Saudi Arabia and Kuwait thought production should be on the basis of proven reserves. Disunity seemed to prevail, and the new organization was belittled by many.

OPEC was not a joke, however. Its pressures did contribute to the fact that the companies never again reduced posted prices, and it was able to achieve new methods of calculating taxes and royalties which added slightly to the revenues of producer gov-

---

[4] OPEC currently comprises four non-Arab states—Iran, Venezuela, Indonesia and Nigeria—and seven Arab states: Kuwait, Saudi Arabia, Iraq, Abu Dhabi, Qatar, Libya, and Algeria.

ernments. Its third and perhaps most important success is not generally known. In the early 1960s, most OPEC countries needed more income and pressed their concessionary companies to produce more oil—even at the expense of production in other OPEC countries. The companies responded in each case that they could not increase production unless the government gave tax rebates. So far as I know, the temptation to undercut its partners was not accepted by any major OPEC country—and I doubt by any minor one. In other words, the organization maintained its solidarity in a period of a buyers' market, and at a time when member-countries, save Venezuela, regarded their reserves as infinite and were generally eager for unrestricted growth in production.

Then, in mid-1967, came the closing of the Suez Canal in the Six Day War. The ensuing oil "shortage" was of course one caused by transport, but the effects were the same as an actual shortage of crude oil. Rapid steps were taken to increase tanker capacity, and the consumer noticed only slightly higher oil prices. But the increase in tanker rates put Libya in a special position by reason of its location. Production there was stepped up rapidly to meet European demand. Libya, in the short run, seemed the ideal answer to all the world's oil problems.

The "short run" was shorter than most had assumed. King Idris was overthrown in September 1969 by Colonel Qaddafi, a fanatic anti-Communist, but also a zealous pro-Arab, who considered Israel and the United States, which he characterized as the sole supporter of Israel, as even greater dangers to Arabism than was communism.

Early in 1970 Qaddafi and his colleagues moved to cut back oil production (then at almost four million barrels a day) for conservation reasons. New and extreme strains were also placed on the tanker market by the closing of the pipeline from Iraq, in a dispute over transit fees, and by the cutting of the Trans-Arabian line. Although most of the losses were made up, reserve stocks in Europe were drawn down. In this situation, the Libyan government demanded, in the spring of 1970, a large increase in tax payments on its oil. After an arduous round of discussions the international companies operating in Libya yielded one by one.

It seemed at the time, and still does, that they had little choice. Libya had $2 billion in currency reserves; its demands were not unreasonable; its officials could not be corrupted or convinced;

and most important, Libyan oil could not be made up elsewhere. The Libyans, it should be noted, did not threaten to cut off oil deliveries to the consumer countries; their only threat was not to allow the *companies* to have the oil unless they paid the higher taxes.

Europeans, at this time, were almost unaware of what was happening and would have been totally unprepared if oil had been cut off. During the negotiations, a top official of a major oil company seriously urged the American government to dare the Libyans to nationalize; if they did, the Europeans would then be told they would have to tighten their belts, while Libya, according to this theory, would be forced to yield soon because it could not dispose of its oil. When it was noted that Libya's currency reserves could keep the government at current expenditure and import levels for four years, the company official stated his assumption that all of this would be blocked by all the European and American central banks. It was an assumption hardly likely to be realized.

But the main reason for not following this course was the fact that the loss of all oil from Libya alone would have meant the drawing down of more than half of the European oil reserves within a year. It seemed unlikely, indeed inconceivable, that France, Germany, Spain or Italy would have allowed that to happen; especially as the goal would apparently have been only to protect the Anglo-Saxon oil monopoly, which they had long sought to break. To have tried to explain to them that they would themselves suffer in the long run, would have been less than futile. We in the State Department had no doubt whatever at that time, and for those particular reasons, that the Europeans would have made their own deals with the Libyans; that they would have paid the higher taxes Libya demanded and that the Anglo-Saxon oil companies' sojourn in Libya would have ended. As for the possibility of using force (actually suggested since by a handful of imperialists *manqués*), suffice it that it was never for a moment considered.

I dwell on the 1970 Libyan demands and their success, primarily because they demonstrated, like a flash of lightning in a summer sky, what the new situation was; to be sure, it was Europe that was extraordinarily vulnerable and extraordinarily oblivious, the United States as a consumer was not yet affected, and the fact that the companies caught in the middle were American and British made for misunderstanding and some bad feeling in the European consuming countries. But these points were incidental to the fundamental fact, which was that a threat to withhold oil could now be effectively employed to produce higher prices. Hindsight suggestions as to how that threat might have been countered, either by the companies or by the American or other governments, seem to me quite unrealistic, and the charge that the State Department by inaction was to blame for creating a new monster is, in simple terms, nonsense. The Libyans were competent men in a strong position; they played their hand straight, and found it a winning one.

So, in the course of 1970, Persian Gulf taxes were raised toward the new Libyan level, and at the end of 1970 Libya made it a complete spiral by a second wave of demands to "balance" the new Persian Gulf prices. In the course of this eventful year, the Department of State necessarily became deeply involved, consulting constantly with the companies and holding frequent meetings with the Libyans in particular, though never as participants or negotiators. Better informed itself, the Department was soon able to keep European governments abreast of OPEC actions, and in due course to help persuade the companies that they should do so directly—so that since 1971 relations between the companies and the European consuming countries have generally been smooth. We have not heard in the last two years any echo of what was said by one European minister in 1967: "American companies brutally conquered our market; if they do not keep us supplied at all times, they will be expelled."

Toward the end of 1970, the producers consolidated new tax demands through OPEC, and began to act as a single group and more stridently. Every OPEC member, with the exception of Indonesia, either made public statements or (more convincingly) told the companies privately that if their demands were not met, all oil production would be stopped and the companies would then have to face the wrath of the consuming countries. An OPEC resolution in December laid down a 15-day time limit for acceptance and called for "concerted and simultaneous action by all member countries" if the negotiations failed. Meeting with the companies on January 11, 1971, the Libyan Deputy Prime Minister left no doubt that what was meant was a cut-off of all oil production. The same message was conveyed directly and through official channels to the American and British governments by two rulers of friendly countries.

The demand for increased revenues, while alarming, had been an economic matter which would not traditionally have engaged the American government. The threats to cut off oil, however, brought the Department of State inevitably into an active and public role. First, Justice Department action was obtained to permit the companies to form a common negotiating front—not be picked off one by one as had happened in Libya. And, in mid-January, following a meeting with the chief executives of the oil companies, Under Secretary John Irwin was dispatched to present American official concerns to the Shah of Iran, the King of Saudi Arabia, and the Ruler of Kuwait. In these talks, Secretary Irwin explained that the United States took very seriously threats to cut off oil deliveries to America or her allies, and that any country which took such action would find its relations with the United States severely and adversely affected. In reply, all three monarchs assured him that the "threats" had been misunderstood, that they were directed solely against the companies, and that the oil would be made available to consumers even if the negotiations with the companies broke down. Later threats by the producing countries were in this sense—a form of pressure on the companies, but not a threat of total nondelivery.[5]

In addition, Secretary Irwin requested an extension of the deadline for negotiations and an assurance that agreements reached with the companies would be honored for their full terms. Both requests were agreed to. The negotiations then continued, and the settlement reached at Tehran in February 1971 provided for tax increases equal to about half the initial OPEC demands: these increases meant a rise of 45 cents per barrel in the Gulf price and of 80 cents in Libya, with a schedule for further increases through 1975.

There was jubilation in OPEC. The triumph and the demon-

[5] The OPEC position was codified in Resolution XXII. 131 (1971); the American view on threats to cut off deliveries has been reiterated on many occasions since, most recently by the author in September 1972. It has been suggested that American representatives virtually invited the threat of cut-off and thus built up OPEC's bargaining position, specifically through statements at a meeting of OECD in Paris on January 20, 1971. (See M. A. Adelman, *The World Petroleum Market*, Baltimore: John Hopkins University Press, 1972, pp. 254–5; also the same author's "Is the Oil Shortage Real?," *Foreign Policy*, Winter 1972–73, pp. 80–81.) By January 20, however, as the above chronology shows, the threats had already been made; thereafter, on American representations, they were modified. As for the thought that the OPEC countries needed to be told how damaging a withholding could be, this seems to me to belong to a bygone view of the capacity of leaders in less-developed countries.

stration of power seemed complete. But there was also, in the circumstances, some satisfaction in the industrialized countries represented in the Organisation for Economic Co-operation and Development (OECD). None had been in any position to hold out against the threat of even a brief suspension, for despite discussions since the Libyan episode, the level of reserves in Europe was still low. The underlying bargaining position of the European consumers was weak, and they knew it full well. Thus, there was genuine relief that the agreement appeared to promise assured prices for a substantial period, and that the consumer, because of lower tanker rates and increased company efficiency, would still be paying less for his petroleum in constant dollars than he had in 1958. In fact, after the OPEC settlement, prices to the retail consumer in Europe, including taxes levied in the consumer countries, went up only three to five percent, while one country, Italy, actually offset the increase by reducing her excise taxes by the same amount.

There was satisfaction, too, with the American role and with the fact that the major consuming countries had been consulted at all stages. The Italians, however, raised for the first time the suggestion that the consuming countries might in future have to play a greater and more direct role in negotiations; this position has since gained adherents in OECD.

Here it should be noted that, if the industrialized consumers were fairly well pleased with the outcome, it was quite otherwise with the underdeveloped consuming countries, which had counted on declining real fuel prices to sustain their economic growth. This group at once expressed alarm, and at least one key country, India, was unable to absorb the increase and was forced to cut back petroleum purchases proportionately. This possibility had been foreseen in the negotiations, and the question of a lower or differential tax for sales to underdeveloped nations had been broached with various OPEC countries, specifically Iran, Saudi Arabia, Kuwait and Venezuela. The idea was rejected, on the technical ground that it might lead to circumvention and resale, more broadly on the plea that the producing countries themselves were underdeveloped. If Europe, America or Japan were concerned about the welfare of India or Colombia or Tanzania, it was argued, they had the means to assist them. The issue has lain dormant since; it is sometimes still raised by Asian, African and Latin American states—without response.

V

In spite of the upheavals in the oil world of the last two years, the Tehran OPEC agreements have been both successful and stable. I say that with tongue only partially in cheek. The main agreements were on taxes and on the posted prices of oil. These have not been changed. The OPEC countries insist that the agreements only covered these matters. When currency values were changed by the Smithsonian accord of 1971, the Tehran agreements were interpreted, under a supplemental Geneva agreement of 1972, to provide for a proportionate increase in payments to the producers. The same kind of increase will presumably result from the recent 1973 U.S. devaluation.

Yet OPEC dissatisfaction was not long in manifesting itself. Various members, in the next half year, started looking at the figures more harshly. They could see large and growing incomes for their governments and were generally pleased. But they could also see that their income per barrel was still low—especially when compared with the excise taxes which Europe levies on its fuel. Much more important, indeed of overwhelming importance to the changing world oil picture, was that the OPEC countries, for the first time, began to recognize and discuss openly the fact that their reserves were exhaustible and should be conserved.

At the Arab Oil Congress in Algiers in May-June 1972, OPEC was castigated for having been too soft, for having yielded too easily and readily to company and consumer government pressures. The OPEC "triumph" thus lasted in the eyes of many Arab observers a scant 15 months. And the idea began to take root that it was important to maximize present revenues but without exhausting what was now perceived to be a wasting asset.

In this mood, the OPEC countries turned their attention in mid-1972 to the question of participation, i.e. a defined percentage share in the producing operations and assets of the international companies. At once there was a sharp difference of view on whether this issue had been laid aside, at least until 1976, by the Tehran agreements. The producer governments took the position that participation was an old demand in no sense relinquished at Tehran, and indeed that the companies had been told explicitly that it would be raised as soon as the price issue had been settled. The company position was that participation had not been discussed and that the Tehran agreements guaranteed the existing concessions in their present form for the full five-year period. Possibly the case was one of an ambiguity that neither side had wished to clarify. Undoubtedly there had been mention of participation, but each side preferred to leave the meeting undisturbed by possible conflicting interpretations.

From a careful study of the Tehran agreements, the State Department concluded that the company position was correct. The OPEC argument, that there was an inherent right to renegotiate the concessions whenever circumstances changed, seemed to us contrary to both Western and Islamic jurisprudence.[6] Accordingly, our ambassadors made representations in Iran, Saudi Arabia and Kuwait, but were met by reiteration that participation was an issue totally outside the Tehran agreements, and that the companies "knew" before those agreements were signed that participation would be next on the agenda of talks.

Participation was also discussed in the OECD, but it was of limited interest, being viewed as an issue between the Anglo-Saxon oil companies and the producing governments. Perhaps the companies were being partially nationalized, but the OPEC countries had given renewed assurances that prices would remain the same. At best, therefore, participation would mean nothing to the consumer countries. At worst, it would mean only a few cents a barrel increased cost.

At any rate, the companies did enter long negotiations on participation. In these the United States played one major role, forcefully noting that it would have to consider compensation based on "book value" as confiscation. In the discussions, it was pointed out that many of the OPEC countries themselves would soon be investing large sums abroad; any principle that meant in practice no compensation might later apply to their own investments. Ultimately, the issue was resolved by a new compensation formula, based on many complex factors. Face was thus saved on all sides.

The agreements reached in Riyadh by the end of 1972 provided for the producing governments to acquire percentage shares starting at 25 percent and working up gradually to 51 percent,

---

[6] It may be pointed out here that a surprisingly large number of oil company officials were already examining the possibility of offering a new relationship to the oil producers. The day of traditional concessions, they saw, had clearly ended and a dramatic new offer to the producers might guarantee another generation of tranquility, as ARAMCO's offer of the 50-50 profit split in the early 1950s had done. This view did not prevail, and participation was only discussed when OPEC demanded that it be discussed.

or an assumption of control, by 1982. The companies were far
from pleased, although the arrangements did give them and the
consuming countries a basis for continuing. Within three years,
the producing governments will be permitted to take their full
25 percent of the oil, and it seems likely that if existing market
conditions continue the governments will be able to dispose of
their rising percentages, including the 51 percent to which they
will be entitled in 1982. The effect, of course, will be to further
increase the return to the producing governments, at least to the
extent of the present margin of profit of the companies' own
production operations.

At this writing, there are several developments which could
reopen the Riyadh agreements. One is the Iranian demand for
total ownership and management of its oil resources now, i.e. for
a conversion of the companies into long-term buyers of Iranian
oil. Another would be the "success" of the Iraqi nationalization
of Kirkuk fields—and by this I mean little or no compensation for
the fields and unrestricted freedom in selling the oil; the third
would be the yielding of the companies in Libya to government
demands for 50 percent participation now. It cannot be said that
any one of these would surely result in the reopening of the
Riyadh agreements in their present form. But resisting change
at this point will not be easy or even desirable.

Regardless of what happens to the current agreements, the
companies will continue to play a major role in transporting, refining and distributing oil. And they very likely will also play the
major role in oil production for the next ten years. Predictions
for longer than ten years in the energy field are daring, but the
companies probably have even a much longer life than that. It
seems doubtful that the national oil companies of the present
OPEC will look for oil in third countries; this action will be left
to the Western companies.

In sum, the international companies will probably go on playing an active role in finding, developing and marketing oil for as
long as it is used as a fuel or as a raw material. But in this role the
companies may increasingly find themselves minority partners
of both producer and consumer governments—and they must
reconcile themselves to the probability that their role in negotiating with the OPEC countries will in the future be more circumscribed than it has been until now.

The idea was first expressed, I believe, by the Italians, that the oil companies should be turned into "regulated utilities"; that consumer governments must have the right to set the prices the companies pay for crude and the prices they can charge for products; and that consumer governments will then allow the companies a fair return on their investment. This has long horrified most of the top company management, and I have no doubt that it would be an undesirable method of finding and developing oil. But there is no doubt that this concept too is finding more adherents in the consuming countries. How the companies react to these pressures, and what they offer as alternatives, will to a large extent determine their future form and their future activities.

VI

As can be seen, OPEC has moved hard and fast in the last three years. One result has been to reduce the position of the companies and to make bargaining more and more a political matter between governments. In economic terms, moreover, the series of agreements create a new price situation which is defined through 1975 only, and thereafter subject to renewed demands and changes.

What, then, is the likely picture of Middle East and North African production and revenue, taking into account reasonable projections of demand in Europe, Japan, and other consuming areas, plus the added share of American consumption that cannot be met through domestic U.S. production?

The Tehran and subsequent OPEC agreements raised the average 1970 tax of around $.80 per barrel in a single jump to around $1.25 per barrel in 1971, with provisions for further annual increases to around $1.80 in 1975. There was no noticeable inhibiting effect on consumption: while some less-developed countries reduced their imports, the imports of the industrialized nations, notably the United States, grew more rapidly than expected. Already in this current year 1973, the United States will be importing something over three million barrels per day from the Eastern Hemisphere. The total gross cost of all U.S. oil imports will exceed $8 billion, although in our balance-of-payments accounts more than half of this will be offset by company remittances and increased exports generated through the purchases.

For 1975, a reasonable estimate of the situation, based on the tax rates flowing from the Tehran agreements and without taking into account any further increases, would be as follows:

ESTIMATED PRODUCTION AND REVENUE, 1975

(Stated in thousands of barrels per day; billions of dollars annually)

Middle East	Production	Revenue[7]
Iran	7,300	4.7
Saudi Arabia	8,500	5.4
Kuwait	3,500	2.2
Iraq	1,900	1.2
Abu Dhabi	2,300	1.5
Other Persian Gulf	1,800	1.0
Subtotal	25,300	16.0
North Africa		
Libya	2,200	2.0
Algeria	1,200	1.1
Subtotal	3,400	3.1
Total	28,700	19.1

After 1976, of course, any estimate of taxes and prices becomes considerably more speculative. The 1970 State Department projection that prices would rise by 1980 to $5.00 per barrel may now be on the low side: sources within OPEC are publicly discussing an increase of $1.50 in taxes in 1976 alone, with "substantial" increases thereafter. If one takes, however, a $5.00 American production cost as decisive for the delivered import price, and deducts company profits and cost of production and transport, the revenue to the producing countries would come to approximately $3.50 per barrel in the Persian Gulf and $4.25 per barrel in North Africa. At these levels, it is generally estimated that consumption would still rise roughly in the same way as had been projected prior to the latest round of price increases; this amounts to saying that a price of $5.00 for delivered crude oil is still below the level that would cause any significant contraction in the use of oil in Europe, Japan or the United States. The startling fact is that world consumption within the next 12 years is now expected to exceed total world consumption of oil throughout history up to the present time.

On the basis of demand trends and the $3.50/$4.25 rates of return per barrel, the picture for 1980 would be as follows:

---

[7] These figures are based on the taxes and royalties in effect prior to the dollar devaluation of February 1973. If the 1972 Geneva agreements on currency revaluation apply, the income figures should be increased about 8.5 percent.

ESTIMATED PRODUCTION AND REVENUE, 1980

(Stated in thousands of barrels per day; billions of dollars annually)

Middle East	*Production*	*Revenue*
Iran	10,000	12.8
Saudi Arabia	20,000	25.6
Kuwait	4,000	5.0
Iraq	5,000	6.4
Abu Dhabi	4,000	5.0
Other Persian Gulf	2,000	3.2
Subtotal	45,000	58.0
North Africa		
Libya	2,000	3.1
Algeria	1,500	2.3
Subtotal	3,500	5.4
Total	48,500	63.4

It must be noted that the estimated production figures are higher than others cited elsewhere in this article. Iran, for example, has said its production will level off at eight million barrels per day; Kuwait has said its will be kept at three million. Iraq will have difficulty in realizing five million unless the Western climate changes, and the others will strain to meet six million. Yet the world with its present habits will need this quantity of oil unless there is a war or a major recession. The only alternative to a shortfall before 1980 will be Saudi Arabia, and its projected production of 20 million barrels per day (set by Minister of Petroleum Ahmad Zaki Yamani as a goal) already seems improbably high.

If production levels fall significantly short of these numbers, there could be a real supply crisis in the world, and competition among the consumers could drive prices even higher. In this and other respects, the projection for 1980 is of course subject to a substantial margin of error. But it does seem likely that the general picture is an accurate projection of current trends, with all that it implies for costs to consuming countries and revenues to the Middle East and North African producers.

VII

With the possible exception of Croesus, the world will never have seen anything quite like the wealth which is flowing and will continue to flow into the Persian Gulf. There have been and still are countries which are richer than any country in OPEC, but there is none which is so small, so inherently weak and which has gained so much for so little activity of its own.

The cumulative OPEC income is even more startling than the annual figures. Let us ignore the income of Iran—for it will have no trouble absorbing funds in its vast development projects— and concentrate on the Arab countries. Their cumulative income from 1973 through 1980 will probably be over $210 billion. Even assuming a 20 percent compounded growth in expenditures (and it should be pointed out that all of the main Arab producers except Algeria are not spending all of their present income; in some cases, they are spending less than half), their cumulative expenditures for this period would be well under $100 billion. Capital accumulations therefore could be the balance—over $100 billion by 1980. At eight percent, just the income from this enormous sum would be $8 billion—larger than the current expenditures of Kuwait, Saudi Arabia and the Federation of Arab Amirates combined.

What will be done with this money will be a matter of crucial importance to the world. The first place for its use must certainly be in their own countries; the second must be the Arab world, which will not, as a whole, be capital-rich. At the Algiers Arab Oil Congress in mid-1972, the proposal was made that the Arabs should solve their "problem" in an inter-Arab agreement whereby the main producer nations would limit their income from oil to the 1972 tax structure. That is, as oil production went up, the increased payments at the 1972 rates would go to the producer governments, but all or at least part of any *increases* in payments per barrel over 1972 levels would go into an inter-Arab development bank for projects in the entire Arab world. This additional money would be, in a sense, unearned. Moreover, such action would be in perfect consonance with Islamic law practice, which demands twice as much *zakat* from income derived from lands fed by God-given rain as from lands irrigated by man.

It was interesting to note the enthusiasm with which this suggestion was accepted by the oil have-nots. It was much more gratifying to see the interest shown by some Kuwaitis, Iraqis and Libyans. Although it should be pointed out that interest shown by individuals is a long way from governmental acceptance of an idea, it must also be noted that both Kuwait and Saudi Arabia are already providing very substantial loans and gifts to other Arab countries.

Yet the sums we are talking about probably could not all be

absorbed in the next eight, ten or 20 years in the Arab world; at least for part of that time they could be more usefully invested in the developed world. And one of the main tasks of the producers will be to find adequate investment opportunities for their funds. This matter was discussed in the spring and summer of 1972 with Arab officials, who seemed interested in investing in the United States. In a Middle East Institute speech of September 29, 1972, I suggested that the enormous capital requirements of the oil and energy industry could be met only by large new infusions from the main capital-rich consuming countries (Germany and Japan), and from the producer countries themselves. I also suggested that Saudi Arabia, Kuwait and Iran might consider investing in the United States in other energy fields and even in non-energy-related industries. Sheikh Zaki Yamani of Saudi Arabia replied the following day that he strongly agreed with the suggestion of Arab investment in the "downstream" oil sector (refining, distribution, etc.), but did not believe Saudi Arabia would be interested in other types of investments.

In a recent meeting in Kuwait it was suggested that Arabs accumulate their money and simply float it from country to country, depending on how each country reacts to Arab problems. The difficulties of such an action are surely underrated, but the fact that it was considered and debated must give us some pause. Frankly, however, it is a problem I am convinced we will never face. I do not believe the Arabs will ever accumulate anything remotely approximating the figure of $100 billion. Either they will spend the money at home or in the Arab world or they will find adequate investments for it abroad. If they do not, or cannot, they will very likely conclude that the oil had best stay in the ground—and this would cause a problem for the developed world far greater than the floating billions.

If finding a use for the money is of great importance to the Arabs, it is of even greater importance to us. There are many trained and sophisticated Arabs; there are Arab engineers who can run oil fields and there are Arab economists who can calculate the value of investments. There are also, unfortunately, Arabs who are venal, who are susceptible to flattery, who could quite easily be taken in by charlatans, and the sky over Riyadh today is black with vultures with great new get-richer-quicker plans under their wings. Whether an Arab is a Harvard Business

School graduate or an illiterate bedouin he strongly dislikes being cheated. If one grandiose project is sold to Saudi Arabia which fails to produce the ingots or pipes or widgets it is designed for; or if it produces them at costs far above the imported cost; or if the Saudi government buys into one shaky American concern which then fails, I seriously doubt that the reaction would be: "We've been had. Too bad. Let's try harder next time." It much more likely will be: "We're still not trained enough to deal with the Westerners. The oil can always be sold—as a raw material if not as a fuel. Let's not increase production further." Or worse: "Let's restrict production."

VIII

So far we have looked at the world oil reserve situation; at length at the recent history of bargaining by the producer countries through OPEC; at projections for the future; and at the situation of the producer countries in the light of all factors. It is time now to return to the question asked early in this article: Can OPEC hold together? The answer seems to me, if not certain, clear enough so that it would surely be foolhardy to bet on a contrary outcome for the next several years at least.

Repeated suggestions that OPEC would not notice its strength, if only the consumers did not refer to it, represent perhaps the single most pernicious fallacy in our past thinking on world oil. It assumes an unsophistication and ascribes an ignorance to the major producer countries, particularly the Arabs, but also Iran, Venezuela and the others which, for better or worse, has not existed in recent years—if it ever did. OPEC economists are fully as capable of making supply-demand calculations as are Western economists. And they reach the same conclusions.

OPEC cannot usefully be compared to other producer cartels. It controls a product which is irreplaceable in the short run, and is vitally necessary to the economies of every technologically advanced country. The main oil producers are not competing with each other for larger shares of the consumer market—as would be the case in other producer cartels. Probably the most important reason for OPEC solidarity is that the key countries, notably Kuwait, Saudi Arabia and Libya, do not need more income; they are unsure of how they could use it if they had it, and they fear the international consequences of acquiring too much wealth.

Almost as important is the recognition of all OPEC countries that their reserves are finite and must be conserved. These proven reserves are indeed very large. Yet, for example, Kuwait's 66 billion barrels today seem much less impressive to Kuwaitis themselves than they did a decade ago. Hence, Kuwait recently stopped expansion and plans to keep production at three million barrels per day. At this level, Kuwait will have oil for a couple of generations—but even this is a short period for a nation; and Kuwait's prospects of finding more oil are very small. Iran has stated that it will limit production to eight million barrels per day before the end of this decade; production will be held there for eight or ten years and then will decline. Increases in Iranian income from oil will only come from increases in taxes per barrel, and it counts on this. North Africa's reserves are not large enough to play a dominant role in world oil in 1980; and the rest of the world will produce whatever it can. This leaves for consideration two countries: Iraq, whose government does not encourage foreign investment and seems unable, on its own, to produce substantially greater quantities of oil; and Saudi Arabia, by far the most important.

In the last analysis, whether Saudi Arabia or any other OPEC country with large reserves would act to disrupt the market is a question of the behavior of men in control of national governments, affected by political factors as much as by theoretical economics. Thus, it is frequently noted by observers outside the area that from an economic standpoint an increase in present income should be vastly more useful than the discounted value of income deferred for 10–20 years—and that with other energy sources in prospect oil may not even command high prices in such future periods. To Arab countries, such arguments are simply not persuasive. In the personal experience of their leaders, past income has been wasted and even current income is not invested profitably. Moreover, just about every top official in OPEC, starting with Perez Alfonso in Venezuela 20 years ago and including Zaki Yamani of Saudi Arabia today, is convinced that his country can sell its oil profitably in ten or 100 years as a raw material (primarily for petrochemicals) if not as a fuel.

The predictions of Western economists that competition in OPEC for larger shares of the market will soon bring down prices are read not only in the West but in OPEC countries. They merely increase the already firm determination to avoid such a development. The producers may want to "maximize" their income but they also recognize that, until there are alternatives to oil as a fuel, this can be done most easily by raising prices. No OPEC country, no matter how great its wealth, is interested in "breaking" world oil prices.

It is difficult to see how these elements of self-interest would be changed or how any of the OPEC countries would act differently if they should now move quickly toward complete nationalization of the producing operations and assets of the Western companies. Bargaining directly with the consuming countries, the producing countries would still be just as disinclined as now to drive prices down; and needing no additional income, would not feel under pressure to increase their market shares.

The Kingdom of Saudi Arabia, without doubt, could destroy OPEC. It could produce oil in much greater quantities than it does today; it could drive the price of oil down to the mythical $1.00 a barrel, and every OPEC country would be ruined. But Saudi Arabia would also ruin itself in the process. Using the economists' expression, Saudi Arabia would not "maximize" its income; it would only "maximize" its production, and even its enormous reserves would soon be exhausted. It is difficult to see what folly could possess Saudi Arabia to take such action; any consumer government that assumed that Saudi Arabia would (or could) do this without an internal revolution would be guilty of an even greater folly.

The "collapse" of OPEC would indeed seem a serious possibility on either of two conditions—if there were discoveries of vast new reserves in areas which could be kept outside OPEC, or if there were an unexpected breakthrough in the development of new energy sources. Both are unlikely to occur; and neither could, even if it occurred tomorrow, operate rapidly enough so that it would necessarily drive down oil prices in the next decade. The world cannot simply wait for or expect such a *deus ex machina* to solve its energy problems.

IX

This article up to now has dwelt almost exclusively on the strengths of the oil producers. The consumers are not without power of their own—or they would not be if they were united. So far they have not been, and they have as yet shown little inclination toward collective action in spite of repeated urgings by the United States. In the fall 1969 meetings of the OECD oil committee, before the first OPEC crisis, the Department of State first raised with the EEC the possibility of a common approach to the energy problems we would all soon be facing. Assistant Secretary of State Philip Trezise, in the OECD meeting in Paris in May 1970, urged that energy problems be considered in a multilateral context, but got little positive response. The general attitude was that the United States was becoming vaguely hysterical as its import needs grew; the United States, they thought, worried too much about losing Arab oil. This was something they, the Europeans and Japanese, did not need to think about. Israel was a millstone around the neck of the United States; this was the U.S. choice; the Europeans and Japanese could make their accommodations with the Arabs. Restrictions on oil deliveries would apply only to the United States; its allies would have much less to worry about. Not every OECD member took this view; the U.S. position was always supported strongly by the United Kingdom, the Netherlands and a few others; but generally American fear of a cut-off of oil supplies was not widely shared.

In the course of the last two years attitudes have changed. Italy has gone through a rather traumatic experience in Libya; 50 percent of her oil company was nationalized before production began. And the French experience in Iraq went sour. France had taken a markedly pro-Arab position in the Arab-Israeli dispute; she had reached oil accords with Iraq which were the most favorable to the producing government of any agreement theretofore signed, and many Frenchmen looked forward to a new French oil empire in the Middle East. But the agreements with the French national company, ERAP, did not measure up to the new OPEC agreements and the Iraqis demanded renegotiation. This very likely will be achieved, and oil certainly will be produced by France in Iraq; but the French have found that the doctrine of changing circumstances is also applied to outspoken friends of the Arabs.

In the fall of 1971, the United States raised more formally with the Europeans and the Japanese the possibility of a joint approach to the energy problem; apart from a general expression of support for the companies in their dealings, no ideas were forthcoming. The subject of coöperation was raised again in the spring of 1972 with the same lack of response. Finally, in October

1972, in both Brussels and Paris, the Europeans and Japanese were told that the United States would need some indication, at least in principle, of their intentions. Did they prefer a purely autarkic approach, or did they think we should try (as the United States strongly preferred) to tackle our energy problems jointly? The European Community, speaking together for the first time replied that it too favored a coöperative approach. The Japanese reply was ambiguous but seemed to be inclined toward coöperation.

The United States has discussed at various times a two-pronged approach to consumer coöperation. The first would be coöperation among the major consumers to find new sources of hydrocarbons and to develop new forms of energy. This could be as simple as expanded exchanges of information, or could go as far as a supranational authority with power to direct research and allocate funds. We have not put any specific plan on the table but have indicated our willingness to discuss all possible approaches. The second and more difficult part would be the formation of an international authority to avoid cutthroat competition for available energy in times of shortage. Such competition could drive prices far higher than we can presently imagine. The producers, in such a case, would need still less production to maintain their incomes and could restrict production even further.

Such competition for oil, of course, has already begun. Various companies are trying to conclude long-term purchase contracts for oil with various OPEC countries. At least three governments have made overtures to Saudi Arabia with offers of attractive long-term contracts, since the Yamani offer of a special relationship to the United States made in his Middle East Institute speech of September 1972. Japan has recently concluded a deal with Abu Dhabi which went beyond the OPEC agreements; and small American companies are now offering the producers long-term contracts with equity participation in their firms. With OPEC production limitations in the future, or even with normal slow growth, with only Saudi Arabia and perhaps Iraq capable of substantial expansion, bidding for supplies could soon get out of hand, and the projected price of $5.00 per barrel in 1980, or even a price of $7.00, could seem conservative.

There was strong agreement in the OECD that a consumer organization (which all agreed should be formed) should not be considered a challenge to OPEC; it would not be designed to drive prices down and certainly not to ruin the producers; it would only be designed to protect the consumers. It could even be used to bring the OPEC producers into closer ties with the consumers. Producer country investments in Europe (and possibly Japan) as well as in the United States should be encouraged. In September 1972 I stated the American position in these terms:

If consumers band together to search for new energy forms or to ration available energy in periods of shortages, this should cause no surprise or offense. If consumers encourage companies to resist further price increases, this should also cause no surprise. Many consumers already believe that the companies have not been adequately vigorous in resisting producer demands, as they could and usually did pass on to the consumer any tax increases. The producer governments have banded together in a well functioning organization. Their immediate adversaries are only the companies—an unequal contest.

Lastly, there is the possibility of some additional measures to build up reserve stocks for bargaining purposes. These are indeed badly needed for their own sake, in Europe and also in the United States. They could have some importance in future dealings with the OPEC countries, although it must be realized now that the enormous financial resources of the OPEC countries give them a considerable advantage in any endurance contest.

X

Consumer solidarity will be necessary if the present trend toward bidding up prices is to be halted. It will be indispensable if political or economic blackmail is to be successfully countered. There are various interpretations of what this means and how far the consumers could go or would want to go in a confrontation with the oil producers, particularly if the issue were exclusively one of oil prices.

In the long run, though, the only satisfactory position for the United States (and to a lesser extent for its main allies) must be the development of alternative energy sources. The United States is particularly blessed with large reserves of coal which can be converted to hydrocarbons, and of shale oil. The United States shares with all nations the possibility of developing geothermal energy, solar energy, and energy from nuclear fission and fusion. But the lead time is long for the development of all of them and some are still purely hypothetical.

Suggestions a few years ago for a vast program of development of new energy sources received no support in the Congress or from the public. Yet, had the United States a few years ago been willing to accept the realities which became evident in 1967 or even in 1970, it might have started sooner on the development of Western Hemisphere hydrocarbons and domestic energy sources.

The potential is there. Venezuela probably has close to a trillion barrels of heavy oil in place, with at least ten percent recoverable by present technology; the United States has large reserves of oil tied up in shale, and coal which could be turned into hydrocarbons in almost unlimited quantities. And there are probably over 300 billion barrels of recoverable oil in the Athabascan tar sands.

Let us not exaggerate all this, however. The shale, the heavy Venezuelan oil, and the tar sands all require capital investment on the scale of $5–$7 billion for each million barrels per day of capacity. Above all the lead time is long—perhaps 15 years, certainly eight—before significant production could be achieved from any of these sources.

On the diplomatic front, we have for years discussed an agreement with Canada which will permit free entry of Canadian oil into the United States. This has lost much meaning by now, for Canada is currently sending us all her surplus oil and has imposed export controls. But we still may reach agreement. We have also discussed a treaty with Venezuela which would permit the development of her heavy oils. We have proposed free entry of these oils into the United States in return for investment guarantees to the companies developing these oils.

Within the United States itself, a wide sweep of actions can be taken to increase domestic energy production and to use energy more efficiently. Finally, there is the question of controlling the rise in oil demand, through reasonable conservation actions. Such measures as the spread of effective mass-transit systems could do much to limit our present profligate use of energy for a host of marginal purposes.

No one action will solve our energy problem, much less that of the entire world. But taken together these steps—collaboration with other nations, the development of alternative energy sources, and controlling our consumption reasonably—could allow us to reduce our imports significantly below those projected in this article. This must surely be our immediate goal.

XI

To look simply at the world's oil reserves and conclude that they are sufficient to meet the world's needs can no longer be acceptable. We could allow ourselves such fatuities as long as we had large spare oil production capacity, and while our overseas imports were small. We can do so no longer. Our security and balance-of-payments problems are large and growing. Whether we focus on today, or 1980, or 1985, it is abundantly clear that we must move on a variety of fronts if we are to avoid a situation which could lead to or even force us into highly dangerous action.

Having argued throughout this article that the oil crisis is a reality that compels urgent action, let me end on a note of hope. The current energy problem will not be a long one in human terms. By the end of the century oil will probably lose its predominance as a fuel. The measures we have the capacity to take to protect ourselves by conserving energy and developing alternative sources of energy should enable us, our allies, and the producer nations as well, to get through the next 25 years reasonably smoothly. They might even bring us smiling into the bright new world of nuclear fusion when all energy problems will be solved. This final note would ring less hollow if we did not remember the firm conviction of the late 1940s that the last fossil fuel electricity generating plant would have been built by 1970; and that in this new golden age, the home use of electricity would not even be measured. It would be so cheap, we were told, that the manpower cost of reading meters would be greater than the cost of the energy which the homeowners conceivably could consume. But perhaps in 2000. . . .

A PLAN FOR ENERGY INDEPENDENCE

By Carroll L. Wilson

I BELIEVE the United States is facing a national energy emergency. It arises from our extravagant and wasteful use of energy and from a shift in the sources of fuels. Per capita consumption is three times that of Western Europe, and we may ask ourselves whether our greater use enriches the quality of life by any such margin. Our cars are twice as heavy and use twice as much fuel as European cars which run about the same mileage each year, and the ratio is getting worse because of the sharp drop in fuel economy on recent models of American cars, owing to emission controls and air conditioners. We keep our houses and buildings too hot and use large amounts of fuel in air-conditioning everything. We have not given a thought to fuel conservation and efficiency since the days of rationing in World War II—an era which only 30 percent (those over 45) of the population can remember. These are some of the reasons why with six percent of the world's population the United States uses 33 percent of the world's energy—and why Europe and Japan are unlikely to be sympathetic to our plight as we ask them to share with us their traditional supply sources in the Middle East.

The costs and perils of dependence upon Middle East nations around the Persian Gulf were eloquently stated by James Akins of the State Department in the last issue of this journal.[1] His analysis of the expected scale of payments to Middle East countries and the inability of the largest producer, Saudi Arabia, to absorb or use a significant fraction of these payments for internal purposes underscores the perils of open-ended dependence upon these nations for our oil. The most critical aspects of the national energy emergency are the shift to such dependence and the enormous foreign-exchange drain it must progressively entail

[1] "The Oil Crisis: This Time the Wolf Is Here," *Foreign Affairs*, April 1973.

by the late 1970s alone. Recent "symbolic" interruptions by some Middle East countries, in protest against U.S. policy toward Israel, may be one hint of what the future holds; the continued hard bargaining on price is another. Although we will have to live through a period of substantial reliance on Middle East oil, it is hardly an acceptable national policy to leave the emerging situation in this highly unsatisfactory state. There are simply too many cumulative problems and dangers involved.

The question, of course, is what *could* we do about it. The time has come to propose solutions. I propose a strategy to overcome this emergency, a program of action to implement such a strategy, the machinery needed for implementation, and an assessment of the global and environmental consequences of the adoption and execution of such a program by the United States. Obviously, the number of variables is immense and only by gross simplification can one define a strategy and program; there should be alternative strategies and plans. But this may be a place to begin.

II

The objectives of my proposal are to achieve, by 1985: first, the independence of the United States from critical reliance on imports of energy in any form—defining critical reliance as anything more than ten percent of our needs; second, energy costs below some target level, in dollars per million British Thermal Units (BTU), which is a common energy pricing unit for all fuels. I suggest as a goal keeping energy costs for premium fuels such as gas or oil below $1.00 per million BTU. This is equivalent to oil at $6.00 per barrel, roughly twice present prices, or to gas at $1.00 per thousand cubic feet, twice present wellhead prices on new contracts. The current cost of coal is very low in relation to its heat content, and the proposed ceiling gives great latitude for its use.

To see how we might reach these goals, let us start by examining the components of energy supply in the United States—past, present and future. Current projections make three key assumptions—that total energy consumption will continue to grow at the rate of 4.5 percent a year that has prevailed in the past decade, that the present pattern of use of particular energy sources will continue, and that nuclear power will be rapidly developed. As we shall see, all three of these assumptions can be challenged. If they were the case, however, the currently projected picture (seen in relation to present and past) would look as follows:

TABLE I

U.S. ENERGY SOURCES AT STATED PERIODS

	Actual 1960–63	Actual 1970–73	Projected 1980–83	Projected 1985
Oil	44%	44%	44%	47%
Natural Gas	29%	33%	28%	20%
Coal	23%	18%	17%	17%
Hydro/Geothermal	4%	4%	5%	6%
Nuclear	.5%	1%	6%	10%

As the table shows, the crux of the problem is that oil has had to assume a large and slowly increasing share of the total. Natural gas appears to have reached its peak and will decline as a proportion of total supply even if higher prices produce increased exploration and discovery. Hydro sources can at most hold their place.

There remains, of course, the question whether present geothermal sources can be expanded to a greater degree and whether new "miracle" sources of energy can be found from solar energy, nuclear fusion, hydrogen broken down by nuclear methods, or any other. In all of these there is hope if we look ahead on a 30-year projection—and in the most promising areas there is justification for much greater research and development effort. But if one puts together the theoretical possibilities and the best available sense of what it would take to develop any of these "miracle" sources to major production levels, the honest judgment at this stage must be that they will contribute nothing by 1985 nor be substantially operative before roughly the year 2000, if then. And we simply cannot wait that long.

Rather, then, we have to look to our present sources of energy within the 1985 time frame. Obviously, we must have the maximum possible expansion of domestic oil and natural gas production, but the increases cannot be large in relation to total need. In addition, we should establish synthetic oil industries based on shale and on coal, building some large-scale plants to demonstrate feasibility and costs and to test features that minimize environmental impact. Such developments might yield a few million barrels per day, and we might require refineries to mix such oil with regular crude oil for a fraction of their feedstocks—even if initial prices of synthetic crude oil exceeded the $6.00 per barrel ceiling target for 1985 energy costs.

Looking at all the technological possibilities, however, it is my conclusion that the best sources of energy that can be greatly expanded in this time frame, at reasonable cost and with an impact on resources and on the environment that we can bear, are nuclear fission and the production of gas from coal through gasification—a process which produces from coal a clean, all-purpose and readily transportable gaseous fuel. For this purpose, some of the necessary technology now exists, but some still requires additional development. Gasification itself has been demonstrated, and technologies are already in use that produce low-BTU gas. However, the technological obstacles to producing gas of pipeline quality from coal are still formidable; a massive crash program of parallel pilot and demonstration plants for the four or five processes that now appear possible should permit construction to start in two to three years on production plants that make use of whichever process or processes then look best.

This selection of technological possibilities is the first element in the proposed strategy. The second—at least equally important and urgent—is a program effectively to reduce the rate of growth in our energy consumption. Actually to lower our consumption substantially is not, I believe, acceptable without far too drastic changes in our whole society. But I believe it is feasible, and should be our target, to achieve and maintain a rate of growth in our energy consumption of three percent per year, rather than the present 4.5 percent. In arithmetic terms, instead of our energy consumption in 1985 being 70 percent greater than it is now, it would be "only" 43 percent greater—a large and critical difference without which no action program can, I believe, do the job.

This is still a drastic target. To achieve it requires a recognition and acceptance that we are in a national emergency. Since shortages are upon us, we will have to begin to practice conservation not because of price but because of shortages. Although the first guidelines for voluntary "sharing of shortages equitably" have been issued by the government, we have no rationing machinery except to give priority to domestic heating and to drop other loads if not enough energy is available. There are not even the rudiments of machinery for rationing fuel. The only serious study of an emergency program has been made by the Office of Emergency Preparedness, which has produced two very useful studies indicating measures that could be taken if the will existed to diminish significantly our energy demands, thereby reducing our dependence upon imported oil. Yet, before the year is out, shortages of gasoline and heating oil in many parts of the country will make it clear that a national emergency exists and that appropriate steps must be taken.

Some of the necessary measures will involve presently extravagant uses and waste, and some an increase in efficiency. Here it is striking to note how little scientific and technical effort now goes into this latter question; a very modest improvement in our present low fuel efficiency may turn out, over time, to be in itself sufficient to bring us close to the three percent growth rate. But in the meantime we must surely cut back painfully.

III

On the whole we do very well in dealing with national emergencies. Many examples come to mind from World War II when we created the machinery; gave it the necessary authority; provided the money; mobilized the parts of the society, public and private, which were needed to overcome the emergency or meet it; energized the program by a system of contracts; and achieved the target results.

A notable example was our action in dealing with the abrupt cessation of the natural rubber supply. We carried out a crash program to set up a synthetic rubber industry, quickly creating the necessary machinery, authority and money. The results were dramatically successful. Another example was the decision to produce an atomic bomb in time to be usable in World War II. The decision was taken at a time when there were four or five possible routes to securing fissionable material from uranium and only some clues as to how to make a weapon from fissionable material. Special machinery was set up with the needed authority, with superb leadership and organizing capability, and within the tradition of mobilizing the private sector by contract. The Manhattan District then conducted that remarkable program of carrying forward simultaneously four different approaches to producing fissionable material and two simultaneous approaches to making a weapon, while building everything from cities to railroads to huge and completely novel factories, all in the space of less than three years. It worked.

Another example of how we can mobilize resources against an explicit target was the space program. In 1960, for reasons then considered sufficient, we decided that we should put a man on the moon before the end of the decade. To accomplish this, we created a special agency with great authority and lots of money and manned it with extraordinarily capable leadership. The fantastically complex and difficult scientific, technical and logistical problems were overcome, and, indeed, we put the first man on the moon in July 1969.

These are a few examples of how we have acted successfully when we have accepted the existence of a national emergency and taken the necessary actions (through Congress and the President) to provide the authority, the money, the machinery and the leadership to meet and overcome it. It is our national style to be most effective in tackling concrete programs, or working toward specified goals. Sometimes that approach is not appropriate as, for example, in solving the problem of cancer; in this case, however, it is the right one.

What might be the action program aimed at 1985—the Decade Program if you will—if we accepted the existence of a national energy emergency and then took the necessary steps to cope with it through meeting the specific targets suggested?

The first element in any such program must concern the use of oil. To limit our oil imports to ten percent of energy requirements by 1985—using now the target three percent annual growth rate to estimate total 1985 energy consumption—would mean that we would be importing no more than five million barrels of oil per day at that time (compared to the roughly 15 million barrels now projected).[2] In the total energy picture shown in Table I, oil (domestic and imported) would have to drop markedly from its projected 47 percent to a proportion of roughly 30 percent in 1985.

This at once suggests the first component of the action program. Thirty percent is roughly the proportion of our energy that now goes to transportation, especially automotive uses—for which, of course, oil is uniquely suited. It will take work to keep our transportation uses down to this proportion, for they are now expanding faster than total energy consumption and this tendency

---

[2] Oil would not, of course, be the only energy source imported. As we know, substantial possibilities exist for the importation of natural gas from Canada and of liquefied gas from Algeria, the Soviet Union and perhaps other sources. Without judging the wisdom of expanding any of these sources, their proportion of total energy is not likely to add much to the ten percent of total energy represented, for this program, by imported oil. We would still be within reasonable overall margins of import dependence.

will be accentuated by lowered efficiency due to tighter emission controls—not to mention the current sales rate of a million passenger cars a month! But if the proportion can be kept down—actually slightly reduced—then it can and should be met from oil, and oil should be withdrawn from other energy uses such as heating. This is a harsh measure but an indispensable one—the keystone of the whole program in fact.

The next component of the action program concerns nuclear power—currently providing one percent of our total energy, and projected in Table I to provide ten percent by 1985. In this respect, Table I reflects technological possibilities with proven techniques, but it does *not* reflect current political realities, nor, in my judgment, the true difficulty of meeting valid safety and environmental objections to the kind of major expansion it would take to achieve the projected figure.

Like others who have followed closely the development of nuclear fission as an energy source for more than 25 years now, I originally and for some time believed that it could, without undue difficulty, become the most important source of energy we have, especially for electricity. But problems have mounted, and delays, restrictions and technical uncertainties have dogged nearly every one of the many steps needed to bring a new nuclear plant into full operation, thus drastically slowing down the nuclear input to our energy system. The determined opposition of states and localities and citizen action groups, plus rising caution by the Atomic Energy Commission, has stretched out to ten years the interval between application for a plant permit and bringing the plant "on line" at an economic power level.

In part, the political forces at work reflect an exaggeration of the problems, or at least a failure to weigh fully the inevitable trade-offs between energy supply and other factors. But these politically reflected concerns do have a substantial basis, both as to safety and as to unnecessary and unacceptable environmental consequences. Only if we deal with these factors can nuclear fission play the role I believe it must play in our total energy picture by 1985.

On safety, a real uncertainty now exists concerning possible accidents which could have disastrous consequences—especially the failure of liquid cooling systems resulting in a meltdown of the highly radioactive core and release of the gaseous fraction of these radioactive products into the atmosphere. A year of hearings by the AEC has not persuaded the critics that current reactor plans are safe against such accidents, and the problem exists as well in the liquid-metal-cooled breeder reactor designs.

As I see it, the only way to meet these objections and so resolve the current impasse is to put all new plants underground. This is an entirely practicable course of action. Studies indicate that placing nuclear power plants underground would add only a small fraction to their cost. The extensive know-how of the mining industry plus that of the underground gas storage industry could be applied in placing such plants in suitable geological formations 500 or more feet underground near load centers. So located, with suitable locks in the elevator shafts to contain and hold back any pressure of radioactive gas in the event of an accident or a meltdown, these plants could meet the requirements for nuclear safety. Placed in a suitably impermeable geological formation, a meltdown, even if it buried itself below the underground chamber level, would not leak radioactive products into underground water or into the atmosphere.

The second big nuclear production problem today is primarily environmental; it concerns the effects of the water discharge from large reactors in heating up streams and larger bodies of water, thus altering the ecology in many harmful ways. Here Europe has pointed the way to the answer—large cooling towers, built on the surface to recycle and cool the hot water discharges with very low net water heating.

Finally, there are problems in the safety and security of handling and transporting plutonium, and in the perpetual storage of radioactive wastes. In these areas, risks cannot be totally eliminated, but they can and should be sharply reduced to an acceptable level by determined action—as we enter an era of massive production, transport and handling of plutonium, which is one of the most toxic substances known.

All in all, the measures required to permit expansion of nuclear-fission plants will not be cheap or easy. But if the necessary steps are taken, nuclear-fission plants should be able to provide roughly ten percent of our total 1985 energy needs at tolerable levels of risk and bearable costs. And experience in this next decade should tell us much about the degree to which we can hope to expand, by the end of the century, our use of nuclear fission, especially through the breeder reactor; in the 1985 time frame, the breeder is not likely to make a significant contribution.

If roughly ten percent is the best we can hope to get from nuclear sources by 1985—the figure used in our original Table I —it follows that there remains a very large shortfall from the proposed reduction in overall oil use. Even if we now assume that total consumption would be less than assumed in Table I, the proportion to be made up is on the order of 15 percent. Indeed, on my own best guess about the amount of domestic natural gas we shall be able to find by 1985, I should think that natural gas (even with some imports) should not be counted on for more than 15 percent of the total, and perhaps as little as ten percent; perhaps new gas reserves will be found on a large scale, but at the moment much expert opinion doubts this. We would do well to plan prudently on a figure not exceeding ten percent, or a total shortfall of roughly 25 percent of the total to be made up from sources other than oil or gas.

Inevitably, we are drawn to coal—and to greatly expanded coal production and gasification as the third central element in an action program. To whatever extent possible, coal as a solid fuel should be expanded in its own right, especially in electric power plants—using processes to remove the sulfur from stack gas such as the Japanese now employ. But for every reason —adaptability, transportability and environmental consequences —gas from coal is particularly important.

Available options for processing coal include conversion to low-BTU gas, high-BTU pipeline-quality gas, oil or various combinations. Technical, economic and time criteria should guide the choices made. But the great advantages of pipeline-quality gas for most uses justify major emphasis on this choice. A massive crash program is needed to move present process options forward. Current estimates indicate that the cost of capital investment in new gasification plants should be on the order of $20,000 per ton of daily coal feed to process coal into pipeline-quality gas.

Any program to increase coal mining must face up fully to the problem of environmental impact. The necessary coal must come overwhelmingly from surface mines, predominantly west of the Mississippi. In the past, such strip mining has rightly acquired a bad reputation. Fortunately, a large part of the coal reserves in the West are located on public lands. Therefore, the federal government is in a position to set the conditions for mining operations. I believe it essential that such conditions include provision for restoring the land after the coal is extracted, putting solid waste from the mining process back underground and creating a land surface that must be at least as stable, fertile and valuable as the original. An allowance of $2,000 per acre for such purposes may be a fair approximation of what it would take, and this cost would have to be considered a basic cost of production. Underground mines must control pollution and use several practices which might increase costs up to a dollar per ton. Similarly, coal gasification plants can and must incorporate controls to avoid air and water pollution. Altogether, while the mere existence of the plants means that the countryside can never be quite the same in the future, the problem of environmental impact can at least be reduced to bearable proportions in view of the stakes involved.

Building up our reliance on coal would involve capital costs for mining production as well as for the gasification plants. In 1970 U.S. coal production was about 500 million tons and accounted for roughly 20 percent of our energy needs. To meet 50 percent of total energy needs in 1985 (at the three percent intervening growth rate) would require a production level of two billion tons per year—a quadrupling of the 1970 level and an average growth rate for the next 12 years of 12 percent per year. Investment needed to produce this basic production increase can be roughly estimated at $10 per ton, or $15 billion. If two-thirds of the increase, or one billion tons, went to gasification, the plant investment would be approximately $60 billion, and there would be a major additional investment in gas pipelines. Finally, for the one-third of increased coal output burned directly in power plants (to replace present oil and natural gas supplies), a substantial railway transport investment would be required, as well as costs of conversion to coal where feasible, and desulfurization of stack gases.

Obviously, such a buildup of coal production and coal gasification is a truly major undertaking, difficult from a technical standpoint and costly and complicated in terms of the mix of private and public effort involved. It is a big job, but no bigger than the Manhattan or Apollo projects—in fact substantially less in proportion to the scale of the American economy in the 1970s and 1980s.

One crucial question remains—the adequacy of reserves. Before embarking on a course designed to make coal our principal source of energy by 1985 and thereafter, we need to assess the scale of our coal reserves and how long they might last. While I have stated my proposal purely in terms of 1985, it is obvious that we would not wish to mount an effort on this scale and then change course quickly thereafter; on the contrary, it is my own belief that we should plan tentatively at this stage to meet not just 50 percent but as much as 75 percent of our energy needs from coal by the year 2000. It is now forecast that natural gas reserves will be gone before 2000 and that global oil reserves will be declining fast (even with less U.S. consumption than now forecast). Thus, coal and nuclear power *could* be our overwhelming energy sources by that time, with coal by then being converted on a large scale to oil for transportation needs. Oil from shale might also have become a substantial source; present reserves of oil shale are such that we could produce five million barrels of oil a day for more than 300 years before such reserves were exhausted. We need not be quite this futuristic for concrete planning—but we do need to assess reserves on the basis of large assumptions, to be sure of what we are doing in the 1985 time frame.

Happily, the coal reserve picture is reassuring even if all this comes true. The current Bureau of Mines estimate (1970) of U.S. coal reserves is 1,600 billion tons. If coal use now moves up steadily to 50 percent of total energy by 1985 and to 75 percent by 2000 (again allowing for a small but steady annual increase in energy use), then total consumption in the entire period from 1974 to 2000 would be on the order of 70 billion tons, or four and one-half percent of known reserves. Exhaustion of reserves would be roughly 100 years away in 2000, even if the use continued to increase at a steady rate.[3]

In sum, coal reserves are ample to meet the projected needs through the balance of this century and to leave us with supplies to last another century. Through the use of coal on this scale, coupled with the restriction of oil supplies to transportation uses and the regaining of our momentum on nuclear power, we could meet the strategic goals stated at the outset: minimal dependence on overseas supplies and reasonable rises in energy costs—to

[3] The actual calculation here is that 17 billion tons of coal would be consumed between now and 1985 and 50 billion in the next 15 years. The latter figure assumes that growth in total energy needs (in terms of BTU content of fuels) would have been reduced to two percent per year, versus the three percent target of the Decade Program and the present 4.5 percent.

levels not over two or three times present rates. This is the best
action program now available. It would get us through this
period and buy crucial time for whatever innovations may develop, while allowing us to continue with expanded coal use if
such innovations do not appear on a large scale.

IV

I have outlined this "Decade Program" first in order to define
the key elements in our effort between now and 1985. These key
elements are essential, they take time to bring about, and we must
get started on them at once.

But as we do so we must also reckon that the required changes
cannot be brought about immediately. The program needs at
least the whole decade to take full effect, and in the meantime—
even if we have cut our energy growth rate to three percent—
we face extraordinarily serious problems. Hence, in addition to
our Decade Program, we must have what might bé called an
"Emergency Program." This would dovetail as well as possible
with the Decade Program but inevitably would not be wholly
consistent with it.

Oil remains the crux of our present problem. The standstill
on new refinery construction, partly for environmental and related political reasons and partly because of unattractive return
on investment, may compel some rationing of gasoline this summer and of fuel oil next winter. And even if new refinery capacity existed today, an adequate supply of crude oil from abroad
could not now be landed without at least one new "superport"
and also large-scale new tanker construction. As for domestic oil
development, the Alaska pipeline is still in abeyance, and offshore exploration is inhibited by state opposition and disputes
with the federal government about royalties. Also significant is
the public belief that all offshore operations are as disastrous
as the Santa Barbara episode (which disregards the large-scale
operations conducted in the Gulf of Mexico and the North Sea
for years without major accidents).

The fact is that we cannot avoid a continuing increase, for
some years to come, in our imports of oil—especially from the
Middle East. In 1973 we shall be importing 3.4 million barrels
a day from the Middle East and North Africa, and two million
from Latin America. These figures are bound to rise—for some
years well above the Decade Program goal of only five million

barrels a day of imports by 1985.

Finally, there is a basic policy question that must be faced—whether in common prudence the United States should now have a strategic reserve of crude oil or refined products to protect against interruptions. Crude stocks are currently below 20 days and refined products in the form of working inventories in the distribution system are less than 40 days—essentially minimum working levels with no strategic reserve. Such a reserve is something individual Americans have quietly urged on Europe for years, and in 1968 the members of the European Community accepted the obligation to build up oil stocks equivalent to 65 days' use. Now it has been proposed that this reserve be raised to 90 days. In the case of the United States, the targets need not be defined in terms of such periods of total oil use, but as our imports increase we should at least have a strategic reserve equal to perhaps 90 days of our imports, to cushion the shock of any interruption for political or bargaining reasons. To urge this does not indicate the slightest degree of hostility to the supplying countries; it is what businessmen all over the world prudently do in order to negotiate on a relatively even keel with suppliers.

Solving all of these emergency problems will take both resources and ingenuity. In the case of refineries, I believe inland sites must be found, and new refineries must adopt available technology which produces virtually no air or water pollution. Such refineries exist in Europe; they can be matched here, and not at excessive cost. Similarly, superports must be built with expensive safeguards—their cost would be perhaps as high as $1.5 billion to unload ten million barrels a day, with additional pipeline costs to bring the oil to inland refineries, and conceivably an investment of $15 billion for tankers adequate to haul the ten million barrels a day from the Persian Gulf. It is a daunting prospect—and underscores the vital importance of preventing our maximum import dependence from going beyond roughly the ten million figure at any time, and the importance of reducing dependence as soon as possible to our target ceiling of five million barrels. The painful fact is that some part of total refinery capacity, and as much as half of the planned superport capacity, will become obsolete or surplus as we carry out the shift to coal and the reduction in the proportion of our energy needs supplied by oil imports.[4] When a problem has been neglected as long as we

---

[4] It seems likely that substantial strategic reserves of crude and refined products may still be important to protect against the effects of important interruptions.

have ignored or misjudged the energy situation, the short-term requirements may not mesh with the requirements for the medium and longer term—and so it is in this case. We have to fix the roof and build a new house at the same time.

V

In short, it will take a two-fold crash program to master the situation, part directed to a transformation in our energy pattern by 1985, part directed to getting along in the meantime. The dual task involves a series of massive new efforts, some of them within the capacity of private companies, some beyond that capacity, some which will be so clearly uneconomical that private companies would be reluctant or unable to undertake them with their own funds. No one can now say just what the mix of public and private effort will be—but what seems absolutely clear is that a much larger public role will be required than now exists, partly to pull together all the strands of both parts of the program, partly to support private effort, partly to undertake those aspects that cannot be handled by private companies.

I see no alternative to new government machinery at the federal level. Accordingly, I propose a National Energy Authority (NEA) with a ten-year life and with appropriate powers to deal with the national emergency. This will mean authority to override obstacles in regard to land acquisition, siting, environmental impact, and óther areas as necessary to carry out the program. This should not relieve the NEA of a very serious obligation to make environmental assessments of its proposed projects and to hold public hearings to develop the best available means to minimize the environmental consequences and risks of the actions it takes, but it would authorize the NEA to proceed with its program and not be stopped by the obstacles which stall so many things today.

Under the NEA it would be essential to create a National Energy Finance Corporation (NEFC) to provide funds for parts of the program which may not be privately financeable, including the superport, a billion-barrel strategic stock and its storage facility, sites for refineries, offshore production units, tankers, coal gasification plants, and gas, oil and coal pipelines. Large amounts of capital are going to be needed. An important obstacle today is that some of these essential investments are not attractive to private capital. In designing the NEA and the

NEFC we have many examples such as the TVA and the New York Port Authority, the Reconstruction Finance Corporation and the Export-Import Bank. There are ample precedents for the kinds of authority needed and the appropriate legislation, controls and accountability.

The NEA should be an independent agency, perhaps modelled on the original Atomic Energy Commission, in any event as resistant to political pressures as that Commission was. I propose that NEA have a ten-year life and go out of existence in 1985 except for the NEFC, which is likely to be needed beyond that time. There are several reasons for this proposal. First, the exercise of emergency powers is anomalous in our system and should be limited to as short a time as required to overcome the emergency. I believe the job will take a full ten years, but can be done in ten years if the program is geared to such a timetable. Second, when the job is done most of the programs should be carried forward by industry on a commercial basis, and necessary continuing governmental functions can be transferred to other agencies. Third, the best period in the life of any agency is the first ten years. After that the sclerosis of bureaucracy sets in and we certainly do not need any more bureaucracies. No one should seek a career in NEA—only the excitement and satisfaction of doing a critically important job and finishing it. Meeting numerical targets and being measured on performance in meeting them through frequent public reports is the kind of a challenge which should attract the kinds of people needed.

The NEA will have to undertake extensive research and development and pilot plant and demonstration operations. It should, for example, underwrite the incremental costs and use its authority to clear the way for the first two or three nuclear power plants which are built underground. It should back the construction of several demonstration units of large offshore oil production operations incorporating the maximum safeguards in technology and procedures and should use these for public education and to provide a model for the industry. NEA can work out with the AEC appropriate joint activities in regard to the underground power plants, waste disposal, plutonium shipment handling and so on.

In addition, in the Program for the Decade and beyond, conservation should be an important component; this might include the creation of a national fuel efficiency service to effect economies in the use of fuels. Currently, there is an almost complete absence of professional interest, activity, or expertise in this subject—whether in universities, engineering firms, business enterprises or the government. A major task of NEA would be to stimulate such expertise and put it to work. As a result of coping with limited fuel supplies during the next few years, we may discover economies which are not only relatively painless but which reveal to us better life-styles. Adopting such life-styles might substantially reduce per capita energy use.

In the Emergency Program of NEA, one of the first projects will be a superport. It may be sufficient for the NEA to exercise the authority to establish the superport and to supplement its financing. Clearly the NEA must work in close collaboration with the oil industry in many of the things it does. It must be shown that gas and oil pipelines can come ashore on their way inland and leave no offensive trace of their transit across the coastline. A second project is to acquire inland sites for oil storage and refineries. It should be noted that even packed closely together a billion barrels of oil storage would take 10,000 acres, or 15 square miles. Inland sites will save our finite coastline for better public uses. Another major project is the question of supplementary finance for tankers—at a time when world shipyards are solidly booked.

The NEFC will have much to do. To repeat, one problem in the financing of facilities such as the superport, tankers and perhaps the refineries is that at the end of the Decade imports are to be brought down again to only five million barrels per day. Thus, the success of the Decade Program may mean a fairly early obsolescence for part of the capacity of the superports and tankers—hence one key need for significant public financing.

VI

In laying out this proposed program, I have indicated some specific steps to minimize its consequences for the physical environment. In some areas we should be better off in the new 1985 situation: our cars should be smaller and have reduced volumes of emissions; most fossil-fueled electric power plants would be taking sulfur out of the stack gases or burning clean non-polluting gas; new nuclear power plants would be safely underground and out of sight save for their enormous cooling towers; most important, a declining rate of energy expansion would make a great difference to the environment all across the board, at least as compared to what we are headed for at our current rate of expansion. This would represent a sensible modification of our past craze for growth, and the environment would be the gainer in some respects.

But not in others. Up to now we have behaved as if we had the luxury to have the best of both worlds. We have not made the tough choices. Now the energy emergency makes us choose, and the choices are few. Some environmental prices must be paid: one or more oil superports off the East coast, and added refineries (however pure) inland; the Alaska pipeline with residual risks that even the safest design and procedures cannot avoid; much increased offshore oil development, and much increased coal mining largely from surface sources—which even with the best possible measures would tend for a time to deface the particular area. I do not minimize these costs, but feel them keenly as one who has been active for several years in the scientific effort in support of national and international environment measures. In each case, the trade-off has been weighed, and it seems to me that the gain outweighs the loss.

VII

What I have proposed is a national program for the United States, calculated on the basis of particular American resources and American needs. One of its major purposes is, of course, an international one, to shorten the duration of the costs, pain and strain—and of the dangers to world harmony and peace—that lie in a situation of growing American dependence on external energy sources, especially Middle East oil. But it is primarily the United States that would be hitching up its belt and putting its energy house in order, by measures that do not in themselves harm any other nation.

Is the program, however, not only national but nationalistic? Would it affect the world energy picture indirectly to the disadvantage of others, whether suppliers or consumers? Does it mean an increase in American autarky, fortifying the tendency other countries now see for the United States to take care of its own needs and let the rest of the world go hang?

The answer to all these questions is a resounding "No." This is most obvious if we look at the relations between the United States and the other major industrialized countries, which are also the major consumers of energy. As things now stand, Western Europe and Japan are inescapably dependent, far more than the United States and far longer into both past and future, on imported oil and gas; if the United States becomes a vastly increased buyer of both, the effect can only be, at best, friction, and, at worst, price wars and preëmptive deals that would cut at the very roots of coöperation between the United States, Europe and Japan. This danger is indeed already visible, and it will take a good deal of statesmanship to avoid it as things stand now; by 1980 or 1985, on present trends, the seeds of strife could be beyond control.

Yet Japan and most of Europe have no alternative comparable to what coal can be for America. Only the United Kingdom, among the major European countries, can meet a significant part of its needs from coal and from North Sea natural gas—and the latter only at the expense of its neighbors' expectations.

Hence these countries should welcome a determined American effort to reduce dependence on the oil sources that are a "must" for them. And the same should hold true for the oil-consuming developing countries, now being badly hurt by the price rises of Middle East oil.

But does this mean that the oil-producing countries would be hurt? I think not. If Mr. Akins and others are correct, the 1980 prospect already assumes that at least two key countries (Saudi Arabia and Iran) will produce more oil, and tap a higher proportion of their predicted reserves, than they may like.[5] To prolong the life of these reserves and to space out the income of the producers can mean a net benefit to most of the producing countries. Their prices will rise in any event in the years to come, but the present prospect of runaway increases in production cannot be attractive compared to a more orderly expansion that prolongs their assets.

Indeed, I would go one step further. I believe that an American program such as I have described could be an essential ingredient in a new approach to the energy situation by the whole international community. On any rational look at the production and consumption of energy all over the world, the United States represents not only a statistical discrepancy and target for the role of villain (six percent consuming 33 percent, and getting greater), but a potential disruptive force in almost every market

[5] Akins, *loc. cit.*, p. 480.

day by day; only if this is brought under control can the United States play any responsible role in the effort that may have to be undertaken within the next decade, or at least by the end of the century—to balance and distribute world energy supplies much more fairly and reasonably than nature or men have ever done to date. For unless we do this there is scant hope for human progress and peace in the long run.

Thus, I propose a program based in the first instance on American national interest. But I deeply believe that this program could make a vast difference to international relations in the next 10 to 20 years, and serve as a step toward a more rational world use of energy for the benefit of man.

THE OIL STORY:
FACTS, FICTION AND FAIR PLAY

By Jahangir Amuzegar

THE multitude of articles, news reports and commentaries on the energy "crisis" in recent months have been chiefly concerned with four basic issues: (1) a growing (and by implication, a worrisome) oil "shortage" in the United States and the industrial world; (2) an intimate (and by implication, an unholy) alliance between the major oil companies and the Organization of Oil Exporting Countries (OPEC) at the expense of the consuming public; (3) an increasing (and by implication, an undesirable) redistribution of oil revenues through higher oil prices in favor of producing countries, giving them significant (and by implication, excessive) controls over future oil supply and foreign exchange reserves; and (4) a need for concerted action (and by implication, "drastic measures") on the part of the oil-short countries vis-à-vis the "oil cartel."

An obsessive preoccupation with the superficial and adversary aspects of these issues has in turn given rise to some unfortunate misunderstandings regarding the real problems facing both oil producers and oil consumers in the next decades. The need for a more balanced assessment of these problems, and for a constructive world view of the situation, has never been so compelling.

II

The genesis of the present energy "crisis" is no mystery. Oil is being depleted much faster than other sources of energy, and its price has been on the rise. Oil suppliers, however, are not the *cause* of the oil "shortage." Rising oil prices are symptomatic of an expected imbalance between potential sources and uses of oil. And the oil demand and supply arithmetic within the whole energy picture is very simple. In the last three decades the world has used up more energy than in all previous history. In the next 15 years mankind is expected to use up as much energy as it has up to now. On reasonable present predictions, more than 70 percent of this energy need will have to be met by hydrocarbons, i.e. 16 percent by gas, 54 by oil. Yet despite such unprecedented demands, the supply of natural gas and crude oil has failed to keep pace because production incentives have been weak and inadequate—reflecting in part a deliberate and deceitfully plausible policy by the industrial world to keep premium energy prices below their true costs.

Between 1945 and 1960 the non-Communist world energy demand expanded at the rate of 4 percent a year. During the 1960s the annual growth rate reached nearly 6 percent. On the basis of past trends the total energy demand may double between 1970 and 1985, reaching over 145 million barrels per day (b/d) of oil-equivalent. Total U.S. energy consumption is estimated to double from 33 million to 63 million b/d between 1970 and 1985. Consumption in the European Economic Community (EEC) in the same period is expected to rise by 93 percent; that of Japan by 156 percent.

To meet such enormous energy demands there are three alternatives: (1) to raise the supply of conventional sources (e.g. coal, crude oil, natural gas and hydroelectricity); (2) to look more seriously into further development of more expensive substitutes (e.g. oil shales, tar sands and nuclear power); or (3) to develop exotic energy potentials (e.g. geothermal, solar power, tidal waves and hydrogen fusion). An increase in the supply of coal and hydroelectricity is time-consuming, costly or replete with significant technical and environmental limitations.[1] Exotic potentials—now in experimental use for heating and power in some countries—are expected to remain marginal, at least for the rest of the twentieth century, because of enormous technological complexities and high costs.

The combined supply of the first two categories in 1985 is now estimated to amount to 20.3 million b/d (of oil-equivalent) for coal; 23.2 million b/d for gas; 14.5 million b/d for nuclear energy; 8.7 million b/d for hydroelectric power; 1.4 million b/d for oil shales and tar sands. The lion's share of the total energy market—54 percent or 78.3 million b/d—will have to be provided by crude oil.

Oil reserves are not evenly distributed among nations. Nor is the thirst for oil. More than 63 percent of total world proven petroleum reserves are located in OPEC territories—mostly in the Persian Gulf area. The rest is chiefly owned by the United States (about 6 percent) and the Socialist or "non-market" camp (about

[1] The share of coal in total non-Communist world energy supply is now expected to fall to 14 percent in 1985, from 22 in 1970, 60 in 1950. Gas and hydroelectricity are to remain relatively constant, at 16 and 6 percent respectively. Only nuclear power is to increase by tenfold, although still no more than 10 percent of the total by 1985.

15 percent).[2] On the demand side, the unevenness is equally striking. With six percent of the world population, the United States consumes almost one-third of all world energy and one-third of global oil consumption; it now produces about 11 million barrels of oil a day and consumes nearly 17 million b/d. The Common Market consumes 13 million b/d and produces only .5 million. Japan produces virtually no oil, but uses 4.6 million b/d. With an inadequate supply of indigenous hydrocarbons, the energy-hungry countries of the industrial world are, therefore, increasingly dependent upon oil imports—America 30 percent, the EEC 90 percent, and Japan almost totally.[3] Even the Soviet Union and China—so far self-sufficient in their energy requirements—may become oil importers by the close of this century.

III

The future imbalance between supply and demand for energy in general, and petroleum in particular, is indeed real and significant. But the present energy "crisis" is not a cataclysmic event. It has been in the making for years, and could have been predicted and dealt with long ago. What is novel in the energy picture is the public's awareness of the possibility of an oil-less world in the not too distant future. This, in turn, is caused by an about-face barrage of corporate advertising designed to sell the "crisis" instead of oil, and by the crucial role of oil imports ($4.6 billion in 1972) in U.S. overall trade deficits. To understand the embryonic origin of the present imbalance in the world petroleum market—chiefly, the U.S. oil "shortage"—one has to examine (a) the behavior of oil prices and profit distribution between 1946 and 1971, and (b) the gradual shift by industrial countries to oil and gas as a major source of fuel, with two unfortunate results: an accelerated depletion (and wasteful use) of premium hydrocarbon resources, and an inequitable distribution of world income.

First, a word on oil prices and profits. By a bounty of nature, the fossil fuel floating underneath the Middle East and North African sands and offshore waters is of such quality and ease of reach as to make extraction costs at the wellhead only a fraction of such costs in other parts of the world—10 cents a barrel on the average for the Middle East, compared with roughly 51

---

[2] The Oil and Gas Journal, December 25, 1972, pp. 82–83.
[3] By 1985 (or perhaps sooner), the U.S. need for oil imports is estimated to reach nearly 15 million b/d or more than 50 percent of consumption.

cents in Venezuela, 82 cents in Indonesia, $1.31 in the United States and 80 cents in the U.S.S.R. in recent years). Since oil of the same quality is bound to obtain uniform f.o.b. prices in the world free markets, Middle East and North African crudes have up to now offered their owners an enormous windfall profit—what economists call Ricardian rent—stemming from the difference in production costs compared with Mexican Gulf suppliers and other high-cost producers.

The postwar history of the oil industry is a story of a continued jockeying among petroleum exporters and the oil majors, to divide (and appropriate) this rent. In the heyday of the seven major international oil companies and the oil boom at the end of World War II, the rent was divided pretty unevenly between the oil-producing countries (18 percent) and the oil concessionaires (82 percent). The consuming countries reaped the competitive benefits of low-price oil in the form of a Marshallian "consumer surplus." The low oil prices also permitted the oil-importing countries to finance part of their infrastructures through import duties on fuel and stiff excise taxes on gasoline, thus siphoning off part of the "surplus." The practice still continues.[4]

The companies' oligopolistic grip on world oil production, refining, transportation and marketing was gradually loosened by several new developments: the entry of independent oil producers in the world market; emergence of the Soviet Union as an oil exporter; creation of national oil companies in the producing countries; and declining political influence of the oil majors on their own governments. With each crack in the oligopolistic structure, a notch was added to the producers' share. The establishment of OPEC in 1960 served as a final turning point in the long struggle by the producers to get their due share. Thus the 18/82 ratio per barrel of oil in 1948 became 32/68 in 1952; 50/50 in 1960; and 70/30 in 1970. Nevertheless, rising volume of production and exports (without much additional new investment required) gave the oil majors a ratio of income to their net Mideast assets of 55 percent in 1970. The ratio of crude oil income to net assets in crude oil production in the same year was nearly 100 percent.

[4] Excise taxes alone on retail gasoline by industrial countries in 1972 ranged from a low of 32 percent in the United States to a high of 78 percent in Italy, with Japan, France, Great Britain and West Germany in the 55 to 70 percent range. In all these cases, taxes charged by consumer governments have exceeded oil producers' share per barrel of oil by more than three and one-half times.

The gradual change in rent-sharing in favor of oil producers was only partly effective in taking from the Caesars that which was not theirs. As long as the oil concessionaires had the prerogative of determining the posted price of oil (i.e. the price on which royalties and taxes were based) the sharing formula was of only small benefit to the owners. The price of a barrel of crude oil (34° API), fixed by the companies at $2.17 in 1948, was gradually and unilaterally brought down by them to $1.80 in 1960 in order to capture European and Japanese markets. Right after its establishment, OPEC managed to put an end to unilateral price determination by the companies. But precipitous attempts on the part of most producers to increase their exports (partly to offset the effects of price reductions and partly for higher total revenues) resulted in further reducing effective oil prices by offers of 35 to 55 cent discounts per barrel below the posted price.[5]

The second aspect of the present energy "shortage" has to do with the excessive and inefficient use of oil. Without doubt, the rapid postwar exploitation of Mideast and North African oil resources and their export at bargain-basement prices to West Europe, America and Japan helped provide the basic underpinnings of fast economic growth and unprecedented material prosperity in the industrial world. But, in retrospect, the costs seem to have been devastatingly high. And therein lies the fallacy of cheap oil, and the paradox of prosperity in the midst of poverty.

The rich industrial countries favored the cheap oil policy because of a false sense of security, as if the world had an inexhaustible supply of energy—as though no end were in sight. By an economic myopia of incomprehensible dimensions, millions upon millions of energy-gobbling products—from impractically big and fast cars to profligately trivial household gadgets—were allowed to flood the market, only to be replaced soon by bigger, faster and more power-thirsty models. Awed by the marvels of high-energy technology and lulled by the borrowed affluence of unfettered growth, the West refused to believe that its immediate energy demands were on a collision course with long-term environmental considerations.

[5] To isolate itself from a deluge of "dirt-cheap" oil imports, the United States imposed restrictive quotas on Mideast oil in 1959, and American domestic prices soon rose to $3.50 per barrel on the average, giving quota-holders a new $1.25 to $1.50 a barrel "windfall" profit for access to the U.S. market. The quotas were removed in April 1973 and replaced by a "fee" still designed to protect domestic producers from foreign competition.

Cheap oil as a matter of national policy was thus responsible not only for a worldwide shortage of energy, but for some possibly irretrievable damage to the earth's ecology.[6] By keeping the Mideast oil price deliberately below its true scarcity value (in terms of production costs in other parts of the world, equivalents in other sources of energy, or replacement costs), the industrial world inadvertently perpetrated four hoaxes on itself and on its unborn generations. The artificially low price of oil (a) discouraged oil producers from searching effectively for new sources of supply; (b) helped hold down prices of substitutes (e.g. coal, gas and hydroelectricity), and likewise dampened their development prospects despite their huge reserves; (c) stifled and/or delayed research in the development of more efficient technology for the economical use of nonconventional energy sources; and above all, (d) contributed to an inexcusably reckless waste and inefficient use of world premium fuels. In the United States, for example, automobiles reportedly use only about 20 percent of the energy potential in gasoline, and 23 percent of their passenger capacity. Factories waste power by useless lighting and inadequate recycling. Residential and commercial buildings use 20 to 50 percent more heating and air conditioning than needed for comfortable but intelligent use. Electric generators use about three BTU's of fuel to produce one BTU of electricity.

In short, the post-World War II miracle of material prosperity and soaring consumption was achieved, partly at least, at the expense of colossal environmental degradation—air and water pollution, soil erosion, nuclear hazards, noise, congestion, junk piles and other material and nonmaterial disamenities brought down upon Spaceship Earth. In some countries the substitution of fuel-based energy for human energy caused serious and protracted unemployment. Backed up behind this facade of material affluence and progress are the intolerably high costs of cleaning and restoring the environment—accumulated costs which, if recognized in time and charged against beneficiaries, would probably have been less burdensome.

IV

If the postwar miracle of GNP growth in Western Europe, Japan and the United States had been achieved mainly through

[6] The same short-sighted policy has been followed in the United States with regard to natural gas, the price of which at the wellhead has been fixed by the Federal Power Commission at about one-third of its full scarcity value.

a foolishly fast depletion of their own energy sources, the trade-off might have looked less pointedly ironic. The staggering retribution which they must now pay to restore the earth's "finite, enclosed, life-support system" might have fit their self-inflicted sins both of omission and commission. But the irony of this economic miracle lies in the manner in which it was achieved —by subsidies from the oil-producing countries, mostly poor and struggling countries, at the expense of *their* limited irreplaceable assets.

Thanks partly to an uninterrupted supply of cheap oil—as low as $1.25 a barrel as late as 1970—the EEC countries and Japan raised their industrial production, boosted their exports, improved their balance of payments, saved their own solid fuel resources and amassed enormous foreign-exchange reserves. But now, not only does the affluent West feel no redeeming sympathy for such embarrassing enrichment at the expense of its unsuspecting and helpless partners; some Western politicians, economists and oil experts are self-righteously indignant about the prospect of having to pay the full scarcity value of imported oil through collective bargaining with OPEC.

OPEC was originally organized by Iran, Iraq, Kuwait, Saudi Arabia and Venezuela in 1960 as a countervailing force to try to resist unilateral action by the oil majors to reduce the posted price of oil, action that was intensified particularly during 1959–60. Later, OPEC was joined by Algeria, Indonesia, Libya, Nigeria, Qatar and the United Arab Emirates. But despite their heroic resolve to stabilize oil prices and to prevent further deterioration of their terms of trade with their rich partners, OPEC members fought in vain for ten long years. It was only under the 1971 Tehran agreement that the basic oil price was raised upward of its immediate postwar level.[7]

The news media accounts of OPEC negotiations since the 1971 Tehran agreement have been mostly concerned with price hikes and income boosts. Not surprisingly, little attention has been paid to four other and more positive features. First, the acceptance by the oil majors in February 1971 of a petroleum price policy based on "collective bargaining" instead of the previous practice of unilateral determination. Second, the introduction of an "escalator

[7] Even the $2.60 a barrel f.o.b. price of crude oil in the Persian Gulf in 1973, however, shows less than 20 percent increase over the 1947 price, while the index of manufactured imports by Mideast countries has risen by more than 50 percent.

clause" or parity adjustment in income calculations—similar to the ones for wages—based on general price-level increases in industrial countries. Third, the establishment in December 1971 of a "real" price for oil based on "stable dollars" and free from exchange fluctuations, putting oil on more or less the same parity with gold. And, fourth, the acceptance in March 1972 by the oil majors of the principle of local equity participation in oil-company assets and profits.

The main thrust of OPEC's struggle for recognition and representation of producers' interests has thus been to see to it that the price of crude oil like other energy prices reflects its true cost, and that the legitimate interests of the owners are protected. This is neither an unreasonable goal nor necessarily a purely self-serving one. This is the way all prices should be set. This is what the environmentalists are asking for. This is what President Nixon has recommended in his recent energy message to Congress. If it looks like a sheep in wolf's clothing now, it is a blessing in disguise for the long-term interests of all mankind.[8]

V

Now, a word on OPEC's rise and its future. There has been ill-concealed apprehension over OPEC's "victories" and their effect on future oil supply and world monetary reserves. Dark hints are made about the possibility of a *"défi Arab"*—an Arab challenge—to the Western corporate structure and international monetary order. Suggestions for remedies have ranged all the way from the innocuous gesture of coöperation among importing countries to the preposterous notion of "a planned takeover of the oil lands." Among other proposals along this competition-confrontation spectrum there has been persistent demand for breaking up OPEC, and putting the "genie" back in the bottle.

The proposal to break up OPEC and remove the oil companies from crude oil marketing (so as to increase competition among oil producers) is, to be sure, incredibly naïve. Apart from the insurmountable political and technical difficulties of such a "mission impossible" (who is going to put the bell around the cat's neck?) the practical effects on reducing future oil prices

---

[8] Recent studies show that supply and demand for energy are significantly price-elastic. Market forces, through scarcity-value pricing, can thus be mobilized in favor of energy conservation instead of its historical plunder. By the same token, it can be shown that a rise in the price of oil and gas may in fact result in a *reduction* of BTU cost, not only through more efficient use but through the development of substitutes.

are far from certain. OPEC is what OPEC does. If it has any strength—and the critics believe it has too much—the reasons must be sought in the awareness, wisdom and determination of its members. It is indeed amusingly paradoxical that the organization itself is often credited by its critics with so much clout in setting oil prices, imposing participation conditions, putting political pressure on uncoöperative nations, and even denying Western access to its resources. Yet its individual member-governments are expected to act impetuously and irrationally in cutting their own throats and those of their former allies after OPEC's fall. Not only do OPEC leaders fully realize the futility of such actions now; even in their sophomore years at Harvard and Cornell they knew that no producer of an irreplaceable and vital commodity (who can sell all he can prudently produce at the going or higher prices) is ever going to lower his price no matter how competitively he may be expected to act.

Oil is just such a commodity in the present energy situation. Even an elementary oligopoly matrix, portraying the behavior of a few rival sellers, suffices to show that for prices to follow an upward trend no formal collusion or concerted action is essential: every smart seller, mindful of the reactions of his rivals, will find it ultimately suicidal to undercut them. Not to grant OPEC leaders this much instinctive sagacity would be the height of incredulity, if not the dawn of prejudice.

Another serious proposal for dealing with the energy "crisis" is confrontation: the formation of an organization of oil importing countries within the Organization for Economic Coöperation and Development or elsewhere to give backbone to the oil companies in any confrontation with OPEC, or to intervene directly in oil price negotiations. Whatever swashbuckling merits this type of confrontation may have, it looks both impractical and counterproductive. Impractical because, as is commonly recognized, the vital national interests of the oil-importing countries (particularly Japan, the EEC and the United States) do not always coincide; and they certainly do not tally with the interests of the oil companies. Japan, in particular, has been lukewarm toward this idea from the beginning. And EXXON officials have gone on record opposing the proposal on grounds of inflexibility, excessive bureaucratization, and undue interference by consuming governments in their business affairs. As *The Wall Street Journal* has put it, "the threat not to buy oil is totally incredible, while the threat not to sell it is only mildly incredible."

But even if such a united front could in fact be established and made effective, the results might aggravate the problem rather than solve it. As is well recognized by oil-industry leaders, the hostile atmosphere that ensues from such confrontations is bound to stiffen each party's position and lead to compulsive actions and reactions that may jeopardize the possibility of rational compromise and mutual accommodation. Some OPEC-member officials have made it clear that they regard an oil-consumer bloc designed as a cartel for purposes of confrontation as an "unhealthy and abrasive" development which is "never in the interests of the consumers."

Confrontation also seems undesirable because in the last analysis it is bound to be counterproductive. It can, at best, reintroduce past injustices (and inefficient use of oil) by denying oil exporters a fair price for their fast-dwindling assets. And, at worst, it can trigger needless interruptions of supply or export restrictions which would be in no one's interest.

There is, however, a third and more statesmanlike approach—closer international coöperation among oil-short and oil-surplus countries both in the intercountry allocation of available supply at reasonable prices, and in a joint endeavor for the development of other, cheaper sources of energy. The exact form of such coöperation is naturally subject to detailed and obviously difficult negotiations. A variant, frequently mentioned in America, is an international oil agreement—modeled after some of the more successful postwar commodity schemes—under which sovereign rights, economic interest and managerial prerogatives of the exporting countries are amply protected in return for an assurance of secure supplies at reasonable prices for the importers.

No matter what specific form and shape such international coöperation may take, however, its ultimate success will depend on the acceptance by the oil-importing nations of two unavoidable realities—unpleasant and unprecedented as they may appear. First, oil-short countries must realize that the era of cheap energy is past, and that they must be prepared to pay the true cost of their daily amenities powered by oil. Oil is relatively clean, easy to handle and still a comparatively cheap source of energy. For some uses, such as vehicular transportation, it is as yet unmatched. As a lubricant, it can perhaps never be totally replaced. It thus demands a price commensurate with its inherent qualities as compared with its substitutes.

The fact that some of the oil-exporting countries are small, sparsely populated, with no need for rising incomes, is legally absurd and morally baseless. "From each according to his need, to each according to his ability" is fortunately not yet a distributive criterion among civilized nations. The majority of OPEC countries are underdeveloped by Western norms. For almost all of them, petroleum is the mainstay of the economy. But oil is an exhaustible resource. Proven world reserves probably will last no more than a few decades at the present rate of exploitation. The OPEC members know that when oil is gone, the companies will be gone too. They are trying now to diversify their economies. They want to secure a decent standard of living for their unborn (and oil-less) generations—generations that shall, hopefully, be of little or no economic burden to other countries. Oil-producing countries are determined to develop their economies, not through foreign aid, not through concessionary loans, not by force, but through an improvement in the terms of trade with their rich partners—through full-cost pricing of their precious assets. They can hardly be denied this.

The second imperative for the success of mutual coöperation has to do with the provision of practical and profitable uses for the oil exporters' surplus investable funds. Much ado has been made of late about certain exponential (and by inference, alarming) projections of future "Arab wealth," and the Croesus-like flow of dollars to the Middle East in the years to come. Depending chiefly on world demand for imported oil during the next decade and a half, price increases per barrel of oil beyond 1975 (the termination of the Tehran agreement), and production policies followed by individual Mideast countries, OPEC's income in 1980 has been estimated at anywhere between $40 and $80 billion, with a cumulative total of some $250 to $360 billion. A third of these amounts is presumed to be saved by the recipients and added to world "excess" liquidity.

While the exaggerated and alarmist nature of these projections is acknowledged by some of the soothsayers themselves, there is no doubt that OPEC members are going to receive increasing amounts of foreign exchange for the sale of their oil assets, and part of the proceeds from these sales is going to be saved. But, for many reasons, this should be considered a welcome development instead of a disaster.

The OPEC members fall into three categories: (a) those who are net debtors and are expected to remain so, at least for the next decade, because their rising oil revenues will still fall short of their capital needs for domestic economic development; (b) those who may be net creditors now and in the future, but whose annual oil production is expected to remain at about the present level, and whose future annual receipts will not increase except for possibly higher oil prices and inflation; and (c) those whose production and incomes are destined to rise, but whose domestic investment opportunities are not likely to absorb their total foreign exchange revenues. In the first category are such producers as Iran, Nigeria, Venezuela, Indonesia, Algeria and Iraq. The second category includes Kuwait and Libya (although the latter may fit partly into the first category as well). Only Saudi Arabia, the United Arab Emirates and Qatar fall into the third group.

Incidentally, as this summary shows, more than one-third of the OPEC members (including Iran as one of its two top producers) are non-Arab. So is nearly 45 percent of OPEC's crude oil production, and almost 25 percent of its total reserves. To treat OPEC itself as an "Arab group," or to identify the revenues of its members as "Arab wealth," is thus incorrect.

The countries in the third category above, plus Kuwait and Libya, may be the ones whose revenues transcend domestic needs. Their combined annual revenues by 1980, in my judgment, might be in the range of $25–30 billion, rather than the higher figures now being estimated in some quarters.[9] Better than half of these projected revenues will probably be spent internally by the recipients, with only the rest available for investment.

Now even a $10 to $15 billion surplus by 1980 (with an accumulation of, say, $50 to $75 billion by that time) may still seem like a lot of money available for speculation. But the caveats are numerous. If the possibilities of "drastic measures" should still loom on the horizon, or if profitable joint ventures should not be found, surplus nations would in all probability rather cut production than increase devaluation-prone reserves to be kept in

[9] My projections are based on the assumption of a 12 million b/d production for Saudi Arabia, three million b/d each for Kuwait and the Emirates, and two million b/d each for Qatar and Libya at the price scales laid down by the 1971 Tehran Agreement. These "middle-of-the-road" projections are clearly below those of James E. Akins (*Foreign Affairs*, April 1973, p. 480); he himself has pointed out that his demand estimates might not be met from the Middle East.

foreign banks, subject to possible blockades. The Parkinson Law regarding revenues and expenditures works just as effectively in the Middle East as elsewhere. And, above all, whatever future surpluses may happen to be, they would look paltry in the context of (a) desperately needed development in the Arab world, (b) investment requirements in other developing sister countries, and (c) joint ventures with industrial nations.

To be sure, for every inhabitant of the "oil-rich" Arab countries there are eight Arabs living in other, oil-less, and relatively poor countries of the Middle East and in North Africa. Their annual per capita incomes range between about $80 (for the Arab Republic of Yemen) and $250 (for Tunisia); only Lebanon can claim as much as $600. For every dollar of increased per capita income in these relatively underdeveloped Arab lands, there is a need for three or four dollars of fixed capital investment. Thus even a modest increase of only $100 a year in income for the 90 million or so oil-less Arabs would require an investment of some $30 billion. And when the opportunities for investment in the West are contemplated, even the wildest estimates of Arab wealth would look quite modest. A "middle-of-the-road guess" regarding capital costs of meeting U.S.-projected energy requirements by 1985 is put at $500 billion. A similar sum may be required for the rest of the world. Why can Arab oil revenues not be attracted into such investment opportunities? And herein lies the importance of mutual coöperation in finding practical and businesslike outlets for future Arab reserves.

For obvious political reasons the West may not wish to see Arab money take a majority interest in General Motors or CBS or Imperial Chemical or Volkswagen. But why should it be difficult to designate industries, activities and degrees of control to which Mideast funds can be invited? The real catch is not the size of future Arab reserves, but how to use them peaceably, prudently and profitably. The West's real worries should not be about the principle of true-cost-pricing of oil, but the security of supply. And here, any workable coöperation between surplus and deficit countries should see to it that the flow of oil to the West not be interrupted under normal conditions, and that adequate provision be made for such an uninterrupted flow in all eventualities.

VI

The real issues in the present energy "crisis" are, therefore, not the ones sensationally publicized. First, oil "shortages" in the United States (and depleted world oil reserves) are not caused by Mideast Midases or their "tax-collecting agents," but by a deliberate (and only in retrospect a short-sighted) Western policy aimed at prolonging the ephemeral luxury of cheap oil. The Middle East cannot be expected to meet the entire world's energy demand; nor can it be expected to subsidize industrialized countries indefinitely. It can only coöperate with other nations toward a more permanent solution. Second, consumers have not been victimized by a collusion between oil producers and oil companies, but mainly tax-whipped by their own governments and partly self-deluded into believing there is no end to nature's patience and generosity. Third, leaving the Cassandras, nervous-Nellies and ax-grinders aside, the prospect of OPEC's affluence should be regarded by everyone as a fortunate and desirable development for its members and the world as a whole rather than an object of Western damnation. And fourth, any attempt to hold down OPEC's oil revenues by "drastic measures" may not only result in fruitless and even dangerous reprisals and counter-reprisals, but would indeed be self-defeating.

Potential coöperation between oil-importing and oil-producing nations should thus be regarded as a triumph of reason and decency and fair play over shortsightedness and greed and prejudice. No measure of saber-rattling and name-calling on either side can obscure the common interests of the oil-producing nations and the consuming public in maintaining a stable and abundant supply of oil at reasonable prices. Up to now, Mideast costs and supply have determined world oil prices as well as prices of other energy sources. In the future, U.S. demand and other energy costs will set the pace in world oil prices. And in this lies the possibility of a rational solution to the world energy "crisis."

THE WAR AND THE FUTURE
OF THE ARAB-ISRAELI CONFLICT

By Nadav Safran

THE 1973 War has had an enormous impact on all the complex of factors that enter into the Arab-Israeli conflict. The study of these changes will take many years and many hands. In this article, an attempt is made to examine that impact in several areas that seem to have a particular bearing on the immediate future.

The war has brought into full view what some specialists had long been pointing out: that the Arab-Israeli conflict is actually a complex network of which Arab-Israeli relations (so far, alas, mainly military) have only been one segment. Feeding into this network, in addition, have been the changing pattern of antagonism and association that makes up inter-Arab relations, the fluctuating rivalries among the big powers with interests in the area, and many features of the internal life of the antagonistic countries. This essay will touch upon each of the preceding dimensions of the conflict.

II

The military dimension of the 1973 War provides ample material for study and reflection at all levels—from tactics to strategy and from grand strategy all the way to the level where war merges into policy. Among the lessons, the following seem to stand out:

First, the Arabs were able to achieve virtually complete surprise for their initial thrust, and this in turn had crucial consequences. It gave them the initiative for a while, dictated to the Israelis the kind of war to be fought at least at several stages, caused the war to be costly and prolonged, made outside intervention necessary and possible, and in all these ways and others determined the general outcome of the war. It has already been pointed out that the failure of Israeli and American intelligence was due not to any dearth of information about the Arabs' war preparations, but to an incorrect evaluation of that information. Israeli analysts started from the premise that Sadat was convinced that Israel enjoyed a great margin of military superiority over any military coalition he could form; consequently, they could only view the vast ostensible war preparations as an attempt to bluff Israel and the United States, and/or to force Israel into going through the psychological strain, trouble and cost of mobilization as a means of pressure on it. Such a conclusion appeared all the more plausible since Egypt and Syria had gone through similar military motions several times in the past. However, had the analysts started from a different—a political—premise, they might well have reached different conclusions. They might then have seen that, given the predicament in which Sadat found himself, any war short of one that was certain to end in quick and total disaster would be preferable to staying still. This observation may sound like wisdom after the fact, but at least one observer proceeding in the latter way had publicly anticipated the probability of war. At any rate, the point of the observation is that the faulty evaluation may well have had a structural rather than an accidental basis—the absence of appropriate or sufficient representation of political analysts in the intelligence-evaluation apparatus concerned.

Next to the general surprise at the fact that the Arabs chose to go to war when they did, people profess to be most surprised by the quality of the Arabs' performance. Conclusions have been drawn to the effect that, in the brief lapse of time since 1967, the Arabs have greatly narrowed the "technology gap" and the "quality gap" between them and Israel and have learned to fight well in a modern war.

This observer has no doubt that the Arabs did indeed fight much better in 1973 than in 1967, but he is inclined to attribute the difference to other reasons. The Arabs were no worse soldiers in 1967 than in 1973, but they fought better in the latter war because they did so under better strategic conditions. Granted that they did learn a few things from the 1967 experience, the most important by far was the necessity for them to preëmpt the initiative and to dictate to the enemy conditions for the battle that were most favorable to themselves. More specifically, they forced the enemy to fight a set battle, where the undoubted courage of their own fighting men and their numerical superiority in manpower and equipment could be used to best effect; and they denied him, at least for a crucial period, the option of fighting the kind of war he favored, and at which he was best, namely a war of rapid movement and envelopment.

Liddell Hart, the outstanding modern student of strategy, spent a lifetime propounding the thesis that creating the right strategic conditions is a much more critical consideration than the quality of the fighters. This was brilliantly confirmed in the record of the fighting in the Western Desert in World War II, where basically the same kind of forces on either side, as far as quality is concerned, experienced dramatic and repeated fluctuations of fortune, depending mainly on the conditions of fighting that their commanders succeeded or failed to create for them. In the end the point was demonstrated on both sides in the 1973 War, for the tide seems to have decisively turned once the Israeli breakthrough to the west bank of the Canal created conditions for a war of maneuver that threatened to pull down the entire Egyptian front.

Thirdly, because the Arabs were able to dictate a slugging type of war, this turned out to be extremely costly in men and especially in equipment to both sides. Indeed, in terms of continuity of action and ratio of forces to battle space, the 1973 War was one of the most intensely fought contests in history.

The intensity of the war, with the resultant rapid running down of stocks of hardware, was one of the main reasons why first one superpower and then the other intervened in the war as equipment supplier. At the same time, the rapid depletion of equipment is certain to impel the parties, if the conflict is not resolved, to seek to provide against such an occurrence in the future by accumulating equipment in much larger quantities than in the past. This means that the arms race could accelerate even more than in the past, with all sorts of deleterious consequences. One is that future wars might be even more destructive. Another is that, as one party or the other fails to keep up with the arms race (which in the key countries has already passed the ruinous levels of 20–25 percent of GNP in cost), it might be tempted to launch a preëmptive war before the odds turn further against it.

Still another possible consequence is that the number of parties involved in the conflict and the degree of their involvement are apt to increase, as the present belligerents are forced to seek more assistance from outside sources. The acceleration of the arms race is apt to involve the superpowers in the conflict even more deeply than they have been in the past. If this should give them a greater measure of control over their respective clients, the latter's independence will have been impaired. If it should not, then the chances of the superpowers becoming directly involved in a future explosion will have greatly increased.

Finally, the war did not involve much transfer of territory, nor did it change fundamentally the relative strategic posture of the parties. But it did make a political stalemate much more difficult to sustain militarily. In the north, the Israelis have improved their prewar positions somewhat, by gaining territorial depth and deploying themselves closer to Damascus and the crucial junction of the borders between Syria, Jordan and Iraq. In the south, however, although the ceasefire left forward Israeli forces in a much more threatening position than forward Egyptian forces in the short term, the underlying positions are less favorable to Israel over any sustained period than the prewar situation.

The explanation for this paradox lies in the vast difference between the normal readiness state of the two armies. The ceasefire left each side with a substantial bridgehead across the Canal and into territory formerly held by the other. The Israeli bridgehead on the west bank is more substantial, deeper and closer to vital enemy targets than the Egyptian bridgehead on the east bank. On the other hand, Israel's capacity to hold the present lines is much more limited than Egypt's. The lines are long and vulnerable for both sides, with each sitting at the other's flank and able to threaten its rear. However, Egypt can use its predominantly standing army to buttress its lines, whereas if Israel wants to do the same on its side, it will have to maintain a high level of mobilization which would get ever more ruinous with time. Gone is the neat Suez Canal line which (barring a repetition of total surprise) could be maintained by small forces in an only slightly strengthened version of the Bar-Lev line.

It follows that unless the present lines are made more "rational" by mutual agreement, they will most probably have to be changed by either war or peace before long. And as of late November the chances of their being made more "rational" by any early agreement are not too good. Israel has, of course, of-

fered to "straighten" them out by proposing a return to the prewar Canal line. However, although this proposal would relieve
the beleaguered III Corps, Egypt is not likely to accept it. Not
only would it nullify the bridgehead that Egypt gained at such
great cost; not only would it make the war appear to have been
in vain by restoring exactly the prewar lines; but also, by so
doing, it would facilitate the restoration of the political stalemate
Egypt had gone to war to break, and broke.

III

One of the most important features of the 1973 War has been
the new pattern of Arab solidarity that manifested itself. A
superficial look may take that solidarity to be no different from
that manifested in the 1967 War. A more careful examination
would quickly show some basic differences, which have very far-
reaching implications for the future.

One of the differences between 1973 and 1967 is that whereas
one "first-circle" Arab country—Jordan—participated only
nominally this time, countries in the "second circle" around
Israel played a much more meaningful role. Iraq sent very substantial forces to the front, as it did in 1967, only this time they
took an active part in the fighting. Kuwait and Saudi Arabia
contributed vast amounts to the war chest, while Libya contributed money as well as Mirages acquired from France. In addition, the three Maghreb countries contributed small contingents,
Morocco's being the most substantial.

A second and much more important difference is that Saudi
Arabia took the lead in putting the Arab "oil weapon" into play.
Of course, in 1967, it and other oil-rich countries did the same,
and even seemingly went farther by placing a total embargo on
oil shipments to the United States and Britain. However, we
know that in 1967 Saudi Arabia cut the flow of oil involuntarily,
under pressure by Nasser, and therefore did not enforce the
measure strictly and cancelled it as soon as possible. In 1973, on
the other hand, it introduced the weapon of its own accord, in
advance of the war, and has now set up a staff and adopted a
systematic, subtle, long-term strategy in order to maximize its
effect in direct and indirect ways.

What accounts for these two phenomena? And what are their
principal implications for the future of the Arab-Israeli conflict?

The first phenomenon—the more active role assumed by countries of the "second circle" around Israel—is probably the consequence of the vast growth of Israeli power in the years since 1967. As the military capabilities of Israel multiplied in these years, the "radiation" of that power began to be felt directly by these countries for the first time. As long as Israel had been hemmed in within the pre-1967 boundaries, surrounded by a ring of Arab states that contained it and threatened to roll it back, countries like Saudi Arabia, Kuwait and Iraq could feel completely safe from any Israeli threat. Whatever contribution they made to the Arab cause against Israel was made purely on the grounds of pan-Arab considerations. But as Israel overwhelmingly defeated the countries of the "first circle" in 1967 and effectively neutralized them since, it demonstrated a previously unsuspected capacity to hurt them in a significant way. From that moment, their concern with Israel began to rest no longer solely on pan-Arab considerations, but also on considerations of precaution; and their support for countries of the "first circle" became an investment in their own security.

Attentive students of the Arab-Israeli conflict will have noticed that what has just been described is merely a continuation of a process that goes back to the very beginning of the Zionist endeavor in Palestine. The Zionist movement and then Israel have had to cope with an ever-expanding combination of Arab forces opposing them and trying to push them back. Each time they defeated one combination, the power they mustered appeared menacing to Arab forces that had previously been on the periphery and impelled them to join the defeated forces in a new combination, and so on. Thus the overcoming of sporadic Palestinian Arab outbursts by the Jewish settlers helped bring about the great Arab revolt of 1936–39. The insufficiency of this revolt brought the general resistance supported by Arab League volunteers and funds in 1947–48. The collapse of that brought the intervention of the surrounding Arab states in 1948. The defeat of that combination in 1967 has brought, in 1973, the coalition of "first-circle" countries backed by countries of the "second circle."

The second phenomenon—Saudi Arabia's use of the "oil weapon"—is explicable in part by its enhanced concern about Israel. But to understand why the expression of that concern was not confined, for example, to helping Sadat finance the war requires further explanation. Indeed, throughout the years since

1967, and even before, Saudi Arabia had staunchly turned down repeated pleas by Nasser and Arab radicals to use oil as an instrument in the service of the Arab cause. King Faisal, in particular, had flatly ruled that "oil and politics should not be mixed." Why then has he changed his policy now?

The answer is that the reasons that had restrained King Faisal in the past have been removed in recent years, while the factors in favor of using oil as a weapon have been enhanced. Previously, Faisal feared that once he had sprung the "oil weapon," others, particularly Nasser, might be able to arrogate to themselves the right to decide when and how it was to be used. Moreover, since Saudi Arabia itself depended on all the revenues it was getting at the time for its own needs, the "oil weapon" was only of very limited use and could indeed be turned around by others to hurt the Saudi regime itself. In recent years, the enormous increase in oil revenues, far beyond current needs, gave the Saudi ruler much more leeway in handling the oil weapon, while the disappearance of Nasser and the failure of a comparable personality to emerge in the Arab world has meant that King Faisal could be sure to retain control of the weapon himself. The one possible exception has been Colonel Qaddafi of Libya, who considers himself to be Nasser's heir and the custodian of Arab nationalism and the pan-Arab cause; but Qaddafi would become a real threat only if he could succeed in his endeavor to extend his base so as to include Egypt. By using the "oil weapon" now and supporting Egypt financially on a large scale, Faisal hopes to minimize the principal appeal that Qaddafi and the prospect of union with Libya have had for Sadat and many Egyptians.

Two crucial implications flow from these developments in the inter-Arab arena. The first is that the greater involvement in the Arab-Israeli conflict of countries that had previously been only marginally concerned with it will make it much more difficult, if not impossible, in the future for the United States to try to contain the Arab-Israeli conflict, if it is not resolved, by means of a "balance of force" between the parties.

Until the war, the United States had viewed the Middle East in terms of two distinct constellations having only limited effect on one another—one centered on the Persian Gulf and one centered on the Arab-Israeli area. Now that concept of balance will have to be drastically revised. The Arab side in the Arab-Israeli

equation will need to be expanded so as to include Arab countries of the "second circle," and even of the Maghreb—perhaps
not by adding up all their military capabilities but by counting
different proportions of various elements of their forces. In the
area of air power, for example, where the capacity of even the
remotest Arab country can be relevant to the Arab-Israeli situation, any attempt to achieve a balance—given the aroused desire
of the Arab countries to acquire substantial air forces and the
availability of means and suppliers—would require bringing
the Israeli air force before too long close to American and Soviet
levels, at least with respect to some weapon systems! Such a
trend might encourage the development of a false or exaggerated
sense of power on the part of Israel and tempt it to adopt rigid
positions or engage in hasty action in local disputes. And if the
whole balance collapses once more, as it already did twice—in
1967 and 1973—then the ensuing war would be so destructive,
and its ramifications would reach so far, that the chances of the
superpowers staying out of it would be practically nil.

However, the greater involvement of previously marginally
concerned Arab countries, while it has certainly added to the
complexity of the conflict, need not make it less susceptible to
settlement, and may indeed make it more so. Countries like
Iraq and Libya may exert pressure in the direction of extremism;
but this pressure is apt to be more than offset by pressure toward
resolving the conflict on the part of countries like Saudi Arabia
and Kuwait. For if the conflict is not resolved now, these countries may find themselves in the position of having to finance
much of the ongoing confrontation on the Arab side amidst a
rapidly accelerating arms race with Israel—while at the same
time holding back oil production, thus forfeiting revenue, in
connection with the effort to influence the United States and
Europe. Five or ten years from now, these countries may have
enough reserves to do both and also meet their own needs. Right
now, their resources would be severely taxed before long by such
a double effort. Hence, as they look at the prospects facing them,
they are likely to apply their weight in the direction of a reasonable and prompt settlement.

IV

Secretary of State Kissinger said that one of the principal
lessons of the 1973 War was that the superpowers could not keep

out of a violent explosion of the Arab-Israeli conflict. For Western Europe as a whole—one does not know about Eastern Europe—the war showed that they too could not remain unaffected in very crucial ways. The consequences in both instances are of momentous significance.

Implicit in the statement of the Secretary of State was an admission of the failure of previously held contrary expectations. These expectations had been based, among other things, on vows that the superpowers had made to each other at the highest levels in Moscow and Washington to avoid any involvement in the Middle East that would endanger their détente; and on the fact that in the interim between the 1972 and 1973 summits the Soviet military presence in Egypt had been all but eliminated.

The expectations of the Europeans, on the other hand, had been based on a sense that they had actually worked out a modus vivendi with respect to the conflict that was apt to shield them from any serious repercussions in case it exploded. That modus vivendi consisted of their deliberately abstracting themselves from any significant practical role in the conflict (leaving matters mainly to the superpowers), and then granting to the Arab side all the political and symbolic support it asked for. In this way the Europeans thought they would protect their interest in Arab oil without hurting Israel too much.

The course of events after the outbreak of the 1973 War did at first appear to conform to the previous expectations of the superpowers and Europeans. Indeed, it seemed for a while that the most important characteristic of the war, apart from the surprise of its advent and the initial course of the military operations, was going to be precisely the fact that the outside world did not seem to care much about it. In contrast to the 1967 crisis, for example, nobody issued, at first, any momentous declarations, violent condemnations, or solemn warnings; nobody alerted or moved forces for a while; and nobody even submitted a ceasefire resolution of any sort to the Security Council for two full weeks after the start of hostilities. It looked as if superpower and West European endeavors to "quarantine" the conflict and insulate themselves from its dangers were working out.

But the European expectation had rested implicitly on one unrecognized assumption, that (as the United States itself expected) the superpowers would stay out. The assumption proved wrong when the United States felt compelled to resupply Israel with arms on a massive scale, and sought to use stocks it kept in Europe and some NATO facilities for this purpose. The Europeans suddenly found themselves confronting a very painful choice they had not anticipated: whether to permit the United States to do so and thus become its accomplices and risk Arab oil sanctions, or to oppose it and put an immense added strain on already difficult NATO relationships. In varying degrees and at a different pace, they all chose the latter. As if that were not enough cause for strain, the United States then proceeded first to "settle" the war with the Soviet Union, and next to engage with it in a confrontation on a global scale, without consulting its allies.

It thus became suddenly apparent to Europe that the Middle East conflict could not be "managed" by evasive tactics and policies, and that unless it was resolved it was bound to place before the European nations truly fateful dilemmas involving, on the one hand, the very foundations of their security since World War II, and, on the other hand, the stuff of their economic existence.

As far as the superpowers were concerned, their involvement in the conflict, contrary to their anticipation, was the result of an effort on the part of the Soviets to take advantage of an unsuspected opportunity, followed by an American effort to ward off the consequences. The process began with the Soviet Union's resupplying the belligerent Arab states with arms and ammunition on a large scale and urging non-belligerent Arab states to join in the war. Why the Soviet Union chose to do so is not quite clear as yet, but a plausible explanation has to do with fluctuating coalitions in Soviet ruling councils. With respect to the Middle East, it seems that these councils had been more or less evenly divided for quite some time between those who urged support for the Arabs' war plans and those who deemed that course too dangerous for superpower relations, and futile because of the demonstrated ineffectiveness of the Arabs in war. The latter view, it seems, had the upper hand at a crucial moment in the late spring of 1972, which led the Egyptians to react by terminating the Soviet military presence in their country in July of that year. Now, as the war broke out and the Arabs, contrary to the "soft-liners'" thesis, appeared to be doing quite well, and as it appeared that the extent of possible Soviet involvement could remain under control of the Soviets themselves rather than the Egyptians, the "hard-liners" were able to win the day with a decision to help the Arabs in various ways, thereby trying to regain the position previously lost through excessive pessimism and caution.

Whether this view of the process by which the Soviets became involved is true or not, the United States sought, at first, to stop the Soviets by means of diplomatic representations, arguments about the future of détente, and perhaps promises to work together on a Middle East settlement. However, in the face of Soviet reticence, and since the intense, slugging character of the fighting meant that the overall outcome of the war could well depend on the quantities of equipment and ammunition available to the belligerents, the United States felt compelled to launch its own massive emergency resupply operation to Israel.

As the fighting ground on indecisively and as the superpowers kept feeding the contending war machines, there emerged for a moment the horrifying prospect of a prolonged war sustained by the superpowers—becoming ever more violent, sucking in ever more belligerents, extending to ever wider areas, and involving ever more destructive weapons. Since Israel, because of its relative size, could withstand this process much less than its opponents, there also loomed the possibility that it might, in a moment of despair, spring the nuclear "last resort" weapon it is supposed to possess.

Fortunately that moment did not last long, because the war suddenly changed character as a result of Israeli initiatives. The success of Israeli forces in breaking through the Egyptian lines to the west bank of the Suez Canal and then launching a wide enveloping operation against vast Egyptian forces gave the war a new, mobile character much favored by the Israelis and opened up at least a substantial probability of a rapid, 1967-type consummation. This was enough to break the deadlock between the superpowers and to lead them to agree urgently on a project for a Security Council resolution enjoining a ceasefire in place and immediate negotiations between the parties on the basis of Resolution 242 of November 1967. Thus, after starting as bystanders and proceeding to become "partners" to the opposing sides, the superpowers went on to become for a time joint arbiters, deciding on the moment and the conditions for the termination of hostilities.

The next step in the superpowers' involvement was as dramatic and grave as it was inconsistent with the one that preceded it. The form it took is well known: a worldwide alert of American forces in the face of alleged preparations made by the Soviet Union for an immediate massive military intervention in the Middle East. The exact chain of events that brought this about is not known at the time of writing, but circumstantial evidence suggests that the following elements may not be too far wrong:

(1) Somewhere along the line, in the course of the consultations between the superpowers that went on throughout the war, the United States assured the Soviets that it did not seek a total victory for Israel and wished to avoid humiliation for the Arabs in order to maximize the chances of a peace agreement, which was the principal objective it had set for itself.

(2) As the tide of the war turned and the Israeli operations on the west bank of the Canal appeared to the Soviets to threaten total disaster for the Egyptians, the Soviets urgently invited Secretary of State Kissinger to Moscow, where General Secretary Brezhnev personally called on him to act in accordance with the assurances given. Kissinger agreed to have the fighting stop before the Israelis utterly defeated the Egyptians, but he insisted upon, and obtained in exchange, Soviet, and ostensibly Arab, agreement to the negotiation clause.

(3) As Kissinger left for home by way of Tel Aviv, the Soviets learned that fighting was continuing beyond the ceasefire deadline and that the Israelis had completed the encirclement of the Egyptian III Corps. Not only was that corps now in danger of imminent destruction, but its collapse could bring down the entire Egyptian front.

(4) The Soviets suspected at this point either that Kissinger had deceived them, or that the United States was unable to control Israel. The fact that the United States agreed to a second ceasefire resolution that enjoined a return to the first ceasefire lines suggested that the latter was probably the case. But this made it all the more necessary, and all the more seemingly safe, for the Soviets to react strongly.

(5) Just then President Sadat, worried about the fate of his entire army, issued a call to the United States as well as the Soviet Union to send in troops to enforce the ceasefire. The Soviets took advantage of the occasion and, apparently, notified the United States in a belligerently worded note that they were about to

send troops to respond to the Egyptians' call.

(6) It was now Washington's turn to suspect that the Soviets had deceived it and had engineered Sadat's invitation as well as other conditions to justify the introduction of large Soviet forces into the area. Even if these forces were not to intervene in the fighting, it was thought that their presence would create an entirely new situation in the area, one which, among other things, was not conducive to peace. Since the Soviets notified the United States prior to taking action, it was thought that they were probing for its probable reaction, and the decision was therefore made to respond in the manner most likely to discourage them.

(7) The crisis was over when the Soviets agreed in the Security Council that a newly formed U.N. peace force should not include troops from the "big five." A decision authorizing the Soviet Union and the United States to send in a small number of unarmed "observers" helped salvage Soviet prestige; at the same time a superfluous threat to have the Soviet air force supply the beleaguered III Corps if the Israelis refused to let supplies reach it by land helped preserve the image of determined defenders of Arab interests which the Soviets tried to project.

The involvement of the superpowers in the war and the forms it took showed that détente had not denoted as much of a change in superpower relations as its advocates had led everyone to believe. Even Secretary of State Kissinger, the architect of détente on the American side, admitted, as we have seen, that his expectations had been disappointed by the turn that events took. The fact that the two giants were drawn into the role of feeders of the opposed war machines could perhaps be offset by the fact that they eventually agreed on ceasefire terms that broke new ground for the prospects of peace in the area. But the confrontation at daggers drawn that followed shortly thereafter has no parallel in the history of the superpowers' involvement in the Middle East, even at the height of the cold war. Possibly that experience will prove to have been a necessary prelude to a real joint effort to bring the Arab-Israeli conflict under control, just as the 1962 Cuba missile crisis turned out to be such a prelude for several other crucial issues in the relations between the superpowers. Whether or not this will prove to be the case will, at any rate, become quite clear before very long because of the other feature of big power relations revealed by the war.

The war, we have seen, demonstrated the existence of a critical triangle between the superpowers, the Arab-Israeli conflict, and Europe. This triangle seemingly gives the Soviets an undreamt-of opportunity to score enormous gains at the expense of the United States. By encouraging Arab intransigence and doing what they can to perpetuate the Arab-Israeli conflict, they could hope to force the United States to reassociate itself fully with Israel; force Europe, worried about its very livelihood, to dissociate itself definitely from the United States; and establish for themselves a position from which they would have remote and indirect control over the flow of oil and could use that control to "Finlandize" Europe and keep it so.

Adopting such a course, however, would entail enormous costs. It would definitely mean the end of détente and everything it portended for the Soviet Union—American trade, technological assistance, investments, arms reduction and so on. It would entail the revival of the cold war in a more virulent form than ever, with all its attendant dangers. It is very likely, judging by some statements made by President Nixon, that the sharpness of the American reaction to the prospect of the Soviets' sending troops to the Middle East was prompted in substantial measure, at least, by fears and suspicions that the Soviets might have been working for that kind of consummation. But whether that is true or not, it is certain that the Soviets' embarking on the kind of course outlined would at one and the same time give many occasions for superpower confrontation and immensely enhance the chances that these would actually take place. Finally, the United States would almost certainly seek to restore the balance on the Eurasian landmass by moving much more closely to China and, together with her, trying to tilt the situation at the other end of the landmass. These are the most important implications of the alternative courses that have been revealed by the 1973 War. Which one the Soviets will choose and which way the world might be heading should become apparent before long from Soviet actions.

V

In no other domain is the war apt to have a more extensive effect than in that of the internal life of the belligerent countries. Yet, for our present purpose, we shall only look at a few aspects of the internal front and will confine ourselves to the key countries. How has the war affected the balance of considerations and forces inside Israel and Egypt, in favor of peace, war or stalemate?

The impact of the war on Israel may be understood in terms of a contest between two currents that have not only divided different groups but also made for strongly ambivalent leanings within individual Israelis.

The first current has tended to draw lessons from events as they actually happened, in order to break previous rigidities and look to new approaches that give compromise and peace a much better chance. The second has tended to dwell on preconceived notions as to how events should have and might have unfolded, and to wish to redo realities in order to bring them into conformity with these preconceptions.

Immediately after the war, the latter current, militant and belligerent, appeared to prevail; but as time went on, the former, more moderate and accommodating, appeared to be gaining ground. As of the time of writing, this trend was increasingly asserting itself. However, it was clear that the process could be interrupted and perhaps even reversed because of a breakdown of the ceasefire. The same could ensue if the pivotal Labor Party were to break up just before the forthcoming national elections, as a result of the post-mortem discussions that were beginning to take place, or because of ill-timed external pressures.

The primary source of the militant current lay in the prewar expectations universally entertained by Israelis that a war on the scale of the one that happened was just "impossible," in view of the overwhelming military superiority of Israel, repeatedly acknowledged by the Arabs themselves. War having nonetheless broken out, presumably because of some irrational, "suicidal," urge of the Arabs, all Israelis were certain of a total, fast, and cheap victory. In reality, of course, the Israelis had to fight extremely hard for 16 days and suffer, for them, enormous losses in order to score a partial victory. But all Israelis felt that this course of events was unwarranted and "unfair." It began with a series of mistakes on the Israeli side; then, when these were finally corrected and Israel was on the verge of achieving complete victory, outside powers intervened. Moreover, these outside powers contrived, after the fighting ceased, to reduce the scope of even the limited victory that Israel achieved, by pressuring it to allow supplies to go to the encircled Egyptian III Corps and trying to force Israeli forces to withdraw to a more confined perimeter.

The result of all this was an attitude that nurtured hopes for a breakdown of the ceasefire and looked for excuses to break it in order to complete the job of winning that was left undone. More important, the result was a mental disposition that resisted any idea or suggestion that did not conform with preconceived notions.

This attitude began to break down enough to give a chance for a countervailing current to start, when it became apparent that Israel was not nearly as free to act as most Israelis supposed. One of the crucial agents of the change was none other than Defense Minister Moshe Dayan, a reputedly tough man who still enjoys immense authority despite some recent setbacks. In his typical no-nonsense way, Dayan answered the leader of the opposition in the Knesset, who had said that the soldiers were very unhappy that Israel was yielding to American pressure to allow supplies to III Corps, by saying that the soldiers did not know that the shells they disposed of today were not there two weeks before, and wouldn't have been there but for the goodwill of the United States.

Once the hope of radically changing the existing state of things began to recede, reality and its lessons began to sink in. A crucial factor was the one major positive feature in the situation—the commitment assumed by the Arab side as well as the Soviet Union to enter immediately into peace negotiations.

One important lesson the Israelis began to learn is that even a militarily inferior opponent might find it advantageous to go to war if he is left with no better options. Israelis had deemed war "impossible" because they thought Sadat could not possibly hope to win. They did not realize that it might pay him to go to war if he had reasonable chances of not suffering a crushing defeat very quickly. Another lesson the Israelis began to learn—one that eminent students of war never tire of preaching—is that war is par excellence the domain of *fortuna,* a notion that had been utterly alien to Israelis, accustomed to think that their brilliant past victories had been the inevitable outcome of "scientific" preparation.

The significance of these lessons may be better appreciated if we recall that Israelis had been strongly divided before the war in their views as to what the minimal aims of their country should be in connection with the post-1967 situation. Among the considerations determining the various positions, the Arab capacity to wage war and inflict damage on Israel was initially an important factor. Evaluations of that capacity on the part of the different groups fluctuated in the course of the fighting that followed the 1967 war; but by 1970–71, when a ceasefire became firmly established, a consensus about the "impossibility" of war and about Israel's chances if it nonetheless happened had begun to prevail. Henceforth, the arguments between the upholders of different positions centered on weighing the costs and benefits of the various courses, without the prospect of war and its possible costs entering into the picture at all. Naturally, this tended to push the entire spectrum of positions in a more demanding, "hawkish" direction. Now that war—costly, cruel, and susceptible of complications—injected itself into the picture, the whole spectrum of positions could not but move, in time, in an opposite, more accommodating, direction.

Another lesson, implicit in what has just been said but worthy of specification because of its importance, consisted of the exploding of the position of those who wanted, and thought it possible, to prolong indefinitely the stalemate that came to prevail after 1970, either in order to avoid having to make choices that could precipitate undesired political splits or in the hope that time would give some kind of legitimacy to Israel's retention of the conquered territories. The war and the events accompanying it showed that the Arab-Israeli conflict had just become too complex—involving too many interests and having too many ramifications—to be susceptible of being kept indefinitely in stalemate.

But probably the most specific, important, and hopeful lesson of the war has been that centering on the relationship between territory and security—the rock on which past efforts at peace have foundered. Immediately after the war, at the height of what we called the "militant" current, Israelis argued that the war demonstrated how vital the territorial factor was and how right Israel has been in insisting on very substantial modifications of the 1967 territorial setup. Where, it was asked, would Israel be today if it did not have the buffer of the Golan and Sinai—if, for example, the enemy had been able to score an initial advance of 15 kilometers not at Khushniyya in the Golan but toward Natanya at the "waist" of pre-1967 Israel?

Since then, Israelis have continued to hold on to this argument, but have simultaneously begun to confront the inescapable paradox that in 1967 their country did infinitely better with its "insecure" boundaries than in 1973 with its "ideal" boundaries. It can, of course, be argued—and it is—that in 1973 Israel had fallen victim to a "Maginot-line mentality," that there had been an unwarranted failure of intelligence, that the Soviets had given the Arabs weapons that allowed them to achieve several tactical surprises, that they went on to replenish their arsenal as fast as Israel destroyed it, and that in the final account Israel would have still won a decisive victory but for the intervention of the United States and the Soviet Union. However, each additional explanation or excuse could only point out more and more factors relevant to security, and thus drive an additional nail in the coffin of the previous Israeli attitude that had made a fetish out of territory. The sum total of the explanations could only underscore the truth that security is a product of a multitude of factors of which geography is one, but which also comprises technology, friendships and alliances, relative size of forces and so on—including alertness and aspects of the opponent's state of mind that can be reached. The explanations would also reveal that there is a measure of interchangeability between these factors, so that one could have less of one and more of another and end up being no worse off than before, if not better.

There are signs that this kind of lesson is being learned in Israel along with others we mentioned, all of which make for the erosion of rigidities that have stood in the way of peace in the past. Given a chance, this sober, moderate current is most likely to prevail, if not throughout Israel, then at least among the majority of the ruling coalition. But there is a danger that this chance may be denied to it by one of two developments: (1) a breakdown of the ceasefire; or (2) a breakup of the Labor Party's own coalition of "hawks," "moderates" and "doves." The former development could result from some breakdown in the fragile agreements that have been reached concerning exchange of prisoners, supply to III Corps, definition of ceasefire lines, blockade of the Bab el-Mandeb Strait, and so on. The latter development might come about as a result of an internal explosion, triggered by mutual recriminations among the various segments of the party over the management of the crisis; or it could be precipitated from the outside, by prematurely putting before the party the necessity to make choices about critical issues.

The impact of the war on Egypt, too, may be viewed in terms of two competing currents, moderate and militant, opposing different segments of the power elite and feeding ambivalent inclinations in individual members of it. In contrast to Israel, both currents in Egypt, while being rooted in the prewar situation, have been shaped mainly by the course of the war and associated events. One current tends to view the outcome of the war as placing Egypt in the best bargaining position it could hope to achieve, and is therefore eager to capitalize on it in order to try to reach a settlement now. The other current believes that the war has shown that Egyptians themselves had underestimated their military capabilities and the outside support they could command, and is therefore inclined to be more reticent and insist on more demanding terms. Both currents are, to be sure, already committed to entering peace negotiations with Israel without insisting on prior Israeli withdrawal. However, the former is likely to be accommodating in order not to forfeit the present opportunity, while the latter is likely to seek a much harder bargain, even at the risk of a breakdown of the peace talks.

At the root of the more conciliatory tendency is the bitter memory of the post-1967 era. After years of struggle to eliminate the consequences of defeat, which saw Egypt's options evaporate or end in frustration one after the other, a stalemate set in that was even more oppressive than the repeated failures. For Egyptian society resembles nothing more than a vast bureaucratic enterprise, which depends entirely on impulses imparted to it from the top to operate with any degree of efficiency. Such impulses had not been forthcoming because the top leadership had been completely preoccupied with the Israeli question. President Nasser might have, had he so chosen, ignored that question for some time, but Sadat did not even have that choice; lacking any previous credit, his tenure of the presidency depended for its legitimation in a very large measure on his being able to resolve that problem. The result of all this was that by 1973 Egypt's economy had been stagnant for many years, Egypt's society was completely demoralized, its polity was a seething cauldron, the credibility of the government had sunk to zero, and Sadat and his entourage had their hands full just trying to survive from month to month.

It was in this context that Sadat was finally persuaded by the military chiefs to go to war. The aim he had set for Egypt was not total victory, which he realized was unattainable. At the very most he hoped to seize a strip along the east bank of the canal reaching out to the passes, which would represent the beginning of the process of liberating the occupied territories, put Egypt in a position to press for the evacuation of the rest, and permit the reopening of the Suez Canal and the resettling of the desolate cities of the west bank. The minimal objective, which made the whole enterprise justifiable, was to stave off total defeat long enough to provoke great-power intervention and international initiatives that would break the stalemate.

When the war ended, Egypt, to the surprise of vast segments of the power elite, had achieved considerably more than its minimal objective, though much less than its maximal objective. The fact that utter defeat in the last days of the war was averted only by a hair's breadth did not detract from the accomplishment. However, it made the moderates feel that Egypt had attained the best possible position from which to bargain for ending the stalemate on reasonable terms.

As for the militants, they had shared with everyone else the frustrations of stalemate, only they had tired first of the diplomatic efforts to break it and had urged military action sooner. In the end it was they who prevailed upon Sadat to go to war, by laying out before him the specter of greater trouble, especially the breakdown of military discipline, if he did not. The course of the war—the ease with which the Egyptian forces overran the Bar-Lev line and established a bridgehead, the very heavy casualties they inflicted upon Israel and especially their success in denying supremacy to the Israeli air force over the battle zone—appeared to the militants to vindicate their erstwhile claims, and to give Egypt some highly credible military options. On that basis, as well as on the basis of the recommitment of the Soviet Union to the Arab cause, the seemingly miraculous effectiveness of the "oil weapon" in neutralizing Europe and setting it at odds with the United States, and the evident eagerness of the United States to seek points of contact with the Arabs, they have argued that Egypt now has ample room for maneuver and substantial prospects of further enhancing it. Therefore, they conclude that Egypt need not settle for anything less than total Israeli withdrawal from all Arab territories and "justice for the Palestinians."

It seems evident from the fact that Egypt agreed to the negotiation clause of the ceasefire resolution, and made no serious attempts to break the encirclement of the III Corps by force, that so far it has been the moderate current that has prevailed. However, it is equally evident that the other, more militant current cannot be ignored and could come to prevail should there be a breakdown of the ceasefire or should the anticipated negotiations tarry too long in coming or give signs of inconclusiveness.

VI

Our panoramic survey of the impact and lessons of the 1973 War shows that a resolution of the Arab-Israeli conflict has at last become a real possibility for the parties directly concerned, and an imperative necessity for all the outsiders that have been involved in it. It is completely understandable, therefore, that outsiders should try to exert all the influence and pressure they can in order to bring about a peace settlement; but these outsiders must beware of defeating their own purpose through misapplied zeal. There are forces on either side of the Arab-Israeli frontline, we have seen, that are inclined in directions favorable to peace—as there are forces that are swayed by considerations that would inhibit the give-and-take necessary for settlement. The involved outsiders should be wary of allowing the latter to prevail *on either side of the fence,* through their pressing on either party formulas that do violence to deeply felt and widely shared concerns, or even through pressing any formula too soon or too late.

Clearly, the most fundamental concern of Israel is ensuring its security; that of the Arabs, safeguarding their sovereignty. The two need not be as incompatible as they were felt to be before the war, if sufficient imagination is applied to the search for a solution and to the conception of the resources that might be used. This is not the place to suggest any specific plan that does so; but we might point out in a general way, and by way of illustrating rather than exhausting the possibilities, that the two concerns can be reconciled in one or more of the following ways:

(1) By bringing in an outside factor to enhance Israel's security enough to have it relax its demands for territorial modifications. One such factor might be a U.S.-Israel mutual defense pact. A few years ago, the author made a proposal to this effect which evoked some weighty objections on the part of Americans

and elicited skeptical reactions from Israelis.[1] Now that the United States has confirmed once more its abiding unwritten commitment to Israel's security, now that it has demonstrated its capacity to uphold that commitment in the most dramatic and effective way, and now that the Arabs have shown in many ways that they accept that commitment as legitimate, providing it does not extend to protecting Israel's conquests, most of the previously expressed concerns should cease to be relevant.

(2) By introducing a flexible time factor into an effort to reconcile the two. For example, starting from a formal recognition by Israel of Arab sovereignty, and Arab recognition of Israeli security concerns, a plan might be agreed upon whereby the actual return of the territories is accomplished in a gradual way. This would be conditioned by the establishment and consolidation of normal neighborly relations, which is deemed by the Israelis to be the best security.[2]

(3) By broadening the conception of boundaries to be settled. For example, in exchange for the Arabs' ceding sovereignty over part of their territories to meet Israeli security needs, Israel might relinquish sovereignty over some of its pre-1967 territory to meet such crucial Arab needs as the establishment of territorial contiguity between Egypt and the Fertile Crescent countries. Alternatively, a similar arrangement might be made that is based on the right of use, while sovereignty is retained intact.

Certainly many additional approaches can be developed. But even the best-worked-out plan can fail if it is not presented at the appropriate time. And right timing is not something that can be planned, but must depend on the intuition and experience of the statesmen.

---

[1] See Nadav Safran, "Middle East; The Fleeting Opportunity," *The Nation*, April 5, 1971, pp. 425–28.

[2] For one model of such a plan, see Nadav Safran, "U.S. Policy, Israel's Security, and Middle East Peace," Hearings before the Subcommittee on the Near East of the House Committee on Foreign Affairs, 92nd Congress, 1st session, July–October 1971.

THE STRUGGLE FOR THE
WORLD PRODUCT

Politics Between Power and Morals

By Helmut Schmidt

ANYONE who, in these weeks and months of the "oil crisis," is asked to forecast the future development of international economic relations and who looks for fixed data and reliable trends to support his forecast will soon run into serious difficulties. Even after the mid-February Energy Conference in Washington, the impression, disturbing in many respects, remains that the world economy has entered a phase of extraordinary instability and that its future course is absolutely uncertain; it may bring stability, but also still greater instability. More integration, closer coöperation, an improved division of labor may increase the overall prosperity of nations. But the future course may just as well be characterized by disintegration, national isolation and the search for more self-sufficiency, thereby enhancing the contrasts already existing in the world.

It would be wrong, of course, to believe that the oil price explosion was the only cause of instability. But the massive increase in oil prices has clearly revealed the actual fragility of this elaborate system of economic relations among the nations of the world, from the structure of their balance of payments to their trade policy. To use energy nomenclature: just as a high-energy neutron breaks through the electrical shielding which surrounds the atom and penetrates into the nucleus, oil has shaken the very foundations of the present world economic system. And just as the neutron may induce oscillation and shatter the nucleus, oil may shatter the laboriously built structure of the world economy. The oil crisis may touch off a chain reaction of destructive forces, but—if properly harnessed and controlled—it may just as well help to improve international coöperation, if all those concerned join in the efforts to find the common denominator of what is going on these days between the Libyan desert and the Gulf of Maracaibo, and if they build a policy of reason on that common denominator.

II

At this present stage there can hardly be any doubt that, long before the explosive rise in the prices of almost all raw materials, international economic policy was moving toward a critical phase. It is no longer possible to ignore the fact that difficulties have recently multiplied, bit by bit, and what is astonishing is that this has happened during a period of worldwide new production records. Whereas, on the one hand, the world economy was experiencing a fantastic boom, there was, on the other hand, growing uneasiness about the institutions, particularly the slowness with which they were adapting to changing conditions, to new tasks and objectives, in order to ensure a greater equality of starting conditions among nations and to enable an undistorted exchange of goods and services among them. The crisis toward which the world economy was moving was not so much one of production as a crisis of its institutions in structural respects. In particular, the rules governing the exchange of goods and services were questioned on an increasing scale.

The protracted ill-health of the Bretton Woods system was one of the most significant symptoms of this development. Under the impact of the cumulative effects of inflation and speculative crises, this system finally collapsed and thus ceased to exist as an integrating factor. Ultimately, the system broke down because it failed to provide the framework for an orderly exchange of goods and services. Bretton Woods benefited some countries more than others—particularly the strong more than the weak—and above all it burdened the international monetary system with the payments deficits of the superpower. And thus it is not astonishing that, finally, a system that initially had been so successful should have produced interventionist policies on an increasing scale rather than greater economic freedom.

Even with imagination and expertise, it is difficult to establish a new and better system. It is difficult to create a supranational standard of value which is not at the same time a national currency, like the dollar, or a commodity used for speculative purposes, like gold. The "Special Drawing Right," as an artificial numeraire without a market price, and with official parities only for transactions between central banks, was to be declared a primary currency reserve and to be made so strong that it could win the necessary confidence. There were to be fixed but adjustable exchange rates. In addition, it was intended to ensure that the extent and duration of payments imbalances should be appreciably reduced, that the facilities for financing such imbalances should be limited rather than expanded. All countries were to be obliged to settle payments balances from their own reserves.

The process of evaluating the pros and cons of the proposed monetary rules is still under way. What has so far emerged, after lengthy negotiations in some of the most beautiful cities of the world—including Nairobi, the modern metropolis in East Africa, and Rome, the ancient metropolis of Western civilization—is at least a basic concept. Luckily, there has also been found an interim solution to the important question of the valuation of the Special Drawing Right: the yardstick is to be the average value of a "basket" of major currencies instead of the U.S. dollar. On the other hand, however, there has so far been no decision on the question of how to finance the payments deficits of the less-developed countries; this question, though at first glance it appears to be of secondary importance from the point of view of monetary policy, is actually very important in the light of recent developments. It is certainly true to claim that, despite open flanks, the understanding for the common cause has increased and that therefore the continents have moved closer together in certain fundamental views. But even if all moral accessories are left aside, nobody—including the author of these lines—would be able to say just when the new system can be put into operation. For nobody, in view of the still incalculable effects of the dynamic changes in the terms of trade, can confidently claim to be in a position to determine new fixed parities and afterward defend them against market forces.

There are more symptoms of this struggle for new and better rules—e.g., in commercial policy. Last year we witnessed a peculiar, and largely unnoticed, formalistic dispute both within the European Community (EEC) and between the latter and the United States as to whether and in what form a connection was to be established between the reform of the international monetary system and the new multilateral trade negotiations (GATT) in Tokyo. France had initially requested that the new GATT Round should not begin until fixed parities had been reintroduced. The other European countries advocated concurrent efforts toward further liberalization of trade *and* monetary stabilization. The United States, on its part, was ready to support this formula of concurrent efforts only if it was clearly expressed that an efficient monetary system also called for a commercial policy prone to adjustments.

All this looked like a dispute on formal issues only. But, at the same time, it was the expression of fundamentally different positions: monetary matters first and trade afterward; or monetary matters and trade at the same time; or trade promoting monetary matters—these are concepts which may call for different approaches on the part of the nations concerned, and possibly the acceptance of economic disadvantages or sacrifices. Meanwhile, this dispute has taken on a purely academic character.

The Conference held last September in the Japanese capital was an example of the above-mentioned concurrency and its ultimate results are still largely incalculable. The opening declaration of Tokyo is by no means the Magna Carta of an open world economy based on division of labor, although any reasonable person will accept the objective that the new GATT Round should promote the further liberalization of international trade in order to raise the standard of living and increase the prosperity of nations. He will likewise endorse the general claim that existing customs barriers should be lowered further and other trade barriers reduced or removed.

But the bureaucratic infighting behind these fine words is still going on, as is the struggle over the prices of raw materials. The wrangling is about tariff headings, preferences and counter-preferences, the purpose and extent of protectionist measures. Here, too, as in monetary matters, national interests play a prominent role. Not all countries, for instance, are as vitally interested in the largest possible degree of freedom for world trade as the Federal Republic of Germany. Thus, countries which have only just begun to build up industries at enormous social cost will not be too eager to enter into free competition with the powerful combines of industrialized countries. On the other hand, even in highly developed countries there are certain sectors whose competitiveness is limited; a case in point is the German clothing industry, which is complaining about low-priced shirts being imported from Formosa and Hong Kong. Such sectors cannot stand up to international competition and genuine social problems are created in the countries concerned when economic activity is running at a low ebb.

Agriculture will probably continue to be a further reservation in the system of a free exchange of goods and services. Agriculture is the spoiled child of protectionism, not only because governments vie for farmers' votes, but also because—understandably—every country is anxious to preserve its own minimum basis for feeding its people. This statement can be proved by hard-and-fast figures if one looks behind the scenes of European as well as U.S. agricultural policy. To the outside observer, the policy of European integration appears to be a puzzling tug-of-war over egg prices or wine quotas. Both in Europe and in the United States, the baffled consumer will often have the impression that relationships between the two are determined exclusively by soybeans and Arkansas chickens. Those who resent the economic power of the United States speak of the American challenge, and there may even be such strange excesses as the claim that the consumption of American chickens results in impotence.

Nor can we be certain that free capital movements are welcomed everywhere. Did not American newspapers, for instance, publish malicious reports on an allegedly unlimited stream of German capital into the West? Some people already saw the place swarming with Teutonic roughriders lassoing American cattle. And was not the United States somewhat vexed about the association policy of the EEC, which was even alleged to be striving for hegemony over the United States? Someone even invented the malicious quip that the Sixth Fleet in the Mediterranean would probably soon have to file an application for association.

Meanwhile, however, it will have been realized from New York to San Francisco how difficult it still is for Europeans to translate their dream of a political union into reality. It is not without protracted and painful labors that the Regional Fund is being created, which so far is the latest of the instruments of European unification, following the Agricultural Fund, the Social Fund and the somewhat ill-fated monetary "snake." And it is conceivable that Europe's failure to tackle the oil crisis by pursuing a common policy will have an impact on the further process of unification.

III

What is the reason for this state of affairs? Why is it that 30 years after Bretton Woods the urgently needed reform of the international monetary system makes so little headway? Why is it that nations find it so hard to soften their protectionist trade systems and to give their trade policies a new, open and equal structure? Why is it that after almost two decades of effort toward European unification, European political union is still unfinished? What is the reason for these disputes about quotas, customs tariffs and posted prices? And the oil problem which now creates new and very strong tensions, is its nature not basically the same?

David Ricardo would certainly not like this state of the world economy and its institutions if he saw it. But he might congratulate himself on the skepticism and foresight he showed in discussing the consequences of the free trade thesis of his teacher, Adam Smith. Admittedly specialization, division of labor and free trade across national boundaries have increased the wealth of nations and caused an immense supply of goods in the same way as the division of labor increased production within a single nation. But the main problem then is to define the laws which determine the distribution of this enormous output; it might be added: which determine the "fair" distribution, the "equitable" price, the "proper" value.

Even today, these "laws" have not yet been defined. The most ingenious theories of distribution in most cases explain only parts of the problem or are infeasible in actual practice. What remains are resourceful bickerings over the results of the joint efforts, a game full of ruses and little tricks, with strategies of threats, attrition and fatigue, of overnight conferences and dissolved meetings, a game of coalitions and cartels. What we are witnessing today in the field of international economic relations—in the monetary field and now in the field of oil and raw material prices —is virtually the same as what is going on between trade unions and employers' associations on the national level. It is a struggle for the distribution and use of the national product, a struggle for the world product.

But whereas the struggle for distribution has hitherto been fought within the framework of monetary and commercial rules, it has now become a struggle over prices as well and has thus taken on a new and in many respects dangerous dimension.

The struggle over oil prices may be followed tomorrow by a similar struggle over the prices of other important raw materials. And since what is at stake is not just pawns on a chessboard, but the peaceful evolution of the world economy and the prosperity of the nations of this world, we need a politically sound philosophy if we are to win this dangerous fight.

IV

It would be a mistake to approach the oil problem with illusions, with a swashbuckling rattle of the sword in the manner of a past century's gunboat diplomacy or in an egotistical overbearing manner. This is no way in which to conduct the distribution combat! Each side, the oil-producing and the oil-consuming countries, must learn to understand and appreciate the other's interests, means and possibilities, since there is no other way of avoiding abortive actions and corresponding reactions. The hectic events of the past nine months appear to indicate that this point has by no means been fully grasped.

Oil consumers would be well advised to examine the oil producers' motives impartially. It is true that, in the Middle East, current political issues have a bearing and that, to this extent, oil is considered a political weapon. But, in essence, the oil price issue is not one of a clash over the Suez Canal, the West Bank or Jerusalem. What the oil producers, and not only the Arab ones, have in mind is to increase their share in that portion of the world product which is created with the aid of oil, the most important raw material for years to come. And they are able to do so to the extent that increased oil prices push up the import figures of oil-consuming countries at a rate higher than that at which the latter are able to step up their prices of exports.

The oil consumers would do well to grasp that this is exactly what is intended and not to allow certain facts to be repressed into the subconscious mind, especially the present distribution of wealth between industrialized countries on the one hand and oil-producing countries on the other. If, for instance, U.S. per capita income in 1971, i.e., a year prior to the start of the present price measures of the OPEC countries, were taken to be 100, the latter countries' figures for 1971 would be as follows: Kuwait 75, Abu Dhabi 49, Qatar 45, Libya 28, Venezuela 21, Saudi Arabia 11, Iran 9, Iraq 7, Nigeria 3, Indonesia 2.

And these figures are by no means a true reflection of the actual level of wealth attained in those countries; the disparity, in real terms, for the bulk of the population can well be assumed to be greater than these figures reveal. And it is this gap in incomes or wealth that alone should be taken to motivate the oil countries' policies.

Seen from this angle, the Western industrialized countries, including Japan, being oil consumers, can hardly avoid acknowledging the merits of the oil countries' claim, seeing that cheap oil was in the past a major factor in the former countries' growth. They should not blind themselves to the fact that the times of cheap oil are past and gone. A posted price of $1.80 per barrel of Arabian oil from the Persian Gulf, as it prevailed in January 1970, will not recur. It will not do so because oil producers, following ten years of systematic OPEC policies and aided by 20 years of careless energy policies on the part of the consumer countries, now have the power—in the form of the OPEC cartel—to achieve by increasing their prices the distribution pattern they desire. They have the power of those who control resources in short supply, resources which are of importance, in limitative respects, to a multitude of production lines in industrialized countries. There is so far absolutely no substitute for oil and its derivatives available at short notice; at the most, a sort of fringe substitution might be possible in alternative fuel power stations. Certain economies in quantities consumed are, however, possible at short notice and that alone would involve considerable changes in consumer habits. In other words: as a short-term proposition, the elasticity of demand for oil and its derivatives is very slight, and thus the conditions are right for an independent price policy.

On the other hand, oil producers would do well not to regard the new independence and power they have in pricing to be a device which is devoid of all limitations and consequences, especially in view of the effects this may have on the very existence of the developing countries. They should proceed with care when marking out their field of action. In doing so they should above all not allow this newly grown consciousness to mislead them when assessing the industrialized countries' economic possibilities. For although there is only a very slight possibility of substitution for oil at short notice, there is a limit to the price that can be charged. In the short run there is at least a point beyond which economic stability would be in jeopardy. And that point is reached whenever the industrialized countries are confronted with intolerable adaptation and reorganization problems incapable of being solved at short notice and are thus driven into employment crises or toward an even higher rate of inflation. In this context, I do not wish even to contemplate a point—at least theoretically conceivable—beyond which the irrational use of force might ensue.

But if we think in terms of five to ten years, the elasticity of the demand for oil will rapidly increase. Oil used for heat-producing purposes will become substitutable as soon as the price of oil equals or exceeds that of alternative sources of energy. However, scope for substitution is smaller in certain sectors of transportation and of the petrochemical industry. In the long run, though, oil could be replaced by electricity even in the field of transportation, for instance if nuclear energy were available to a greater extent, and long before that coal will have been assigned a larger role as a basic material in the chemical industries.

For these reasons, oil-producing countries would not only be gravely misjudging the power they wield but also be jeopardizing their own interests if they were to try to attain maximum absorption on a short-term basis. It would run counter to their own long-term interests if oil-producing countries were to pursue a price policy that would drive Western industrialized countries onto the verge of, or even right into, crises: you do not kill the goose that lays the golden egg. Extreme, supermonopolistic absorptions simply are no sensible strategy if the object is to narrow the income gap between the group of industrialized countries and the group of oil-producing countries. But the most important aspect is that such a policy would force the industrialized countries to resort to sweeping crash programs designed to direct their entire resources, their entire sophisticated technology to the substitution of oil or to the exploitation of unused oil reserves (sands, shales). Consequently, in the long run the effect for the OPEC countries might well be reversed. As far as the interests of the oil-producing countries are concerned, the optimum solution would therefore not lie in a *short-term maximum* absorption but rather in an absorption that is *achievable and tolerable on a long-term basis.*

With this in mind, a major question mark remains over the present oil-price policy. Price increases have been so exorbitant that, as a result of changes in incomes and demand, serious repercussions, particularly on employment, cannot be ruled out. In addition, the oil-producing countries have obviously been unaware of the strain which they impose on a fragile monetary system through their sudden withdrawal of purchasing power.

Therefore, even if one recognizes—as I do—that producer countries have a good case for claiming a greater share, there will have to be negotiations on the size and terms, because a new equilibrium cannot be the result of monopolistic practices and mechanisms, but will have to be brought about by balanced judgment and advance planning. Producer and consumer countries will have to sit down at the same conference table. In those talks, the oil-consuming industrialized and developing countries should not be forced at short notice to lower their standard of prosperity at the expense of their social stability. It should on the contrary be in the interest of the oil-producing countries, as well, to ensure that they can satisfy their requirements by being able to draw upon industrialized countries' national products that are in a process of growth and possibly even undergoing structural changes for the better.

At the same time, the problem of the use of the enormous monetary purchasing power now accruing to the oil-producing countries should be discussed, since this will have repercussions on the employment situation in the industrialized countries and on the extent of unavoidable structural changes. The search for solutions will certainly not be facilitated by the fact that there is no homogeneity of interests in either group. Some of the oil-producing countries such as Iran and Venezuela will—at least on a medium-term basis—be in a position to utilize the accruing purchasing power for, say, internal investment projects destined to expand their own production capacity. To this extent they will become importers of industrial goods and consequently trigger off a corresponding demand for export goods in the industrialized countries. Here lie welcome chances for economic and technological coöperation aiming at an accelerated industrialization of the oil-producing countries; this approach will require the development of coördinated programs. Other countries such as the sheikdoms of the Persian Gulf, Saudi Arabia and possibly Libya will—even on a medium-term basis—not be able to absorb the additional purchasing power within their own frontiers. They will, in other words, not increase their imports and consequently not bring about an increase in demand for export goods; they will invest their monetary capital in other countries rather than spend it. This will result at first in the accumulation of huge, readily disposable amounts running in billions, which could well flow back to the industrialized countries as capital imports. Such amounts might also be made available to countries of the Third World which in turn could use them for buying export goods from industrialized countries.

The situation on the part of the oil-consuming countries is equally differentiated. Some of the industrialized countries are more seriously affected than others, the degree varying primarily according to the extent to which they are dependent upon oil imports and according to the previous position of their current account and their balance of payments in general, and finally, according to their export capacity. Countries with a current account surplus, i.e., countries which have so far not used their entire national product internally for consumption and investment, but have made part of it available to other countries, thereby acquiring monetary claims, are hardly expected to run into difficulties. This applies, for instance, to the Federal Republic of Germany, whose current account surplus is quite substantial. For the Federal Republic, even the increase in oil prices will presumably not result in a current account deficit. German export industries enjoy a high reputation in potential purchasing countries. In addition, the Deutsche Mark is backed by a very large monetary reserve so that any lean period could easily be overcome. The effects of the increases in oil prices on income will of course also be felt by countries with a strong monetary position.

Other countries whose balance of payments have hitherto been in equilibrium or have already shown a deficit, particularly a number of less-developed countries, may well run up such huge deficits on current account that they might very shortly be facing enormous financial gaps resulting in an immediate and urgent necessity either to step up exports or to reduce imports. Such a situation is extremely dangerous for the future of the whole world economy. But it would be a great mistake if each individual country within the group of oil consumers were now selfishly to try to solve its payments and employment problems by pursuing beggar-my-neighbor policies at the expense of its trading partners. Any relapse into largely bilateral bartering would be just as dangerous as any reintroduction of trade restrictions. Nor should there be any competitive devaluation. After the Washington Conference, we can only hope that, however justified the concern about specific national problems may be, the common interest will not be forgotten. Otherwise, an arrival at the point of no return cannot be ruled out.

The present flexibility of exchange rates may well facilitate the adjustment process, but it should not be allowed to lead to excessive downward floating. Any current account deficits that would remain if a compensatory increase in exports cannot be achieved at short notice might well be financed from the surpluses of oil-producing countries. The point would be to release capital flows of more or less the same size as the various current account deficits of oil-consuming countries. A large-scale concentration of investments in a few individual countries would create well-nigh insurmountable difficulties both for the latter countries and for those which fail to balance their current accounts for lack of capital imports. Should the earnings of the oil-producing countries, rather than being invested on a long-term basis, remain "mobile" as a whole and be capable of being moved at short notice out of one currency into another and from one investment outlet to the next, there would furthermore be new serious risks for the monetary situation.

Of course, a certain portion of the investment-seeking oil funds will find its way to consumer countries automatically: in the form of direct investments, investments in securities, credits and bank deposits, either direct or via existing or new Euromarkets. Countries which would not automatically obtain an adequate share of these monies might remedy the situation by offering investment incentives or possibly by issuing foreign currency bonds, though there should be no free-for-all in the field of foreign bonds.

If, in the choice of countries in which to invest oil funds, preference were to be given to those with strong currencies, the latters' private sector investment outlets might prove insufficient. If so, it might be advisable to examine whether public investment outlets could be expanded. Above all, the countries concerned would have to ask themselves whether they were in a position to act as "marshalling yards" for international capital flows. They would have to try to offset inflowing liquidity by capital exports and this might entail the willingness to accept financial risks. Two countries that might be capable of undertaking this very difficult task could, for instance, be the United

States or even the Federal Republic of Germany. Such a "marshalling yard" could help to direct the capital outflow selectively into those countries which—as a result of the oil crisis—are faced with major balance-of-payments problems. In the first place, however, this task would be a matter to be tackled by multinational institutions.

v

No matter what action the industrialized countries may take to wipe out balance-of-payments current-account deficits, the fundamental problem as such will remain unsolved. A process of shifts in patterns of income has been set in motion on a huge scale. The questions facing the industrialized countries are what strategy they should reasonably pursue and whether they are well advised to rely on capital imports in attempting to come to a long-term solution of their internal employment and financial problems. During a transitional phase this surely should be possible and might even be necessary in order to give the industrialized countries concerned time to adapt.

What will probably be unavoidable in the long run is a process of structural changes which would, among other things, increase the export capacity of those industrialized countries whose exports now flow at a low level. This results from the pressure of the Third World's dire needs. These would increase if the now-beginning process of transfers of purchasing power were to be strictly confined to industrialized countries on the one hand and oil countries on the other, especially if the released investment-seeking oil billions flow back in the opposite direction. The developing countries are in danger of being left high and dry. Their very existence is threatened by increasing oil prices because they do not have as high a net product as the industrialized countries to draw upon. For those who view the prosperity gap between the rich and the poor of this world with concern, every effort must be made to see that the oil producers place that portion of their additional purchasing power which they are unable to absorb at home directly at the disposal of developing countries to make effective the latter's demand for imports from industrialized countries.

The international organizations, too, will have to join in the efforts to channel the investment-seeking funds of oil countries to where they are needed to lessen the differences between levels of income. The International Monetary Fund (IMF), the World Bank, the International Development Agency and the regional development banks will in the future have to rely on those countries much more than before when seeking to obtain lending funds, even if—as I hope—the industrialized countries do not reduce their development assistance below its present level.

In the long run, therefore, the oil countries will also be facing the problem which now is accompanying development assistance rendered by industrialized countries. Mere financing of credit to developing countries will not be sufficient in the long run. The rate at which most countries of the Third World are accumulating capital resources of their own is so low that it is hardly possible to set in motion an accelerated process of self-development merely by offering them assistance in the form of credit, because most of their gain in productivity is eroded by their commitments to pay interest on, and repay the principal of, loans.

Thus, in the long run, there will have to be more genuine transfers of real resources in order to provide the less-developed nations with a genuine basis for continued self-development and thus also to decrease social and political tension. The oil-producing countries are now succcessfully making the most of their market position for obtaining a larger share, in real terms, in the world product. This share is considerably larger than all the development aid being provided by industrialized countries. Thus, some of the oil producers are automatically beginning to share in responsibility, a responsibility that they cannot shirk.

Obviously, the developments sparked by the increase in oil prices can hardly be brought under control unless there is a change in consciousness of the matter in public opinion. What is needed is a fundamental change in patterns of behavior both among individuals and among nations. This also applies to the question of a less wasteful use of each country's own resources and its attitude toward economic growth. The richer nations will have to realize that the product of national labor will not invariably be fully available for domestic distribution. It will not be easy to make the general public lastingly conscious of this fact.

Developments along these lines have already started in Europe. Of course, the model of the European Community is not capable of being applied automatically to other parts of the world. European integration is an historically necessary process that must be measured against European criteria. In principle there is already a substantial levelling out of differences in resources between the countries of Western Europe. The huge gap between incomes in the industrial centers on the line from Hamburg via the Rhine to the Rhône, including Northern Italy, on the one hand, and major parts of Southern Italy, Ireland and Scotland on the other, will stand up to a comparison with the corresponding gap between certain industrialized countries and certain developing countries. The United States has a comparable North-South problem. From the very outset of the move toward European unity there was no doubt whatsoever regarding the fact that political integration would have to keep step with a planned and controlled transfer of funds from the stronger to the weaker nations. Up to and including 1973, for instance, the Federal Republic of Germany, the main provider of finance for the European Community, had paid some DM9.5 billion— or approximately \$3.5 billion at the current rate of exchange— net to other nations out of tax revenues. My country, whose financial capacity should not be overtaxed in the process, looks upon such payments as the cost of the integration venture.

On a worldwide scale, it will not be possible to reduce the differences in the levels of wealth unless the more advanced industrialized nations develop their own resources in close coördination with one another and with the primary-producing countries. If they fail to do so, the result might be social storms which could even seriously jeopardize world peace. If it can be assumed that most of the developed countries with a high level of prosperity have a great preference for peace, and that most of the less-developed countries have a high preference for increased wealth, there must be a level on which a convergence of preferences would stabilize the international political situation at a higher level of prosperity for both the wealthier and currently poorer countries. It would, therefore, serve the efforts to maintain peace on a worldwide scale if a comprehensive policy of economic coöperation were to be pursued rather than a policy of economic "apartheid."

Seen from this angle, time is short for working out sensible new rules for monetary affairs and trade. And seen from this angle, the cost of the peaceful development of the world economy will now have to be charged and paid.

THE ECONOMIC CONSEQUENCES
OF THE ENERGY CRISIS

By Gerald A. Pollack

THE quadrupling of oil import prices in one year, quite apart from Arab supply cutbacks, has greatly increased the urgency and gravity of the questions that were lurking in the shadows even in the earlier, balmier days of the energy crisis.[1] No less an authority than the managing director of the International Monetary Fund (IMF) has warned that the combination of oil shortages and price increases in 1974 is likely to produce "a staggering disequilibrium in the global balance of payments ... that will place strains on the monetary system far in excess of any that have been experienced since the war." And Treasury Secretary Shultz has stated that the recent oil price increases raised "literally unmanageable" problems for many nations.

These, then, are the questions that confront us:

— Can the international monetary system sustain a transfer of wealth of such unprecedented dimensions without extensive disruption or even collapse because of intolerable balance-of-payments strains?

— Will the consuming countries be able and willing to absorb the immense investments the oil-producing countries may wish to make?

— Will new financial mechanisms be necessary to assure reasonable stability?

— What will happen to currency values?

— Will the consuming countries be able to make the necessary internal adjustments without severe dislocation and with no lasting impairment of growth?

— Will the increase in oil prices further accelerate the inflationary spiral?

— How severe will be the impact of higher prices on living standards?

— How will the resource-poor Third World be able to cope with

[1] The views expressed in this article are solely my own and do not necessarily reflect those of Exxon Corporation or of the individuals whose assistance is acknowledged below. Important contributions were made by my colleagues Kerin D. Fenster, James W. Hanson and John F. Kyle. In addition, I have benefited from discussions with Sterie T. Beza, IMF; Samuel Pizer, Board of Governors, Federal Reserve System; and F. Lisle Widman, U.S. Treasury Department.

the oil crisis, and what will be the political consequences for the industrial countries?

II

The starting point for an analysis of the monetary impact of the energy crisis is the quantum jump in import bills implied by higher oil prices. For the United States, Europe and Japan, oil imports this year may be nearly $50 billion more than in 1973. What will happen beyond this year is highly conjectural, depending on the responses of supply and demand to sharply higher prices in the consuming countries, and on the pricing and production policies of the nations that make up the Organization of Petroleum Exporting Countries (OPEC). If demand does not fall off appreciably when prices rise and if supplies remain tight, import bills will keep rising. By 1985 they might well approach $200 billion, some $150 billion more than in 1973. The OPEC investable surpluses may total nearly $100 billion by the end of 1974, and could cumulate to almost $500 billion by 1980 and more than $600 billion by 1985. These magnitudes would seem to be enough to scuttle any monetary system.

There are plenty of unknowns as we set out to forecast the outcome. But there are also a number of knowns which, if we sort them out, can help to advance the analysis.

(1) Although all importing countries will be transferring wealth to OPEC, the payments problems that may result will primarily involve financial relations among the importers.

(2) An OPEC decision to export more oil than they need to pay for imports is a decision to invest abroad.

(3) There are no limits in any financial sense on the absorptive capacity of importing countries for OPEC funds, but there may well be psychological and political problems.

These somewhat surprising conclusions will become clear if we trace through the financial flows set into motion by higher oil import bills. To the extent that the consuming countries can increase their exports of goods and services to the producing nations, higher oil imports will entail neither balance-of-payments deficits for the former, nor surpluses for the latter. But we already know that even the most rapid increases of imports by the OPEC countries must necessarily lag far behind the explosive growth of their income. And the entire excess of OPEC income over expenditure must necessarily flow back to the importing countries so as to eliminate the payments gap between themselves and OPEC. In other words, the payments flows from the importing countries as a group to OPEC must be exactly offset by reverse flows of funds for imports and investment from OPEC.

Now, how can we be so sure that what flows out will flow back? Consider this: when a U.S. company makes a payment to, say, Saudi Arabia, what happens is that title to a dollar account in a U.S. bank is shifted from a U.S. resident to a foreign government. This money actually never leaves the United States, but convention would have it that the funds flow to Saudi Arabia and then return. By simply endorsing and depositing the U.S. importer's check, Saudi Arabia increases her investment in the United States. And this foreign investment will stick to her like a burr until the Saudis spend it on imports or, to raise an unlikely possibility, give it away as grant aid to developing countries. These are the only ways their foreign investments can be drawn down. To be sure, they can switch out of dollars into deposits in other currencies. Or they can switch out of bank balances into stocks, bonds, direct investments or real estate abroad. Or they can buy World Bank bonds or lend to the International Monetary Fund (IMF). But these are all different forms of foreign investment, and shifts from one into another do not alter the total.

In this perspective, note that OPEC purchases of gold, Rembrandts, and industrial equipment, for example, count as exports, not investment. They draw down bank balances abroad and leave no claims against the industrial countries once they have been shipped to the OPEC nations. They are, of course, forms of *domestic* investment for the OPEC countries. But here we are speaking only of investment forms that involve claims on foreigners.

In the long run, domestic investment by OPEC will feed back on the balance of payments, for example, by generating locally produced goods that can displace imports or gain a foothold in foreign markets. Indeed, given their small population base, industrialization of the Gulf states would necessarily make them dependent on the export markets of their oil customers for profitable operations. This, in turn, would provide the oil-importing countries with new, possibly important, bargaining power for future negotiations with the countries concerned.

The second and third startling propositions follow from this analysis. There are only three ways OPEC could avoid investing abroad: first, to spend their entire oil export earnings on imports; second, to trim back oil exports to the level needed to pay for the imports they want; and third, to give immense gifts of money (grant aid) to their oil-poor Arab neighbors and other countries. Given the enormity of their income, the first solution would be possible only if oil prices were slashed deeply. The second solution could be difficult to implement in view of the counter-pressures the importing countries might exert to safeguard their vital interests. Besides, some OPEC members at least might decide that, at present prices, oil in the ground will not long be better than money in the bank. The third solution is simply not going to occur. Even if OPEC were to provide foreign aid in amounts many times the $1 billion annual sum volunteered by the Shah of Iran on behalf of his nation, their coffers would scarcely be dented. Even more to the point, the Shah proposed to lend the money—in other words, to make foreign investments —not to make outright grants.

These conclusions carry a number of important implications. For one thing, they set to rest any concern that the OPEC nations might deny the importing countries the capital flows needed to redress imbalances. For another, they suggest that OPEC demands for investment vehicles that would safeguard them against inflation and devaluation—vehicles that do not now exist anywhere—do not have to be taken quite as seriously as they have been in some quarters. It is reasonable to suppose, however, that OPEC will take the attractiveness of investment opportunities in the industrial countries into account when deciding on how much to produce and export. In particular, special inducements might be necessary for OPEC to invest in ways conducive to international monetary stability. But the essence of the problem is OPEC's willingness to produce and export oil. There is simply no way of getting around it: above a certain level, an OPEC decision to export oil is a decision to invest abroad.

III

If foreign investment is inevitable, perhaps we should lean back and enjoy it. That there are no general absorptive problems follows from the fact that the investment initially involves no more than the transfer to foreign ownership of bank balances that already exist. Now, to be sure, there could be disturbances in the capital markets if OPEC's portfolio preferences differed greatly from preëxisting patterns. This could involve significant changes in interest-rate relationships or price-earnings ratios, for example. And shifts in the location of funds from the United States to small countries like Switzerland could give rise to troublesome inflationary pressures, if the governments concerned attempted to hold their exchange rates steady, or to severe deterioration in their trade balances, if they allowed their currencies to rise.

Indeed, this latter contingency may be a psychological barrier to the willingness of some countries to absorb foreign investment. A strong mercantilist tradition still pervades our world, equating trade surpluses with virtue and deficits with sin. Higher oil prices will, by themselves, push the trade balances of most, if not all, industrial countries into deficit. To prevent simultaneous downward pressure on their currencies, they might individually accept offsetting capital inflows. But to go beyond that, to allow inflows of foreign investments that would push their exchange rates up and accentuate their trade deficits could well be unacceptable.

In some instances the limits of absorptive capacity may be set by political rather than economic considerations. The industrial countries might not be prepared to accept massive ownership of home enterprises by foreign investors, especially if those investors are not a large and diverse number of foreign individuals or companies, but a handful of governments with political fish to fry. And OPEC attempts to focus their investment interest on a limited number of securities could raise antitrust problems as well as the possibilities of disturbances in the equity markets.

Actually, the likelihood that these problems will occur has faded with the recent price increases and embargoes. Even before they declared economic war on the industrial world, the OPEC nations had a passion for anonymity in their investments. Now, they may be even more leery of having visible hostage assets abroad. Far better, from this point of view, to put funds into the Eurocurrency market, where they can circulate throughout the world without anyone being the wiser as to their origin.

IV

Now, let us return to our initial question. We began by asking whether the international monetary system could sustain the prospective immense transfer of wealth to the OPEC countries, and have concluded, so far, that the payments problems, if any, will be *among* the consuming countries, not between them and the OPEC countries. But there is less comfort in this than meets the eye. The essential question then becomes whether imbalances among the consuming countries will be so great as to tear the system apart. After all, the consuming countries, as a group, could all be in equilibrium at the same time that each of them suffered horrendous, but offsetting, imbalances. On the other hand, there would be no balance-of-payments strains for any country if it should happen that the OPEC countries placed their investable funds abroad in relation to the payments needs of each. But this is more than can be reasonably expected. Some countries are obviously more attractive than others as places to invest or as producers of the things the OPEC countries want to buy. Thus, some consuming countries stand to get more offsets, others less. How, then, are things likely to sort themselves out? Will new financial mechanisms be necessary to assure reasonable stability?

Let us see what is needed and what we can expect of existing mechanisms. The essential problem among the consuming countries, once their equilibrium is disturbed by more expensive oil imports, is to move to a new structure of trade compatible with the altered flow of international investment funds. In this process, exchange-rate movements are likely to be the main equilibrating force. They will rise for countries receiving capital inflows in amounts that exceed the increase in their oil import bills. This will make those countries less competitive internationally. Their exchange rates will continue to rise until the deterioration of their trade balances becomes large enough to offset the extra capital inflows. Countries that fail to attract sufficient capital will experience the reverse process. Thus, if market forces are allowed to work, each country's trade and capital accounts would seesaw to a new equilibrium.

This is all right as far as it goes. But it raises as many questions as it answers. For example: Just how much adjustment in trade balances might be required for individual countries, and how much change in their exchange rates? Will free market forces be permitted to operate if some countries face a severe deterioration in their trade balances and marked changes in their currencies? Would the capital flows that induced these changes in trade be stable, or would they slosh around across currency boundaries preventing trade adjustment, indeed, disrupting trade and investment?

There is certainly a danger that free market forces will not be permitted to work themselves through and that the industrial world will retreat to protectionism. We have already spoken of the pervasive mercantilist ethic that holds trade surpluses to be the essential goal of foreign commerce. Now, the industrial countries as a group cannot help being in an overall trade deficit. This would go against the grain, even if the deficit were evenly distributed among all. But that some might have to bear a disproportionately large share of the total deficit might seem wholly unacceptable. To avoid this contingency, the nations so threatened might resort to competitive devaluations or trade restrictions. The ·new era of floating exchange rates has heightened the danger of predatory currency practices, both by breaking the IMF rule that any country's exchange rate adjustment requires multilateral approval and by facilitating currency manipulation. At the same time, the energy crisis has increased the motivation for competitive devaluation. Before the crisis, devaluation could only aggravate the problems of over-full employment and rampant inflation confronting most countries. But now, with recessionary tendencies in evidence, devaluation may appear more attractive as a way of maintaining output in the face of shrinking demand —at the expense, of course, of other countries. This conjures up disquieting images of the 1930s.

The maintenance of a multilateral, outward-looking trade and payments system may therefore be conditional on capital flows that go quite far toward offsetting the bulk of the payments strains resulting from the energy crisis. As was said earlier, it would be possible for OPEC to prevent each and every consuming country from experiencing any balance-of-payments strain whatsoever, by the simple expedient of channeling their investments to each in accordance with its need. In practice, how close to this result is the outcome likely to be?

So far, the OPEC countries have demonstrated a preference for investing in the Eurocurrency market, rather than in national money markets or directly in securities. There, they find both anonymity—a valuable feature to governments anxious to avoid creating "hostages" abroad—and high returns on short-term deposits. The Eurocurrency market is a highly efficient mechanism for financial intermediation. The funds deposited there are quickly re-lent to commercial borrowers and to governments. Britain and Italy, through borrowings by their public authorities, have already drawn on this large pool of international liquidity to finance their balance-of-payments deficits. And on January 31 France announced intentions to borrow around $1.5 billion in the Eurocurrency market specifically for the purpose of helping to pay for the higher cost of oil imports. (Finance Minister Giscard d'Estaing reportedly expressed hope that similar actions could be taken by the Common Market to recycle Arab funds to the European nations that will need them.)

But governments need not borrow directly to use the resources of the Eurocurrency market for this end. Tight money conditions, for example, might induce their residents to borrow abroad rather than at home, thereby giving rise to the desired capital inflows. In general, since no one can know better than the deficit country concerned what its financing needs are, any institution like the Eurocurrency market that can recycle OPEC surpluses in accordance with the initiatives of the borrower should go far toward reducing payments strains.

The U.S. money markets could also perform this function if, directly or indirectly, Arab funds flowed into the U.S. money or capital markets—something that has evidently not yet occurred on a significant scale. If the OPEC countries acquired U.S. bank balances, or bought stocks, bonds, industrial property, etc., the liquidity of American financial markets would be increased. Interest rates here would tend to fall. This would attract foreign borrowers at the same time that relatively higher foreign interest rates encouraged American investors to place their funds abroad. Similar recycling mechanisms would be activated if London, Zurich, Frankfurt or any other financial center were favored by the OPEC countries. The ability of market forces to induce such intermediation has been greatly enhanced by the termination, at the end of January, of U.S. and Canadian controls on capital outflows, and by an easing of restrictions on capital inflows by a number of European countries and by Japan.

Other institutions could also help in the recycling. The IMF, for example, with its resources augmented by OPEC funds, could play a significant role in easing payments strains—a role for which it was originally designed. The World Bank and the Bank for International Settlements in Basel could help. And loans among central banks could also make a contribution.

It is one thing to identify mechanisms, and another to say that they will suffice to do the job. As things stand, the Eurocurrency market has several defects for present purposes. In essence, there can be no assurance that the allocation of loans based on such commercial banking considerations as creditworthiness and relative interest rates will coincide with the requirements of balance-of-payments equilibrium. Thus, for example, the Eurocurrency market is not well suited to resource-poor or politically unstable developing countries with low credit standing. Here, a partial solution, at least, may lie in World Bank borrowing from the OPEC countries and re-lending to the Third World. Such recycling through the World Bank, for which there is already some precedent, will receive new impetus from the announced intention of the Shah of Iran to invest in World Bank bonds a portion of the $1 billion in aid funds that he pledged to make available this year. In addition, the Arab countries have already spoken of establishing a development lending bank of their own, and the Shah has proposed a new international development fund whose capital would come jointly from oil-exporting countries and the major industrial nations. But what about countries which, realistically speaking, have no prospects whatsoever of repaying a loan? Such countries—and there are quite a number—would be outside the circle of recycling funds. Their situation would be further aggravated by the likely reluctance of the industrial countries, now preoccupied with their own problems, to continue aid at existing levels, let alone contribute the added amounts the poor countries need to pay for oil.

Another problem with the Eurocurrency market is that funds placed there tend to be on short-term deposit, while the debts required to ease the payments strains of oil imports will need to be relatively long-term. This problem might be resolved through normal market processes bringing the terms desired by borrowers and lenders into closer alignment. But given the enormous speed of the Arab investment buildup, these processes might not work quickly enough.

And finally, what can be said about the danger of financial instability resulting from sudden and massive shifts of funds out of particular money markets and across currency lines? Note that this threat would not be confined to possible actions by OPEC countries. In the complicated system of intermediation sketched above, the financial boat could be rocked by any of the many borrowers, creditors, or speculators within the system, anywhere along its chain. It has often been said that OPEC's self-interest in seeing their investments prosper would deter any destructive moves on their part. The same would apply to the other actors on our stage. And yet one might wish for greater reassurance. Financial panics have occurred in the past, even though those who precipitated them lost what otherwise might have been saved.

This question of financial instability may turn out to be the biggest of the threats posed by the energy crisis. Recurring upheavals in the foreign exchange markets could trigger protectionism and bring about a severe contraction in world trade, conjuring up visions of another world depression. Accentuating the dangers here are the incredibly large OPEC surpluses that are in prospect and the extraordinary rapidity with which they will accumulate. Existing mechanisms and institutions are simply untested in handling international transfers on this order of magnitude. It is as if we asked whether, after having safely lived for nearly three months in the skylab, our astronauts could survive for another five years in outer space.

This question, moreover, puts into useful perspective any efforts at quantifying the balance-of-payments implications of various oil price and volume scenarios. In a nutshell: we could envision a cumulative OPEC surplus, including investment yields, of around $450 billion by 1980. Suppose this estimate is wrong and that it will turn out to be around $550 billion; or suppose that it is only $350 billion, or even less. Would the higher or the lower figure be materially different with respect to its implications for international financial stability? I submit that it would not, that we have taken a quantum jump into a new world that is qualitatively, not merely quantitatively, different from the old.

Recognition of the potential for instability in these extraordinary financial flows underlies the various suggestions that have been made for averting the dangers by tying up Arab funds in nonliquid form. In this connection, oil consultant Walter J. Levy has suggested buying oil now and paying part of the cost later. Also in this category is the suggestion that the IMF provide new, value-guaranteed instruments to OPEC to sop up their liquidity and then recycle it to the oil-importing countries. Secretary Shultz has suggested consideration of a new kind of multinational joint venture—a type of mutual fund, as it were—which would employ expert investment management to channel OPEC funds into a diversity of profitable investment outlets in the consuming countries. The investing nations, which would be encouraged to "commit sizable funds for extended periods," would "maintain control over some basic decisions concerning the volume and distribution of the funds." And Secretary Shultz's proposal of lower oil prices would, of course, reduce the size of the financial problem to begin with. Only time will tell whether reasonable stability can be maintained without the help of such special instruments.

But one essential point must be kept in view. The key to the viability of the international monetary system is not some stroke of inspiration in inventing a new investment vehicle with such irresistible features that it will swallow up most of OPEC's funds and neutralize them. No paper certificate or financial contract can go beyond the underlying willingness of the OPEC governments to coöperate now and in the future, changing circumstances notwithstanding. At best, such certificates provide a convenient channel for coöperation. It would no doubt be a costly channel as well, because OPEC may insist on features that no government has been willing to offer in the past—including maintenance-of-value guarantees for inflation and devaluation. Moreover, OPEC's willingness to accumulate such assets does not involve a once-and-for-all decision, but rather daily decisions because, as long as oil flows, funds flow to the producing countries. Considering also a natural desire for investment diversification, it seems likely that any special arrangements would absorb only a fraction of the funds at OPEC's disposal. Therefore, even though they can help, there is no guarantee that they would suffice to make the difference between monetary stability and instability.

Now, let us try to pull these threads together. On the positive side, the OPEC surpluses necessarily remain within the financial markets of the consuming countries, and the existing institutional framework would seem more or less capable of the intermediation necessary to channel funds to the point of need, at least within the industrial world. On the other hand, there are uncertainties as to the ability of existing institutions to cope with the immense magnitudes we envisage, the ability of the resource-poor developing countries to keep their heads above water, and the stability of a financial system so heavily dependent on international lending. No doubt, this list of problems could be expanded greatly.

The long and short of it is that no one can be sure that the financial side of the oil crisis is manageable. Perhaps the best that could be said is that, if the consuming and producing countries can coöperate in working out solutions, there is nothing about the institutional structure that would preclude a happy ending. Regrettably, the comfort inherent in this idea is somewhat marred by the history of international monetary coöperation.

V

Despite the uncertainties, what can be said about the outlook for individual currencies? Major imbalances would remain for the United States, Europe and Japan after the initial increase in oil import bills has been partially offset by oil industry profit remittances, shipping earnings and the like, and by higher exports to the OPEC countries. Unfortunately these calculations do not take us as far as we would like with respect to exchange rates because, as we already know, these will be driven by the engine that recycles capital. And there is really no way to predict the ultimate destinations of OPEC funds.

It must also be remembered that, in forecasting exchange rates as in forecasting stock prices, it is not enough to be right about the underlying forces at work. One must also predict correctly the psychology of the people who make the markets. And these people—foreign exchange traders, investors, businessmen and speculators—will probably be watching the trade and current account positions of the major countries rather than the capital accounts. This is both a matter of conventional analysis and of necessity—because while trade data are released monthly, information on capital flows is fragmentary and incomplete if it is available at all.

A "first-round" look at the magnitude of the deterioration that is likely to occur in trade and current account positions reveals that all of the consuming areas are hard hit. The rapidity of the escalation in oil prices, however, has struck particularly heavily at Europe. If OPEC incomes had reached their high levels gradually, Europe, as principal supplier of OPEC's imports, would have been able to offset a substantial part of its high oil import bills with a large volume of exports. But OPEC's import spending simply cannot keep up with the explosive growth of oil income. Consequently, over the next few years at least, money that would have been spent on imports, largely in Europe, will instead flow into the capital markets.

The initial response of exchange rates to the oil crisis that erupted with the Arab-Israeli war already provides us with a frame of reference for further analysis. To be sure, the market reaction so far has been based not only on the effects of more expensive oil, but also on the possible repercussions of the disturbances caused by embargoes and cutbacks. The latter, we hope, will be short-lived. In any event, the markets reasoned that the United States was most favorably situated, with relatively low dependence on imported energy, a strong initial trade position, and favorable prospects for attracting funds. And Japan was seen at the other end of the spectrum. On fundamentals, these judgments seem realistic.

To be sure, some tempering of optimism about the dollar became evident in the foreign-exchange markets when the United States and some other nations ended their controls on capital exports and imports, respectively, at the end of January and when the oil imports of other leading countries proved to be somewhat lower than had been expected. Thus, toward the end of January, the dollar came within less than one percentage point, on a trade-weighted basis, of recovering its decline relative to Smithsonian rates. However, by the end of February, it had receded to a range roughly midway between Smithsonian levels and the nadir it reached early in July 1973.

On the other side of the coin, the major European currencies and the yen first declined substantially relative to the dollar, since last October, and then recovered about half of their losses. The pound, having risen less earlier in 1973, also fell less. And the lira, having participated in the earlier decline of other European currencies, has failed to share appreciably in their recent strength. That the pressures were great is reflected not only in the magnitude of the changes, but in France's defection on January 19 from the attempt by seven European countries to maintain fixed exchange rates among themselves while floating jointly against other currencies. France was unwilling to commit any more of her dwindling reserves to the defense of her weakening currency.

For the time being, the foreign exchange markets will probably continue their erratic search for new sustainable relationships, a process that is likely to involve abnormally large day-to-day fluctuations. This instability does not yet reflect the actual impact of Arab funds, but rather the anticipatory adjustment of positions by dealers, traders and investors who traditionally dominate these markets. It should not be surprising if, after their vigorous comeback relative to the dollar, the European currencies and the yen receded somewhat in the near term, in step with the march of monthly trade data.

The longer-term outcome will be dominated by capital flows and therefore defies prediction. The fundamentals are ambiguous. Europe will probably be the main beneficiary of the rising trend of OPEC import spending. Indeed, on the somewhat unrealistic assumptions that this trend will continue its steep ascent and that Europe will keep its high export share, OPEC's trade surplus with Europe would be falling rapidly by the late seventies and actually turning into deficits by the mid-1980s. By 1980, Britain could well have joined Norway in being self-sufficient in energy. All of this suggests that the European exchange rates should strengthen toward the end of the decade. We should also be leery of underestimating the long-term potential of the yen. The ingenuity of the Japanese, their productivity, their export orientation, the likelihood that an easing of restrictions would greatly increase the inflow of foreign investment—all of these suggest that the yen, too, may recover its luster toward the end of the decade.

On the other hand, the United States may be favored by the rising tide of capital flows, either directly or as a result of the intermediation of the Eurocurrency market. Moreover, the dollar will be reinforced to the extent that "Project Independence" bears fruit and leads to an acceleration of energy production from indigenous sources.

But this leaves the long-term outcome very much in doubt. At this point, we simply cannot forecast how trade and investment flows might sort themselves out and what exchange-rate movements would be required to do the job. However, one thing is clear: the chances of an early return to fixed exchange rates, which were bleak even before the oil crisis, are now zero. Present and prospective international reserves will simply be no match for the rapidly rising volume of international liquidity resulting from the immense outpouring of funds to oil producing countries. These funds, once mobilized by fears of loss or expectations of gain, or by political considerations, could quickly sweep over even the strongest defenses like tidal waves. Faced with this possibility, no country is likely to risk the loss of its reserve assets in an attempt to hold back pressures that, in the end, probably cannot be contained.

VI

Let us turn to the question of domestic adjustments within the economies of the consuming countries. How much dislocation and how much impairment of growth might there be? Analytically, there are two problems. The first is the transitional problem of adjusting the structure of production to reflect the changing pattern of consumption. Examples would be to shift automobile output away from gas-guzzlers toward compacts, or even to decrease automobile production and improve mass transport systems. The second problem is to maintain a full employment economy in the face of a worldwide tendency for consumption to decline and savings to increase. This is conceptually the more difficult problem to understand, although it is not necessarily more difficult to resolve than the other. The problem is, in reality, simply our old question of ability to absorb OPEC funds in a different guise. We have already concluded that, in a financial sense, there is no problem of absorption, because the funds earned by OPEC do not represent new money that must somehow be shoe-horned into the world's money and capital markets, but money already there that simply changes title. In an economic sense, however, the question is this: will the industrial countries be able to translate into productive, job-creating activities at home the financial savings of the oil-producing countries available to them? Unless they succeed, they face a lasting increase in unemployment and retardation in growth.

Let us examine the dynamics of this problem. Because crude oil prices have risen fourfold in the Gulf over January 1973 levels, consumers in the importing countries will have to spend a larger percentage of their incomes on petroleum products. If they spend a larger percentage on oil, however, they will have less to spend on other things. And, since the increased expenditures for oil accrue primarily to OPEC governments—that is, to nonresidents—total spending by residents on domestically produced goods must fall. This drop implies, in turn, a tendency for domestic employment and output to fall.

Some of this pressure toward higher unemployment will be offset by increased exports to the OPEC countries. Some of it, too, will be offset by a tendency on the part of consumers to maintain their living standards in the face of the higher oil prices by reducing savings, and by a tendency for wages to rise somewhat in response to higher prices. On balance, however, not all of the initial drop in demand for domestically produced goods is likely to be offset. Thus, the entire world will probably experience a tendency for the share of consumption to drop and for that of savings to rise, with the savings increase occurring primarily in the OPEC countries. If income and output are to be sustained in the industrial world, OPEC's extra savings will either have to be translated into investments or into spending for consumption. The latter alternative would counteract the tendency for world-wide savings to rise by offsetting OPEC's higher savings with lower savings—possibly even some outright dissaving—in the industrial countries.

Is solving this problem difficult? No, at least not in concept, because it is essentially the Keynesian problem of overcoming demand inadequacies. This has been studied and understood so thoroughly by several generations of policy-makers that success in developing future solutions could normally be assumed. All that is required, in principle, is that the governments of the consuming countries follow expansionary policies to stimulate domestic demand and offset the drop caused by the diversion of spending from domestic goods to foreign oil.

In the present situation, however, there is a new, complicating factor. When the consuming countries look at their trade balances this year, virtually all of them should find that they are running deficits. Normally, the prescription for such deficits is contractionary monetary and fiscal policies. This would tend to reduce imports and increase exports, thereby eliminating the problem.

To counteract the effect of lower demand, however, expansionary policies are needed. Thus, the instinct to safeguard the trade balance will be in conflict with the instinct to maintain full employment. The logic of the situation is that the latter instinct will prevail, but that will not necessarily happen immediately and, indeed, cannot be taken for granted even in the long run.

VII

Now, let us turn to the inflationary consequences of higher oil prices. These are no easier to fathom than the retarding effects of higher oil prices on demand and output. To be sure, one would have to be blind not to perceive the direct inflationary impact of the jump in oil prices. And it is also apparent that higher oil prices will pull up the prices of coal and other forms of energy, and spark demands for higher wages by workers attempting to keep up with inflation. For the United States, these developments will probably add about two percentage points to the GNP deflator in 1974, and a little more than three to the cost-of-living index.

Beyond these more or less immediate effects, however, lurk others that are more difficult to trace. Structural changes will be necessary within the oil-importing countries that will surely involve shifts in consumption patterns, for example, to smaller cars and better insulated homes. There may also be shifts from the production of consumption goods to investment goods as a joint result of two forces in that direction: on the supply side, an increase in world savings associated with the transfer of wealth to OPEC nations with low absorptive capacities; and on the side of demand, an urgent need in the consuming countries to step up investments in their energy industries, in particular, and, more generally, a need of some years' standing to expand industrial capacity.

Changes in relative prices provide the necessary carrot-and-stick inducements that are the traditional means for bringing about desired shifts in employment, production and investment patterns. But prices have been increasingly "sticky" on the downside, for a variety of reasons. This means that price increases will have to play a proportionately larger role in the adjustment process, and this is clearly inflationary.

In addition to these possible developments, the balance-of-payments strains resulting from higher oil prices will undoubtedly generate pressures to increase international reserves, through stepped up creation of Special Drawing Rights (SDRs), revaluation of monetary gold stocks, or other means. This, too, would tend to be inflationary.

Moreover, there is a danger that the success of OPEC in raising oil prices will inspire attempts by nations producing other essential materials to form cartels of their own. This might conceivably occur in copper, aluminum, coffee, tin, natural rubber, timber, and even such items as tea, cocoa and pepper. Some, but not much, comfort can be gleaned from the conclusions of a recent study by Bension Varon and Kenji Takeuchi published in this issue of *Foreign Affairs*. In essence, these authors found less potential for increases in the price of non-fuel minerals than existed in the case of oil, because of both market factors limiting the ability to raise prices and greater difficulties in forming an effective cartel.

Finally, currency changes will be inflationary or deflationary for individual countries, depending on whether their exchange rates move down or up. For the world as a whole, however, the effects of currency changes on inflation should be essentially neutral because the experiences of individual countries will tend to be canceled out in the process of aggregation.

As against these inflationary tendencies, only a few counter-forces appear present. First, there is the deflationary impact, which we have already described, of the wealth transfer itself. In depressing consumption, it will tend to restrain price increases. Second, a shift toward more investment should, in the long run, moderate inflation. And third, after giving inflation a boost with their initial quantum jump, energy prices may subsequently slow the inflationary spiral by rising more slowly than other prices, possibly even by declining from present levels.

On balance, it would seem that the oil crisis has set in motion a number of forces that, in combination, will increase inflation not only in 1974, but also beyond.

VIII

Even if the monetary system should get through the energy crisis with its feathers unruffled, which seems unlikely, and even if there is no long-term damage to the growth and inflation prospects of the industrial world, which would take a bit of luck, I don't think that we can count on getting by with no skin off our collective backs. The transfer of wealth to oil-producing countries cannot fail to take its toll on the living standards of the industrial world, although even here some of the real burden could be shifted to future generations.

What impairment of living standards means in this context is having less of the nation's output available to its own people. And this is a different matter from employment or economic growth. An example will make this clear. Suppose that the OPEC countries were able to spend every cent of their higher incomes, and that what they wanted to buy in the United States was precisely those things which Americans could no longer afford because of higher oil prices. In that case, no one would lose his job or suffer a loss of money income, the existing structure of output would be maintained and, with it, the country's growth rate. But income in the United States would buy less, and output that would have been enjoyed by Americans would be shipped to the OPEC countries. We can estimate roughly what this would amount to in quantitative terms. If, indeed, the United States paid for the increased cost of oil imports with current output, the transfer would entail roughly the same burden as a ten percent increase in personal income taxes.

Now, consider the opposite extreme. Suppose that the OPEC countries did not wish to spend any of their money for imports, and that their entire income went into investments abroad. In this case, there need not be any change in jobs, incomes, growth or even consumption in the industrial countries. For illustrative purposes, suppose that the higher cost of imported oil were offset by tax cuts in the consuming countries. This would maintain their consumers' purchasing power. The resulting government deficits could then be financed by drawing on the capital accumulations of OPEC. The real burden of the wealth transfer would then occur in the future, not in the present.

In reality, the actual outcome will be somewhere between these two extremes. In the early years, while OPEC import spending remains low in relation to income, the current burden of the wealth transfer may be light for the industrial countries, and their future output will be mortgaged. Later, when OPEC expenditures rise to meet income, the current burden will intensify.

IX

Now, let us say a few words about the effects of the world oil crisis on the Third World. To oversimplify for this purpose, we can effectively split the globe in half, carefully cutting to include West Africa and Latin America in one semi-sphere, and East Africa and Asia in the other. In the western half, there is enough indigenous energy or exportable mineral wealth to leave many of the countries relatively unscathed by the rocketing energy import prices.

In the eastern half, where nearly one billion people already struggle on a per capita GNP of $100 to $200, the consequences will be acutely felt. In most cases, local energy supplies are minimal or not readily expandable. Energy imports are large relative to mineral exports or indeed total exports. There appear to be few opportunities for efficiencies or a reduction in luxury imports to counterbalance the substantial impending increase in the import bill. What oil these countries purchase will be paid for dearly in terms of imported capital equipment and therefore future growth forgone, and what oil they forgo importing will result in current GNP losses. Thus, the eastern half of the Dark Continent will become darker still and the nations of the subcontinent of Asia will no longer merit the adjective "emerging." These latter countries represent those very dominoes to which the United States has paid such profound attention during the cold war. It seems unlikely that the industrial nations or the oil-rich Arab states will be willing to provide financial support on the scale that could well be necessary to avoid political violence and anarchy in these countries.

X

This article has ranged broadly over the domestic and international implications of the recent extraordinary increases in oil import prices. Difficult internal adjustments will be necessary in the economies of oil-importing countries, but serious harm to employment, growth, inflation and living standards can probably be avoided at least in the industrial world. In many developing countries, however, the consequences will be severe, if not ruinous.

The resource-poor Third World is not the only area of particular vulnerability to the impact of the energy crisis. The Achilles' heel of the entire world economy may turn out to be the international payments system. The financial flows associated with more expensive oil are so immense as to threaten intolerable balance-of-payments strains and currency instability. While technical solutions to many, if not all, of the financial problems can be devised, it remains to be seen whether international coöperation will be up to the task of implementing them. The price of failure could be high. To fail would be to risk competitive devaluations and trade restrictions that would amplify recessionary tendencies already set in motion by the energy crisis.

U.S. TRADE POLICY:
THE NEW POLITICAL DIMENSIONS

By William Diebold, Jr.

NEW tremors in the world economy threaten to put a stop to the painstaking efforts by which American trade policy is being, with much uncertainty, adapted to modern times. The danger should be fought off—but that will require still more adaptation.

After a period of unprecedented continuity, from 1934 to the mid-1960s, American foreign trade policy entered a time of great uncertainty. The implications for the world economy were serious, since American policy had been the lever by which a high degree of trade liberalization had been achieved. The strong unilateral action taken by the United States in the summer of 1971—ending the convertibility of the dollar into gold and imposing a surcharge on imports—dramatically suggested how disruptive an American turn to clear-cut economic nationalism might be. In retrospect, it can also be seen as a watershed beyond which American policy made a new start toward the further liberalization of world trade. Ambiguities, uncertainties and obstacles remained, other countries were slow to respond, but a process was under way. Now, suddenly, the entire effort is imperilled by new, dramatic events that seem likely to bring out the worst in everyone.

The questions are not just those of Watergate, foreign oil, Russian wheat, the wounds of Vietnam, traumatic reactions in Japan, and the year of Europe that was, though all these are part of the picture. To understand the present position, we need to look not only at recent events but at some fundamental changes in the political dimensions of American foreign trade policy. International relations, domestic politics, and changes in the nature of international trade policy itself are all involved. A few new developments are clear-cut and have predictable consequences for trade policy. For the most part analysis runs up against developments that are more sensed than demonstrated, and must deal with vivid events that may not have anything like the same significance in the long run that people now ascribe to them. The best that one can do at this point is to try to clarify the issues. In international economic affairs, "thinking makes it so" more often than is generally realized. Therein may lie the difference between a zero-sum game (in which one nation or group gains only at the expense of others) and a game in which all can gain if they do the right things. Both kinds exist in the world economy, and it helps to know which one is playing.

II

Let us start with some points that were already clear before mid-1973. Since the end of the Kennedy Round in 1967 it has been clear that the politics of international trade policy will never be the same again, at least as regards the trade among the industrialized countries with market-oriented economies. In about 25 years, North America, Western Europe and Japan dismantled most of the structure of tariffs, quotas and exchange controls that restricted the large share of world trade that they carry on among themselves. In other ways as well these economies became more open to one another. While some important tariffs remain, any further progress in trade liberalization among these countries will have to concentrate on the impediments loosely labeled "nontariff barriers."

Differing greatly from one another in form, purpose and effect —the list includes subsidies, customs classification, "buy-American" laws, tax rebates on exports, and conserving endangered species, among other things—these trade-distorting practices cannot be dealt with by the sweeping and more-or-less uniform methods that have been so successful in reducing tariffs and eliminating quotas. Often the interference with trade is quite incidental to so worthy a purpose as enforcing the pure food and drug laws or making automobiles safer. Hidden protectionism exists side by side with perfectly overt efforts to keep foreigners from dominating certain industries.

Many of these practices can only be dealt with by agreements on rules and principles that will then have to be applied to cases in a continuing process of international negotiation. Rulings that one subsidy paid to a shoe company is acceptable while another violates an agreement will lack the drama or political force of a commitment to abolish tariffs (as in the Common Market) or even just to cut them across the board (as in the Kennedy Round). Even more important, the fact that so many nontariff barriers are connected with the regulation of national economic activities means that foreign trade negotiations will impinge directly on domestic issues and on what may already be serious struggles among politically important interests. Consider, for example, disputes about environmental controls that raise production costs at home. Should fear of foreign competition influence the decision? While it has not been easy to remove tariffs, this kind of choice sounds more thorny.

Of the remaining tariffs, some may prove no harder to remove than those already dismantled (these things are often more formidable in anticipation than in practice). Others may present great difficulties because they shelter economic activities that governments have been reluctant to expose to international competition—for good reasons or bad. If these tariffs are not to be left standing, governments may well try to work out international arrangements to deal with the difficult problems of adjustment they will face. Gradual liberalization and assistance to workers for changing jobs might be accompanied by temporary arrangements limiting competition and by agreements on the international structure of an industry, under which, for example, two countries might specialize in making components while a third puts them together.

Even if governments indulge one another and leave the existing protection of "hard cases" intact, they will not escape the problem of adjustment. The structure of production is always changing, probably more rapidly than in the past and often in big, irregular jumps as technology decrees larger units of production. The new trade flows threaten established producers. Governments are pressed to erect new trade barriers. Unless these are to become permanent, something has to be done to help bring about adjustment. Once again a combination of international acceptance, help and pressure is called for.

These observations add up to the conclusion that future international trade negotiations are going to be politically more difficult than those of the past. If they are to bring about further trade liberalization, or even just to maintain what has already been accomplished, governments will have to commit themselves to a close and sustained process of coöperation. Much of what has to be done will be complex and tedious, without the glamor of striking accomplishment. When issues are dramatic that will be because they seem to jeopardize someone's job, and perhaps even national security. The international trade negotiations will, more than ever before, involve problems that already cause domestic controversy and that are not generally thought of as being the proper business of foreigners. Unfamiliar questions will arise that cannot be dealt with by such simple principles as that we should reduce tariffs reciprocally. And all this will go on continuously, without many moments of high political feeling that can be used to get public support for measures that promise long-run gain at the possible cost of short-run sacrifices.

III

The second clear-cut change in the political dimensions of trade policy lies inside the United States.

After Vietnam, Watergate, and arguments over presidential privilege and impoundment, the first question about trade policy was whether there was any chance that Congress would give President Nixon the extensive, and to some degree discretionary, powers he would need if he was to enter into a period of hard bargaining. The initial, though partial, answer was remarkably positive. The Ways and Means Committee reported and the House passed by a substantial majority a trade bill that gave the President most of what he asked for (except in the matter of most-favored-nation treatment for the U.S.S.R., which raises a separate set of questions). Why the House endorsed this strong move in the direction of further liberalization instead of adopting something like the restrictive Burke-Hartke bill is a matter of considerable interest that will have to be passed over to get to the second question: How would the difficult relations between the President and Congress affect the way the United States tried to deal with the complex matter of nontariff barriers?

In the great procedural innovation of the Hull Trade Agreements Act of 1934, Congress granted power to the President to reduce tariffs when he could satisfy the standards laid down in the law. This made tariffs a subject of international negotiation in a way that they could not be so long as Congress interpreted its constitutional mandate to regulate foreign trade to mean that every specific change in the tariff had to be made by legislation. That method naturally made domestic considerations dominant in almost every specific issue. Repeated renewals of the Trade Agreements Act have made the 1934 innovations established practice, but have also tightened or loosened the rein on the President. The question for the future is what procedure should be used to deal with nontariff barriers.

The variety of such barriers makes it hard to imagine writing criteria that would cover all of them. The links of many of them with other kinds of activity make it unlikely that any Congress would delegate all its power over them to the President. He would in effect become legislator as well as executive and could alter domestic arrangements to conform to international agreements. But if no power was granted and every case had to be treated on an ad hoc basis and if Congress had to go through the normal legislative process every time an American trade-distorting practice was rooted in a statute, the prospects of trade liberalization would be very poor.

President Nixon asked for some delegation of powers, particularly to deal with measures already linked with other trade barriers and presumably having no other purpose than protection. Much more important was the proposal that if the President negotiates an international agreement on trade practices that would normally require legislation, he should lay it before Congress with an explanation of his purposes and the advantages of what was proposed to the United States. If within 90 days neither house of Congress had disapproved the agreement by a simple majority, it would become law. The House made some modifications in this procedure but accepted its basic feature. If the Senate accepts something like this (and otherwise there can hardly be any broad trade negotiations) a new era will have opened in American trade policy.

To use the new procedure, any administration will plainly have to work much more closely with Congress during trade negotiations than has been usual in the past. Otherwise, it will not know what measures are likely to be acceptable. To a degree, the law already anticipates this, as Congress must be notified of use of the new procedure three months before any agreement is submitted, thus giving an opportunity for advice and consultation. It does not take much imagination to see that members of Congress will use their part in the new procedure to influence matters beyond those for which their assent is technically required. That would be natural in any case, but the nature of the international agreements encourages it. American agreements affecting nontariff barriers will often be closely related to other understandings in which foreign concessions are balanced against American measures that lie within the President's power. Moreover, American interest groups will press Representatives and

Senators to make their assent to specific agreements dependent on other features of the Administration's trade policy as well. Obviously one can spin these connections out indefinitely. How far they will in fact be carried, and to what effect, depends on circumstances. Carried too far, no one will gain, because the international bargains, too, will have their limits. Nevertheless, to a degree not known in recent years, it will be prudent for the executive to keep in close touch with Congress, which feels about the fait accompli much as nature does about vacuums.

Well done, this process may involve some members of both houses in the negotiating process sufficiently to make them fully aware of the reasons for striking particular bargains and perhaps to give them some sense of shared responsibility as well. Indeed, the course of wisdom may be for an administration to find ways of working with at least part of Congress along a much wider front than just that provided for in the new procedure for dealing with nontariff barriers. This presumably is already foreshadowed in provisions in the House bill that are intended to make the participation of congressional advisers in international negotiations more meaningful than it has usually been. In addition, the President is called on to explain many of his specific actions and this should create opportunities for the expression of congressional opinion.

There are some difficulties on the congressional side. Neither the House nor the Senate will always accord foreign issues the same importance the executive does. A division of labor among committees anchored in the past, no longer corresponds to the requirements of contemporary trade policy. There may, therefore, be a need for some new organizational arrangements on the congressional side. A Joint Committee on Foreign Trade Policy would not only cut across the separate characteristics of the two houses but also the widely diffused committee responsibility in each chamber for the many different issues that come into modern trade policy. Beyond the organization of Congress lie questions about new kinds of "steering committees" bridging the gaps between Cabinet members, White House and the loci of power in Congress.

Will even the best arrangements work? Among those whose minds go back far enough, there is a negative reflex related to the horrors of congressional tariff-making in 1931 and before. Others draw back from the prospect of conducting delicate or technical negotiations through delegations that include members of Congress who—unlike most negotiators—have independent political power and at the same time cannot escape a special sensitivity about certain subjects, depending on the make-up of their districts. It is also no exaggeration to suppose that sometimes otherwise reasonable bargains will be put askew by someone's burning interest in a matter remote from trade policy, such as Soviet emigration, the stationing of American troops in Europe or the status of Okinawa.

All these dangers are real. If they all eventuated, American trade diplomacy would be hobbled. But if that is what Congress intends, it has shorter and more direct ways to accomplish it. So one must assume that there is a wish to make the new arrangements work. There are, after all, members of Congress who appreciate the disadvantages of being too closely drawn into the intricate process of trade negotiation and who know that influence may in the long run be gained more by reasonableness than by the arbitrary assertion of will. In any case, there is no real choice. The constitutional and legal systems of the United States require the two branches of the federal government to work together in both foreign trade and domestic legislation. When those two subjects have merged as much as they have in the present interdependent world new ways have to be found to get around old difficulties.

IV

Outside the United States, there are also changes in the political dimensions of international trade negotiations. Western Europe and Japan were transformed from weak spots in the international economy at the end of the war to major centers of strength by the 1960s. For both, foreign trade was economically more important than for the United States, but for reasons that are now fairly well understood neither was inclined to take the lead in improving the international trading system. Indeed, in the post-Kennedy Round period, their preoccupation with other problems exacerbated the rather widespread American sense that others were not carrying their share of the burdens of managing international matters, and that the coöperative system the United States had worked so hard to create was a one-sided affair that gave the United States no advantages when it was weak though it had forgone privileges when it was strong. The troubles with the international monetary system added to the difficulties, with foreigners seeing the dollar as privileged while Americans came to regard its function as a world currency as rather burdensome.[1]

The dramatic action of the United States in the summer of 1971 and the language that accompanied it served a double purpose. For other countries, it was something like the blow on the head by a mallet traditionally required to get the donkey's attention. For the United States, it started a process that set the dollar free, raised the exchange rates of other currencies, and led to further floating so that eventually—and perhaps only for the time being—adjustments took place that reduced the strains that were setting in around trade policy. As time passed the U.S. balance of payments strengthened, American resentment eased, and pressure to demand one-sided concessions from the rest of the world dropped. Europeans and Japanese acquired a greater interest in access to the American market for their products. But they did not quickly change their attitudes. Fear that the United States would link economic issues with security arrangements and political coöperation caused Europeans to hold back. So matters teetered back and forth, but it became ever more apparent that in one way or another trading arrangements of the world would have to become the subject of serious international negotiation.

Some deep-seated factors abetted immediate considerations in creating this widespread reluctance to push ahead with the process of international economic coöperation. One was general affluence, which seemed to make people more willing to bear the cost of misusing resources rather than face the political strain of adjusting to large changes. The great reduction of trade barriers that had already taken place meant that the gains that could be expected from further liberalization seemed small compared with those of the past. Malaise and discontent, common to the industrial countries, made governments and people focus on issues that seemed far more urgent than the distant promise of good results from international negotiations. The feeling grew that governments were rarely as well occupied as when they were knitting up their raveled societies. For those looking after the domestic welfare, international interdependence seemed a source of constraint and distraction. For some people nationalism took on a benign hue, while the gains of past international

---

[1] The process is described more fully in William Diebold, Jr., "The Economic System at Stake," *Foreign Affairs*, October 1972, pp. 167–180.

coöperation were more or less taken for granted.

At the same time, it became a commonplace to say that economic issues were coming to occupy a larger place than ever in international affairs and thus had become "politically" more significant. Whether it makes any sense to call the welfare of a people "economic" or "political" may be beside the point, but the commonplace has probably earned its status by being largely true. But then what? Will governments now pay more attention to devising policies that will contribute to the welfare of their people? Or will they try to give reality to the old cliché and make economic policy the handmaiden of foreign policy, letting the ends of the latter dictate the means of the former? The questions suggest quite different courses of action, but not everyone who subscribes to the thesis of the increased political importance of economics seems to realize this. Part of the difficulty is that policies directed toward the long-run economic welfare have to come to terms with the world as a whole, while foreign policy measures more often than not have to deal with specific countries. Economic measures used to serve the latter purpose often seem contrary to the former. They are also likely to induce others to use economic influence in the same way. When this process gets going, we are only one step away from the rivalries of bloc-building, and rather far from the benign nationalism that is mainly concerned with domestic welfare.

These unresolved tensions—hardly new but more prominent in the last decade than in the years right after World War II—provide still another change in the political dimensions of foreign trade policy, and one that cannot be so sharply characterized as those that have been set out before. Perhaps because these issues are not posed in quite the same way in foreign offices and chancelleries, ministers of the main trading countries in the world—and quite a few others as well—were able to put their names to the Declaration of Tokyo in September 1973. Hardly a guarantee of what could be accomplished, that carefully negotiated document announced a comprehensive and complex set of negotiations under the aegis of the General Agreement on Tariffs and Trade (GATT), aimed at reducing trade barriers further.

V

Even before it was signed, and more markedly right afterward, striking events took place which raised questions about

whether the Declaration of Tokyo provided an adequate framework to deal with the biggest problems that were besetting international trade.[2] Before long, people began saying that it looked
as if the world had once more prepared itself to fight the battles
of the last war. In fact, however, there was a lot more to it than
that.

A sharp increase in world demand for farm products during
1973 was accompanied by substantial price increases and the
running down of American stocks. There was a sharp reaction
in the United States against massive sales of grain to the U.S.S.R.
What were once seen as welcome gains in the export balance
began to be regarded as a domestic deprivation. Up to a point
the shift seemed to improve the prospects for successful trade
negotiations between the United States and the European Community, by extracting the venomous teeth of the American in-
sistence on gaining a freer access to the Community's protected
farm market, which Europe was not about to provide. Anything
that strengthened exports made it easier for American negotiators to agree to balanced bargains. More generally, rising prices
and fears of shortages might encourage a recently manifested
willingness to remove import barriers to ease inflation. As part
of their efforts to fight inflation during the early 1970s, governments in Western Europe, Japan, Canada and the United States
on several occasions unilaterally removed tariffs and quotas to
increase domestic supplies and reduce the strains on prices. The
logic of such a step was obvious, but it was rare that it should be
transferred from the textbook to policy.

Unfortunately for these happy prospects, the other side of the
farm boom of the summer of 1973 was the erection of new trade
restrictions. The United States imposed export embargoes on the
shipment of soybeans—its greatest export crop—and other feed-
stuffs. This too was a response to inflationary pressure and a not
unnatural one. Not altogether unprecedented, the step was un-
usual enough to be quite disturbing. It upset many expectations
in the United States and abroad about the nature of interdependence, once more shook the Japanese, and encouraged those who
thought the European Community's Common Agricultural Pol-

[2] For help in clarifying my views on the questions discussed in this and the remaining
sections of this article, I am grateful to the members of a Current Issue Review Group
at the Council on Foreign Relations where some of the issues were discussed in early
1974. In helping prepare material for that group and in many other matters concerned
with this article, I had invaluable help from Helena Stalson.

icy should be more rather than less protective.

Dependability of supply became the focus. The subject was not entirely a new one to Americans who had been debating whether it made sense to offer credits to the Soviet Union to be repaid in oil and gas in years to come. Neither the Americans nor many other trading nations had thought to ask the same questions about themselves. GATT had rules on export limitation but not much attention had been paid to them. And no one, it seemed, had tried to work his way through the problem systematically. Should countries be free to impose export controls at will? Or were there to be criteria about the degrees of inflation and shortage that would justify controls? Did it make any difference whether there were contracts? Should there be rules about allocation between domestic demand and exports or only among foreign customers? Were traditional trade flows to be treated differently from new or exceptional ones? Plainly, there was something to be added to the agenda set out in the Tokyo Declaration. And if nothing else had happened, perhaps that is just what would have been done. But before that point had been reached, other commodity problems were blotted out by concern over energy. Difficulties there had been building up for some time—but then came the oil embargoes of the fall of 1973.

Dark visions arose in the cities of the industrial world—cuts in power, cuts in production, cuts in employment, the very prescription for depression or at least recession on a scale unknown since the end of World War II. And if those who controlled the supplies would release them at a less-than-recession-causing rate, what did one have to pay—or do—to become a favored customer? The cost of oil, it was freely predicted, would so burden the balances of payments of the consuming countries, and particularly Japan and Western Europe, that all hope of trade liberalization would be lost. Not only could they not import more freely but the diversion of demand from other things to pay for oil would sharply contract trade among themselves. At the same time, each would be fostering its own exports to get the wherewithal for imports. Competitive devaluation would be the order of the day. The Japanese would try to push billions of dollars worth of quickly marketable consumer goods into Western markets to earn dollars. Market disruption would be apparent; governments would not let imports create unemployment; new barriers would be thrown up and they would generate retaliation. A trade war among the major industrialized countries was just around the corner.

The situation did not make for calm judgment, and soon the difficulties with energy amplified existing concern about the possible scarcity of raw materials generally. Old fears revived and were reinforced by much recent discussion of the long-run depletion of irreplaceable resources and the pressure of man on his environment. With the loss of precision and qualification that seems unavoidable when the vulgarization of careful work (and perhaps some not so careful) takes place, proper concerns for the future become nightmares of the present, as in Goya's picture of the dream of reason that produces monsters.

The new circumstances seem almost enough to put all past trade policy on a shelf, if not to destroy it completely. Certainly if there is a serious recession the only trade policy problem for some time to come will be how to keep to a minimum the damage that will undoubtedly be done to trade relations among all countries. This will be extremely difficult, and regaining lost ground afterward will be even harder. Similarly, if the oil producers stick together and the oil consumers find no better way of conducting themselves than to scramble for favors, there will be trade warfare. And the zero-sum game that they will have made out of trade is likely to carry over into the rest of their relations as well. In such circumstances one could say that trade policy has taken on a new political dimension—but that will be equally true if the extremes of recession or trade warfare are avoided.

VI

Put another way, new political dimensions for trade policy arise from the need to give far more attention than anyone thought necessary in recent years to energy and raw materials and their possible scarcity. Some of these issues can be sketched in a single article but not in any depth. Yet even at a very general level, the discussion of what trade policy may have to become is subject to two very considerable limitations.

The first is uncertainty. We do not know whether a major problem of scarcity exists or how long it might last. The energy cartel is real enough, and dear instead of cheap energy is a probability for the future. The great surge in raw materials prices is impressive but we can be less sure what it portends. There have been raw materials booms before and, while there are good reasons to suppose that this one will have some durable effects, to say what they are is guesswork. A general rise in raw materials costs presents a different set of problems from those of shortages of individual materials. The expectation of specific scarcities may itself induce at least partial solutions. To many shortages, the market provides an adequate response, and it is rare for producers to organize as effectively as the Organization of Petroleum Exporting Countries (OPEC).[3] With so much uncertainty, it would be rather foolish to embark on a complex series of international negotiations to work out potentially acceptable principles for situations that may not arise. But it would be even more foolish not to have prepared for such situations if they do arise. Consequently, a double-track policy has to be devised, one track to be followed if things go along much as they used to, the other to be ready if the fears of 1973 and 1974 become realities.

The second major limitation is that if one is trying either to avoid scarcity or to find the best way of living with it, the main weapons are almost certainly not to be found in trade policy. They concern production, investment, conservation, limits on consumption, research and development, and national or international agreement on the principles of equitable sharing and distribution. Here one must recognize that markets do not do very well in giving price signals about the scarcities that may exist a decade hence—nor are the projections of the most affected industries likely to be more reliable than they have proved in the case of energy. Thus, if we have reason to expect scarcity, the market's function in allocating, guiding and balancing demand and supply has to be supplemented by the acts of national, international or private entities in a position to influence production and demand. To find and insert the public interest, vital though it is, is not easy.

But all such measures will have trade elements, and trade policy can be important; while it cannot by itself ensure the avoidance of scarcity it can help the equitable adaptation to it. It is not easy to tell, however, just how trade policy should fit together with other measures. Surely a "trade policy for scarcity," which people say we need, cannot ignore the need to use resources efficiently, which is the basis of the argument for re-

[3] See Bension Varon and Kenji Takeuchi, "Developing Countries and Non-Fuel Minerals," in this issue of *Foreign Affairs*.

moving trade barriers.

Subject to these limitations, it seems clear that one new objective of trade policy in a time of scarcity must be to provide for "access to supplies"—a concept that looks like a reasonable counterpart of the "access to markets" that is provided by removing trade barriers. The thought is not new; access to raw materials on equal terms was one of the main features of the Atlantic Charter. Roosevelt, Churchill, and their advisers were worried about the cartels of the interwar period, the restrictive policies of some colonial powers and the belief that German and Japanese aggression was fueled at least in part by their drives as have-nots. But of all the great principles that found some kind of expression in the postwar economic arrangements, this was the least honored and least well defined. There were shortages right after the war and during the Marshall Plan; the Korean War called forth international allocations; the Paley Commission predicted an increasing American dependence on imported raw materials. These predictions came true. The United States continued, for a time, to have pieces of a raw materials policy—stockpiling, barter for supplies of surplus agricultural products, tax laws favoring mineral exploration and extraction—but for the most part the subject disappeared from the agenda of international negotiations and U.S. foreign economic policy. There seemed to be no problem so far as the consumers were concerned. It was the producing countries which complained that they could not sell enough at high enough prices.

Now the industrialized countries are worried and they talk of access to raw materials. But the old slogan sounds a bit hollow. Why should the producing countries pledge allegiance to this high-sounding principle at the moment when they are being told that their possessions are scarce, their bargaining power has grown, and the ability of the industrial nations to avoid recession and the ruin of the coöperative attitudes that have grown up since the end of the war depends on not falling over one another in a scramble for raw materials? If the hewers of wood and the drawers of water are suddenly told that they are in fact operating a public utility of vital importance, they are not likely to respond by simply working harder. And if they are also poor countries, the sensible question they ask themselves is: "How can I use my new-found advantages to get a larger share of the good things of the world?" It seems unlikely that much of the answer will be found in reverting to a principle that the rich countries have extracted from their memory books and dusted off for the occasion.

There are tangible benefits that the industrial countries can offer, but these have their limitations. How to provide guaranteed markets at remunerative prices has been discussed for years. The problem has been to interest sellers in these arrangements when exports are strong and profitable and to interest buyers when the products are plentiful and the prices low. The industrial countries may now be readier than they were in the past to make commitments, but by the same token the sellers are likely to think it is better to wait. The industrial countries can also offer access to their markets for other exports of the producing countries. This approach is promising if a country has a variety of things to export, but it does not fit a number of raw materials-producing countries, on the one hand, or Singapore and Hong Kong, on the other. There is a good deal of talk about getting access to raw materials by offering to help the producers to industrialize. This is plainly desirable but no great concession; those well enough off to buy have long been able to command the technical resources that are needed to develop industry. Still, the approach would be a healthy one, and still greater progress could be made if the rich countries would promise to open their markets to the products of the industries yet to be built in the raw materials-producing countries. A start might be made by shifting more processing industries to producing countries.

All of these approaches will probably fit one situation or another. None will fit all. They hardly add up to a raw materials trade policy. They may reduce the incentive to producers of other materials to emulate OPEC, and they may help one country or another to assure itself of supplies of certain raw materials. However, even otherwise constructive economic measures can be manipulated to the detriment of third parties. That is probably what will happen if the industrialized countries pursue purely national policies.

To avoid this, some people will prefer a more general approach, such as that embodied in the chapter on commodity agreements in the abortive Charter of the International Trade Organization (ITO) back in 1945–47. Reflecting the dual experience of the 1930s with raw materials cartels and the instability of raw materials markets, these provisions still read rather well as principles. They defined the circumstances in which restrictive arrangements could be made, limited their duration, and suggested the best methods to be used. Consumers and producers shared responsibility for running the agreements; there was a trade-off between stability of prices and markets and access to supplies. After the ITO failed, these principles were discussed further, but one reason they have never been widely followed up is that it is so hard to get governments to apply them to cases. Apart from the differences in national interests, commodities differ greatly from one another; devices that would work well in one case are unworkable in another. The last surge of American interest in commodity agreements came at the beginning of the Kennedy administration, but its only accomplishment was the coffee agreement, a rather special case.

Although the long-run objective must be arrangements that satisfy both producers and consumers, the difficulty of reconciling their interests means that trade policies based on coöperation among the consuming countries alone also need to be explored. The energy difficulties have shown how hard it can be to get consuming countries to work together even when their common interests are clear, but few commodities touch as many political, social, and economic nerves as energy. Moderate steps aimed at avoiding the emergence of new OPECs may be easier to arrive at than the hard decisions of dealing with them once they have shown their strength.

Even in dealing with a cartel once formed, consumers are not powerless. With the present changing situation, this is not the time to try to describe possible strategies, but it is at least worth noting that the history of international cartels is one of failure. Someone cheats; some outsider becomes too important to be ignored; the value of selling more becomes greater than that of holding the price line; prices are held too high to keep the market from shrinking; new producers appear; substitutes are developed; technology permits users to get more out of the same quantity. All these possibilities apply to OPEC. But before *something* happens to make monopoly less monopolistic, the cartel works, consumers suffer, and Mr. Micawber looks the fool if all he does is wait for what turns up. When each consumer "does something" on his own, so long as he acts separately he is really only acting the way competitors are "supposed to" in the face of a monopolist. He is at best the most intelligent rát in the maze, perhaps better fed than the others but still at the will of whoever is in charge.

True, there are separate national actions that can help the common cause of the consumers. High prices cut demand and bring forth new supplies, whether of oil or substitutes. New supplies may mean new suppliers. One's increase in self-sufficiency frees supplies for others; fading markets may beguile a producer into selling more than good cartel management says he should (or than his less needy partners want him to). All increases in world supplies do consumers some good. But such gains—which may be slow—will be cold comfort if they are accompanied by the strains resulting from the interplay of wholly separate national trade policies. Unless there is an agreement on self-restraint, trade barriers will be used as bargaining weapons, as devices to exploit (or resist) monopolistic positions and as means of granting discriminatory favors. The zero-sum approach will tend to dominate; the use of measures resembling economic warfare in one field will stimulate them in others.

Thus, if disputes about energy and raw materials are not to poison all relations, there will have to be continuing exploration of ways to reconcile real and imagined conflicts of interest. This will require extensive discussions between producers and consumers, among consumers and among producers. Even such often-scorned marshmallows as international study groups have a place. They may be a little less vulnerable to partisan manipulation than national or industry-based studies. But before much can be accomplished by this approach, the United States has to arrive at at least the rudiments of a national trade policy on raw materials. This it lacks.

VII

A start has been made under the impact of the energy crisis. The United States, President Nixon has announced, will aim at creating the capability of self-sufficiency. How quickly this can be done, how best and at what cost are matters of great debate. But whether something resembling self-sufficiency in energy supplies is achieved in five, ten or fifteen years, it is not too early to consider the kind of trade policy that goes with such an energy policy. At first glance, zero trade seems the natural counterpart of autarky, but that is neither logically necessary nor very realistic. There is no need to rule out exports—of coal, now in solid, perhaps later in gaseous form, nuclear materials, and maybe some day something else. But decisions will have to be made as to whether exports are to move only when domestic demand is fully met even if long-term contracts have to be broken.

Even the policy toward imports is not obvious. They could be either forbidden or encouraged. If world prices are lower, imports might be taxed to protect the domestic price level, or American energy producers might be subsidized. If the costs of achieving self-sufficiency in energy make American manufactured goods less competitive in world markets, should exports be subsidized and compensatory taxes put on imports? Ways might be found to put the "capacity" for self-sufficiency on a stand-by basis so that American users could buy the cheapest energy in the world while the country could be kept immune to blackmail. All this sounds like a prescription for a great deal of government intervention. Such issues may sound recondite, but they must be faced before too long.

Whatever, in the years to come, may prove to be the most intelligent American policy concerning energy supplies, it will not be sensible to apply the same standards to all raw materials. Self-sufficiency is not physically possible for some, the creation of substitutes not economically sensible for others. With regard to some materials—not to mention farm products—the United States will probably remain an exporter. In this mixed position, there is both strength and weakness for the United States. It may be possible to devise a selective policy that will both fit American needs and be acceptable to other countries. But if so, this will be because the United States has learned to accept that even as it is heavily dependent on others for many key raw materials, so others are entitled to rely on the United States in food and other areas. This is a condition of interdependence that the United States has not consciously thought through.

Two examples will illustrate some of the problems of a mixed policy. Some people are already asking: "How can I persuade anyone to favor liberal trade measures if the President calls for self-sufficiency in energy?" Will the public—or Congress—believe that it is right to protect the coal miner's job if the autoworker is told to find something else to do when the new plants in his "simple" industry are located in Algeria or Mexico? Internationally, the choice of self-sufficiency—the acme of "going it alone"—can easily be made to appear as a kind of non-coöperation that makes working together on other matters impossible. In fact, though, U.S. self-sufficiency in oil would ease the problem of others by removing American demand from the market. Much depends on how this approach is conceived. Secretary Kissinger's speech of February 12, 1974, laid out in some detail a program of cooperation with other oil consumers which was broadly compatible with concurrent American efforts at achieving self-sufficiency.

The second example concerns uniformity of rules. As consumers of energy annoyed at the Arabs, Americans find it easy to champion "access to raw materials." In that mood they will support international agreements to limit the use of export controls. But is not easy to imagine enthusiastic congressional support when it becomes clear that any uniform rules would operate to prevent the United States from limiting the purchase of food by others in the American market—even if such purchases meant that the supply on the supermarket shelf would be reduced and probably more expensive.

To be sure, rules do not have to be uniform for all products but what the United States withholds in one category is likely to be matched by what other countries are unwilling to agree to in other matters. Again the rest of the world might easily view the Americans as hypocritical. (In ITO days, it used to be said that a commodity agreement was a cartel that the U.S. Department of Agriculture wanted to belong to.) There is bound to be trouble if American support of sharing turns out to apply just to the goods that move in international trade and takes no account of differing levels of consumption. Secretary Kissinger seemed to recognize this when he admitted that the United States was "the world's most profligate energy consumer."

A U.S. trade policy adequate to the new needs of the world must deal not only with subjects already touched on in this article, such as access to raw materials, the use of export controls and commodity agreements, but also with many other questions. Among these are stockpiling, national or international, against shortages, natural or man-made, and a whole collection of domestic measures, not least the tax laws, which in a rather higgledy-piggledy way now help shape national performance in these matters. If security of supply is to be an element in policy —and it usually is, at least with regard to some materials— criteria have to be developed regarding the nature of security when the supplier is foreign. Is security geographical, political, or economic? Should some foreign producers be helped, encouraged, and made more secure by being tied more closely to the American economy than others? Would more security be gained by leaving producers on their own? The further one pushes these different lines of questioning, the more political dimensions of trade policy one discovers.

This is not a particularly attractive prospect. The knitting together of the economies of the industrialized countries in the first quarter-century after World War II was in large part due to the sheltering of trade measures from the disturbances of short-run international politics. Thus it was possible to devise rules that were well understood by a limited and generally like-minded group of nations.

In dealing with raw materials problems we do not yet have agreed rules and we are working with a very different cast of characters. For a number of reasons, only some of them concerning the value of trade, the most important trade policy accomplishments of recent decades have concerned the exchanges among the industrialized countries of the northern hemisphere. The problems of the developing countries have been set aside in a special category. Conceived first as a form of the classical infant industry problem, and then seen more broadly as a facet of development, the trading practices of developing countries were exempted from the common obligation of reciprocity and from most other rules as well. Still later, the developing countries were conceded a special position, receiving from most countries preferential tariff treatment, though of a circumscribed kind. They have benefited rather little from this special treatment. If in fact we are entering a period of widespread raw materials scarcity, many developing countries may benefit. But not those that lack raw materials. As they industrialize, these poor countries—the new Japans to come?—are concerned with quite different kinds of trade issues. Some energy producers have already entered another category: rich but underdeveloped; and some of their income comes from poor countries without energy resources.

The line-up for dealing with raw materials problems is clearly different from anything we have seen before. Canada, Australia and the Soviet Union are among the major producers. So is the United States. Japan and the countries of Europe (Eastern as well as Western) are far more heavily dependent on imports of raw materials. But the division between producer and consumer, importer and exporter (which is not necessarily the same thing) differs from one product to another and according to whether food is in question or not. No existing international economic organization quite encompasses the issues. GATT, UNCTAD, FAO, OECD all deal with some of them. It would be a shallow approach to concentrate on drawing up the terms of reference for yet another organization. Before we know what needs to be done, there will have to be quite a few sets of negotiations of different sorts, in different places, about different issues.

The lines are not drawn—except for the time being in energy. For the rest, shifting coalitions, the essence of balance in a changing world, arise naturally in world trade in raw materials and foodstuffs. American policy should make the most of that fact. To do so will require us to break a good deal of new ground. In the process, trade policy will acquire still other political dimensions. Perhaps the most important long-run question is whether this new mix of producers and consumers—among whom the distribution of wealth and power is shifting markedly and will be quite different in the future from what it was in the past—will be able to discover a broad enough area of common interests to accept arrangements that can be seen to give all parties a reasonable share of the continuing benefits of coöperation, even if at any given moment someone is held back from making the most of his short-run advantages.

VIII

Though we are dealing with long-run developments, the analysis has short-run implications. Some are domestic. A trade bill lies before the Senate. What shall be done with it? There is no doubt that interest has flagged. "The Senators," one hears, "will see no point in legislating about nontariff barriers or the authority to bargain with Europeans and Japanese when the real question is how to get oil supplies and whether the copper producers are going to follow the example of OPEC. The bill is as good as dead." If it can be saved, according to this view, this will only be by writing in provisions to deal with the new and frustrating problems that beset us. Abroad, one hears that governments have no time to think about trade negotiations under the Tokyo Declaration; the real question is how to assure supplies, what imports to restrict, and what exports to push to obtain the wherewithal to pay for them. In any case, the foreign governments need make no decisions about the older program as long as the Senate does not put the United States in a position to negotiate.

Understandable as they are, such attitudes are wrong-headed. They are out of focus as to the continuing importance of trade among the industrialized countries. Even with huge price increases in raw materials and food, trade among them will long remain one of the largest segments of international exchanges, and the terms on which it takes place will require attention. The consuming countries can hardly be expected to work together to avoid a scramble for energy and other scarce resources if they cannot accommodate one another as they adjust to rather brutal changes in the world economy. This they will not be able to do if each can take with impunity whatever measures he wishes, however damaging to the trade of others. Unless they recognize an interest in coöperation of the sort envisaged in the Tokyo Declaration and can act on it (which requires American legislation), they can hardly be expected to do anything except strike at one another when that seems necessary.

That the proposed American law and the Tokyo Declaration do not deal adequately with all the requirements of the new situation is clear. But they cannot be adequately modified in the short run. The issues are too complex. An agreement among the main consuming countries on some language about access to raw materials would mean little without long negotiations with producers. But the energy difficulties show that the consumers are far from agreement on anything. Even if we think of the Senate bill as merely stating American policy, it cannot quickly be made into a good instrument for dealing with raw materials problems. This article has suggested some possible approaches. All are controversial. None will work if the ground is not well prepared, within the bureaucracy, in Congress, among interest groups, and in public opinion. As both a great consumer and great producer of raw materials and food, the United States has harder choices to make than many other countries. To postpone passage of the trade bill until the United States decides what it really wants in these new fields has nothing to recommend it.

Two things might usefully be added to the bill. Provisions concerning the use of export controls have been proposed by several Senators and accepted in principle by the Administration.

It would also be reasonable for Congress to indicate concern about the problem of raw materials and foodstuffs and to recognize the inadequacy of the legislation and the Declaration of Tokyo in this regard. The President could be directed to do something about the problem. (He might get in first by announcing such activity.) Perhaps broad principles could be set out to indicate the sense of Congress in the matter, though here the ground is made treacherous by current confusion and short-run preoccupations.

If such a bill were passed, what could be done with it? Probably not very much very soon, but one suspects that would have been true in the absence of an energy crisis as well. For the reasons set out earlier, significant negotiations among the industrial countries are likely to be slow—but without the U.S. legislation, hardly anything could be done. Its defeat would almost certainly be taken as a sign that the United States was not seriously interested in coöperation. The most immediate advantage of passing the bill would be to equip the President to deal with the multitude of trade issues that are bound to arise as each major trading country adjusts itself to the substantial changes in the world economy resulting from higher costs of energy and perhaps other raw materials as well. From a longer-run point of view, the main advantage of passage of the bill may well be the consolidation of the work—intellectual and political—that has gone into it. Even if disturbances in the world economy postpone the comprehensive negotiations envisaged in the Declaration of Tokyo, there is an advantage in recognizing that the major features of the bill embody steps that need to be taken sooner or later if the United States is to cope with the trade problems of the modern world. The constellation of forces that has brought matters to the present state cannot be put into suspended animation. Not to legislate now is to reopen for an indefinite period all the doubts that made the United States such an unhelpful presence in world economic issues between the late 1960s and the latest crises.

While no one could seriously argue that passage of the trade bill is the most important decision before the U.S. government in 1974, failure to pass it would needlessly muddy the waters just when a new current is running that may once again put the United States in a position of constructive leadership. Some of the powers given the President in the bill may well be usable in dealing with countries other than our main trading partners.

They will not suffice to cope with all the issues raised by the energy, food, and raw materials problems in the short or long run, for reasons already made plain. Uncertain as it is just how these problems will develop, the shaping of contingent national policies concerning them has a new priority. It will be done best if it is accompanied by international explorations, through whatever channels seem most promising. The aim should be to find how much common ground there is between the United States and other countries, both producers and consumers, on how the world's raw materials economy should be ordered in the long run.

More is involved than just securing adequate supplies for American needs or avoiding unnecessary disputes with friends. Secretary Kissinger struck just the right note when he told the international oil conference in February 1974 that all countries were affected by the problem before them and that the partial solutions any one of them could find would be inadequate. The United States sees it "as a matter of enlightened self-interest—and moral responsibility—to collaborate in the survival and restoration of the world economic system." It has taken some time for the United States to get back into that frame of mind, and any observer would be excused for saying he would like to wait and see whether the mood persists and what its practical consequences may turn out to be. It is rather sad that phrases such as Kissinger used should sound somewhat old-fashioned, for it has been as plain as plain can be for quite a long time now that the absence of such attitudes contributed greatly to the danger of collapse of the system of international economic coöperation that has brought such extensive benefits to the participants since the end of the war.

In the past, the main difficulties arose among the main beneficiaries of the system, the industrialized countries. Now, in energy and raw materials, the problems arise in the sectors where coöperation was weak, and the challenge comes from countries that benefited less than those which were considered to be in the seats of power. Perhaps the new challenge will sharpen people's consciousness of the importance of protecting the old arrangements. Inevitably it poses a new problem: to build a new system, covering neglected areas, accommodating a changed distribution of power, dividing benefits more equitably than in the past and—above all—providing effective ways of dealing with common problems, ways that convince those whose stakes and power are great enough to upset the system that they are better off not doing so.

This task is an additional political dimension of trade policy. Still another is connected with the reassessment of the American position in the world. Much has been said since the end of the Kennedy Round about the changed distribution of power and the impossibility of the United States' any longer providing the kind of leadership that had shaped the postwar world economy. This correct diagnosis was often taken to support the false conclusion that, therefore, there could be no effective American leadership at all. The new situation opens new possibilities.

Though one can hardly take seriously the view that in some Machiavellian way the United States has manipulated the oil crisis to restore the dollar to its old prominence and otherwise give Washington a helping hand, it is certainly true that the United States has proved less vulnerable than Japan and the European countries. The same is likely to be true of raw materials more generally. While an American effort to go it alone would be highly undesirable, for the United States as well as the rest of the world, this disparity in strength confers both bargaining power and responsibility. As a leading industrial power, the United States can speak as a consumer. As a major producer and exporter of raw materials and foodstuffs, it can see the other point of view. For its own welfare it needs to broaden its concept of trade policy to deal effectively not only with more problems but more countries. Others may come to the same view. As André Fontaine remarked in *Le Monde* of January 23, 1974, the counterpart of "everyone for himself" is "God for the strongest."

One cannot be very optimistic. What has to be done is difficult; short-run achievements may be more in the nature of staving off worse results than demonstrating impressive gains. But if, instead of trying to find some new rules to live by, governments act as if the conduct of international economic policy is a zero-sum game, they may prove themselves right.

DEVELOPING COUNTRIES
AND NON-FUEL MINERALS

By Bension Varon and Kenji Takeuchi

OVER the past three years, a dramatic change has taken place in the world market for one key raw material, oil, whose production and reserves are heavily concentrated among the so-called developing countries of the world. Now, as part of the energy crisis, the developed countries of the world face the certain prospect of very much higher fuel costs in coming years, and the continuing threat that adequate supplies may be withheld either for political reasons or in a process of rather one-sided bargaining with the key producer countries in the now-famous OPEC grouping (the Organization of Petroleum Exporting Countries).

Inevitably, the question arises whether a similar transformation may be in store for one or more of the widely traded minerals not used for fuel. From the standpoint of the developing countries that produce substantial shares of these minerals, such a transformation represents a hope—after successive disappointments with aid flows, transfers of know-how, trade liberalization, and international commodity agreements—that they may now succeed in obtaining from advanced countries increased resources through the operation of the market in changed circumstances, and possibly through alliances emulating OPEC. Conversely, for the consuming countries, such a prospect could be alarming, raising the specter that to the already astronomical amounts they have to pay for oil will be added heavy increases for their other mineral needs, not to mention the chance of having on occasion to do without.

However viewed, the future terms of trade in non-fuel minerals can be deeply significant for individual countries, for the overall balance of economic power in the world, for the welfare of very large numbers of people. To what extent is a transformation in prospect?

It is not a question to be answered simply or with firm conviction. Each of the nine major minerals to be examined in this article—iron ore, bauxite, copper, manganese ore, lead, nickel, phosphate rock, zinc and tin—is affected by factors that cause it to differ greatly from the oil situation, and mostly also from

others in the group. Moreover, as *The Economist* has wryly re-
minded us, recent history is sprinkled with cases where a change
in price factors operated to turn prophecies of scarcity into
realities of glut; even in the medium term of five to ten years,
predictions of resource supplies and markets are especially affected by too many unforeseeable elements to be subject to assured linear projections. This said, only by initially making such
projections, however tentatively, can one see the lay of the land
and identify and assess the elements that could change what
happens.

II

These nine minerals account for 85 percent of the estimated
value of world production of all non-fuel minerals; they are also
the non-fuel minerals of export interest to the developing countries, accounting in 1970 for 12 percent of the aggregate exports
of developing countries. By comparison, oil in 1970 accounted
for 31 percent of these aggregate exports.

For the period from now to 1980, current forecasts by the staff
of the World Bank look for world requirements of these minerals to increase, in the aggregate, at rates approximating those
experienced in the last ten to 15 years. The needs of developing
countries should grow at an accelerating pace, offsetting a slowing down in the dramatic recent growth rate of Japan's import
demand for raw materials. And there is the crucial overall projection—now perhaps in more doubt than it would have seemed
last October—that economic activity in the OECD countries,
which are of course the major consumers by far, will grow by
about five percent per year in real terms over this period.[1]

Naturally, this projected growth in demand is uneven among
the group. Demand for *bauxite, nickel,* and *phosphate rock* is
anticipated to increase faster than economic activity generally
(to have, as economists put it, an elasticity of demand greater
than unity, or one). Bauxite demand is expected to expand by
nine percent per year (faster than that of any mineral including
petroleum), nickel by six percent, and phosphate rock (most of
it used in the fertilizer industry) by 5.5 percent annually (seven

[1] The members of OECD (the Organization for Economic Coöperation and Development) are Australia, Canada, the United States, Japan, Austria, Belgium, Denmark, Fin-
land, France, Germany, Greece, Iceland, Ireland, Italy, Luxembourg, the Netherlands,
Norway, Portugal, Spain, Sweden, Switzerland, Turkey, the United Kingdom and Yugo-
slavia.

percent in the first half of the decade, four percent thereafter).
Demand for four major minerals, *iron ore, manganese ore, copper,* and *zinc,* will expand at rates of 4–4.5 percent a year, while
the growth rates for the other two minerals considered, *lead* and
tin, are estimated to be considerably lower, namely three percent
and 1.2 percent—in line with trends which have already set in
for those two commodities.

It should be noted that these forecasts refer to demand for
virgin ore or for primary metal only; they do not include demand for scrap—or rather assume that recovery from so-called
secondary sources will account for roughly its present percentage
of total supply. For the majority of these minerals, scrap is indeed a major source of supply—40–45 percent of U.S. iron, copper, and lead metal requirements come from secondary sources.
While the proportion of demand met from such sources is technically augmentable, a case-by-case examination of the prospects
for this, particularly the economic incentives, does not yet indicate that scrap ratios are likely to change so markedly as to inhibit the growth of demand for virgin materials significantly in
the foreseeable future. For example, while according to some
studies the scrap ratio in aluminum production in the United
States can be increased from the current 17 percent to nearly 45
percent under an active recycling policy, there is at present little
incentive to do so, since bauxite is one of the most abundant minerals. Yet the assumption of "no major changes in recycling" may
turn out to be wrong even in the seventies, since interest in recycling can be fueled not simply by economics but also by environmental considerations to which public opinion may become
increasingly sensitive.

The above forecasts also assume no major change in rates of
substitution—this on the basis of a case-by-case examination and
giving special weight also to economic considerations. This assumption, too, while justifiable at present, may prove to be fallacious, since trends in substitution are determined, among other
factors, by unpredictable technological innovations in product
development and processing. The development of non-silver
photographic processes or of alternatives to lead in increasing
the octane of gasolines, for example, may alter the demand and
price outlook for these two metals significantly.

Except to the extent that one metal is simply replaced by another, unforeseen developments in both recycling and substitu-

tion would tend, of course, to slow the growth of demand for
new resources. In the longer run, moreover, a third and much
more powerful force may be operating to reduce the growth rate
in demand for minerals. This force is the dynamics of economic
growth itself, and especially the trends within the present group
of developed countries. Historical experience shows, and cross-
section studies confirm, that as an economy grows and matures, its
requirements for most raw materials per unit of GNP (their
"intensity of use") tends to decline. Nowhere is the evidence
clearer and more convincing than in the case of steel, the demand
for which influences the trends of a number of minerals. A recent
study by the International Iron and Steel Institute (IISI) found
that significant growth in "steel intensity" did not occur until
income reached $300 (in 1963 prices) per head, the minimum
level required before an economic takeoff can be expected.
Thereafter, as rapid industrialization sets in, steel consumption
is propelled upward faster than GNP; eventually, however, at
an income level of around $2,500, steel intensity begins to decline,
as the industry sector is extended into sophisticated spheres and
the service sector expands in relative importance. Taking into
account the relative size of those national markets now at the
$2,500 level or above, and of those which will enter or remain at
the $300–$2,500 level, one arrives at projected growth rates in
demand for non-fuel minerals over the next 30 years that tend to
be considerably *lower* than those just projected for the next ten
years.

What then of availability and price? In terms of processing
capacity, the meeting of the projected increases in demand does
not appear to present serious problems, or indeed to require
extraordinary investment; in the case of iron ore, nickel, and
possibly one or two other minerals, existing capacity or capacity
under construction is probably already sufficient for estimated
1980 requirements.

The reserve picture is more diverse. For phosphate rock, iron
ore, bauxite, nickel, and manganese ore, world reserves are by
any estimate ample. (Estimated proven iron ore reserves increased sevenfold in the last 25 years and are deemed sufficient
to last for at least 250 years at current levels of consumption and
for at least 100 years at exponentially growing demand; potential
ore reserves are triple the size of proven reserves and well distributed geographically.) Copper, lead and zinc fall into an

intermediate category, with proven reserves now sufficient to last for only 30 years in the case of copper, and somewhat less for the other two. However, it should be noted that copper is currently being mined at progressively lower ore content and yet at costs rising only moderately in real terms, as a result of new extractive technology. (Because of increasingly strict pollution control standards, smelting costs, in contrast, have recently increased substantially.) Among significant minerals, the only ones whose reserves are tight or critical are silver and tin. Intensified explorations have failed to uncover significant new resources. There are, however, enormous hoards of silver in private hands which can be brought into the market by higher prices. In the case of tin, demand growth has already been forced down to about one percent per annum through substitution.

Finally, as one looks to the longer term, the mineral potential of the oceans becomes relevant. It is now clear that it is enormous, specifically for the nickel, copper, manganese and cobalt contained in the so-called manganese nodules scattered over vast areas of the ocean floor. And the technology of seabed mining appears to be rapidly approaching the point of feasibility at bearable cost. The politics of developing the mineral resources of the seabed are complicated and so far unresolved.[2] But there seems little doubt that a major contribution will come from this source well within the presently calculated life of the reserves of such minerals as copper. And for the relevant materials the seabed potential must of necessity hang over the market, for the future if not in the short term of the next five years.⁻

This brings us to prices. For major minerals, these have been unusually high (especially in U.S. dollar terms) in 1973. The main factors responsible for this phenomenon have been (a) currency adjustments (early 1973) including the uncertainty that preceded the adjustments; (b) the coincidence of sharp upturns in industrial activities in all major developed countries; (c) serious supply problems in several major minerals arising from pollution control problems in the nonferrous metal smelting industry. Each of these was temporary, which would suggest that the price rises are by and large of a short-run nature. On the other hand, the dramatic recent increase in oil prices, and resultant energy costs, may raise substantially the cost and price

[2] See Seyom Brown and Larry L. Fabian, "Diplomats at Sea," *Foreign Affairs,* January 1974.

of some processed minerals—and in cases such as bauxite affect the return of countries which handle primary processing.

Nonetheless, if one looks at the prices of the raw minerals themselves, economic forces now suggest that these will be lower in real terms in the next few years than they have been in 1973. If one takes 1967–69 as a base period, then it can be estimated that only silver, zinc, and phosphate rock prices will rise faster than the rate of inflation assumed in this exercise—that the "index of the wholesale prices of internationally traded goods" will rise by 5.25 percent per year between 1967–69 and 1980. Since mineral prices are notoriously cyclical and unsynchronized (due mostly to supply factors, such as investment cycles, labor strikes, and calamities), such a forecast does not attempt to describe the shape of the price trend, only to suggest the general level of prices by the end of the period. Under this forecast, prices of bauxite, nickel and lead would hold their values in terms of 1967–69 constant dollars, while prices of copper and iron ore may decline slightly, and those of manganese ore and tin significantly.

Silver prices will register the sharpest gain in real terms, nearly 50 percent, between the late sixties and 1980, reflecting the chronic shortage of "new silver" and in order to bring out sufficient supplies from hoarded stocks to meet industrial demand. Zinc prices will follow with an increase of roughly 30 percent over the same period as a consequence of a shortage of smelting capacity (rather than ore) attributable to the problem of pollution control. In the case of the two commodities at the other end of the list, manganese and tin, real prices could decline from their 1967–69 base by about 30 percent and 20 percent respectively, reflecting sluggish demand (for tin), actual or potential overcapacity, and already-approved releases from the U.S. stockpile. The new stockpile objectives call for release of seven million tons of manganese ore, equivalent to total developing countries' output in 1971. The U.S. tin stockpile totals about 250,000 tons, compared to annual world consumption of 185,-000 tons in 1970–72; 43,000 tons of this, equivalent to 80 percent of average U.S. consumption per year, have already been approved for immediate release (though disposals to date have been limited), and congressional approval for the disposal of an additional 157,000 tons is being requested. Accelerated disposal of U.S. noncommercial zinc stocks, too, despite their more modest volume (equivalent to two and one-half months' world consumption) may have an impact on the market, but in this case perhaps a healthy impact, by holding prices in line with prices of substitute materials, especially aluminum and plastics.

III

On the basis of our projections of demand/supply balances and the price trends outlined above—and *without* taking into account possibly higher rates of inflation and the impact of higher energy costs—the conclusion is that developing countries' exports of these nine major minerals are likely to increase from $4.8 billion in 1967–69 to $15.2 billion in 1980 in nominal (or current) terms, rising by ten percent annually—or to $8.2 billion in constant dollar terms, rising at a rate of 4.6 percent per annum, as shown below.

Estimated Value of Developing Countries' Exports
(millions of dollars)

	Average 1967–69	*1980 Value in current dollars*	*1980 Value in 1967–69 dollars*
Copper	2,281	8,000	4,315
Iron ore	811	2,460	1,325
Tin	565	930	500
Bauxite/alumina/ aluminum	450	1,475	800
Phosphate rock	220	800	430
Zinc	130	600	325
Silver	132	525	285
Lead	113	215	115
Manganese	98	195	105
Total	4,800	15,200	8,200

The picture that emerges from the trends spelled out above can be considered neither especially bullish for the developing countries nor threatening for the industrial countries. For the latter, the increased burden on the balance of payments of paying for non-fuel minerals will not be insignificant; moreover, since the United States in particular is dependent on external sources for steadily larger proportions of its mineral needs, the projected burden could rise more steeply after 1980.[3]

[3] One study by the U.S. government has estimated that the United States would have to pay $44 billion per year for its non-fuel, mineral imports by the year 2000. U.S. Department of the Interior, *Mining and Minerals Policy, 1973*, Second Annual Report of the Secretary of the Interior under the Mining and Minerals Policy Act of 1970. Washington, G.P.O., June 1973.

Nevertheless, it is important to keep the size of the trade in non-fuel minerals in perspective. For the developing countries as a group, for example, a growth in foreign exchange earnings of $10.4 billion in current dollars between 1967–69 and 1980 would be less than one-tenth of the increase now projected to arise from petroleum exports in the much shorter period from 1973 to 1980—and this without assuming that the dramatic price increases of December 1973 are maintained. While the forecast suggests that mineral prices will do generally better in the 1970s than in the past, this will serve only—for most minerals—to arrest the downward trends experienced in the 1960s. Moreover, real prices for some will continue to decline; it should be noted that for the last five to six years, the inflation adjustments obtained by many mineral-producing countries under existing contracts or through bilateral negotiation has been on the order of 2.5 percent per year—far short of the 6.2 percent yearly increase actually registered over this period in the index of wholesale prices of internationally traded goods.

To repeat, the above analysis warns against the lumping of petroleum statistics and non-fuel mineral statistics—predictions that the import bill of consuming countries for "raw materials" might be X billion dollars by 1980, which are not explicit about the high ratio (currently at least 8:1) between projected oil import costs and the total costs of non-fuel minerals, are grossly misleading. In addition to distorting the import picture, the lumping of statistics overlooks the fact that while roughly half of the oil revenues will accrue to five resource-surplus countries (namely, Saudi Arabia, Qatar, Abu Dhabi, Kuwait, and Libya), the projected revenue from non-fuel minerals will go to as many as 40 developing countries, nearly all of which are in great need of capital and most of which face increased oil import costs themselves.

IV

The projections presented above have been based on market forces as they currently exist, without the operation of special new pressures by the producing countries in particular. It remains to consider whether, in the light of the remarkable success achieved by the OPEC grouping since 1971 in altering the terms of trade for oil (and recently in withholding supplies), any similar success could be achieved by producers' alliances among developing countries rich in other minerals.[4]

Obviously, the political urge to form such alliances is there. A sense of disappointment at their overall treatment by the industrial countries is almost universal among developing countries. For the producers of minerals, there is moreover (as for oil) the keen sense that their minerals are non-renewable, an asset that should produce the greatest possible return and if possible have its useful life stretched out. Hence, it is only natural that producers should seek to change a situation in which, by and large, the sellers of non-fuel minerals are competing, diffuse, and unorganized in the face of relatively few and well-organized buyers on behalf of the consuming countries.

The four principal producers of copper (Zaire, Zambia, Peru, and Chile) have long worked together in CIPEC (based on its French name, *Conseil Intergouvernemental des Pays Exportateurs de Cuivre*—the Intergovernmental Council of Copper Exporting Countries), and currently there are widespread reports of intense consultation among the producers of other key minerals. The very least that can come out of the current energy crisis is that the producers of all minerals (and of key agricultural commodities as well) will be far more alert to the market situation and far more aggressive in seeking to alter it to their advantage.

But when it comes to assessing their chances of major success, the present prediction must be very cautious. Even the strongest political urge, or the most adroit management, cannot alter certain basic factors that, in our judgment, severely limit the possible accomplishments of producers' alliances in non-fuel minerals.

The key economic fact is that, while demand for most non-fuel minerals is price-inelastic in the short run (i.e., not reduced in proportion to price increases), this is not necessarily true over the long run, certainly not to the extent that holds for oil. Calculations based on historic experience for tin, aluminum and copper, for example, suggest strongly that in the long run the drop in demand more than offsets any price increase, so that the total

---

[4] The question has received wide interest recently and several views on it have been expressed in the professional and daily press. See, on the one hand, C. Fred Bergsten, "The Threat from the Third World," *Foreign Policy*, Summer 1973; a more negative view is contained in "State Doubts Imitation on Cartel in Oil," *The Washington Post*, February 8, 1974; and Philip H. Trezise, "How Many OPEC's in Our Future?", *The New York Times*, February 10, 1974.

return to the producers eventually becomes less than before the price change. Although the econometric measurement of price elasticities is a tricky process leading to differing estimates of individual cases, there is little disagreement on the broad point about short-term and long-term price elasticity.[5]

The reasons are threefold—stockpiles, recycling possibilities, and the use of substitutes—none of which, of course, apply to oil in anything like the same way as yet. All have already been referred to in this article, and the projections for the period to 1980 have assumed no major change in recycling or the use of substitutes.

First, the availability of stockpiles tends to mitigate the immediate impact of supply curtailment—although in times of anticipated protracted scarcity, these might not be released freely enough to improve effectively the short-term situation. Stockpiles, especially those of the United States, have long affected the price of tin, and to a lesser degree manganese and zinc. If these are maintained, the cushioning effect should continue. On the other hand, if the United States were now to dispose rapidly of its stockpiles, their hangover effect on the market would disappear, and after a period of depressed prices the result might be some tendency for prices to increase in the longer term.

The point, however, is that it is not necessary for all three factors to be at work at the same time. *Any one* of the three tends to place a ceiling on prices that would be much lower relative to current price levels than has been the case for the recent price rises of petroleum.

Thus, whereas oil is completely dissipated when consumed, recyclable metal scrap is generated continually in the major con-

---

[5] The common arithmetical measure of elasticity is the ratio between the extent of a price change and the ensuing change in demand: thus, if a price rise of 10 percent produces a demand decrease of the same percent, the elasticity is said to be (minus) 1.0; if the same price rise produces a drop in demand of only 5.5 percent, the elasticity is (minus) 0.55 (and the producers as a group have a higher total return); at elasticities *above* unity, or one, the total return to the producers is less than before the price increase. Applying these measurements to selected minerals, one finds that while the short-run elasticity of world demand for tin has been in the neighborhood of 0.55, the long-run elasticity is estimated at about 1.25; and whereas the short-run price elasticity of U.S. demand for aluminum or copper has been about 0.20, the long-run elasticities are around 1.35 in the case of aluminum and above 2.50 in the case of copper (all figures are, of course, minus). See, for example, F. E. Banks, "An Econometric Model of the World Tin Economy: A Comment," *Econometrica,* Vol. 40, No. 4 (July 1972); Charles River Associates, Inc., *Economic Analysis of the Copper Industry* (U.S. Department of Commerce Publication, PB 189 927, March 1970); and Charles River Associates, Inc., *An Economic Analysis of the Aluminum Industry* (Cambridge, Mass., March 1971).

suming countries, adding to the already vast reserves of so-called secondary sources. While recovery from some of these sources would take time, accelerated recycling is possible for a wide range of materials, including aluminum, copper and lead. The real determinants of the pace of recycling are economic, basically whether prices are such that consuming industries find it advantageous to "dig into the scrap reserve." Environmental considerations may enter in, but recent events suggest that they too may be modified in response to changed economic circumstances. As for the potential impact of the "energy crisis" on recycling, it appears to vary sharply from case to case; for aluminum, where new production is highly energy-intensive, the incentive to use scrap may increase because of the energy input already embodied in it; for steel, on the other hand, the use of scrap requires more energy to process than does "hot metal" (molten pig iron). All in all, price remains the main factor affecting the amount of recycling.

Thirdly, the possibility of substitutes represents a real threat at any time to the effective maintenance of substantially higher prices. Such substitutes can replace the basic mineral as a source for the metal, the metal itself, or the metal-containing product altogether. (For example, bauxite can be replaced by other materials in making aluminum, aluminum can be replaced by tin in making cans, and cans can be replaced by plastic or glass containers.) Current or potential substitutes are available for the majority of minerals, among them nearly all of the nonferrous metals.

While these assessments can be countered by arguments that some of the very substitutes may be in short supply or high-priced (like plastics at this time due to the oil crunch), or that their supply too may be controllable by producers' alliances, it should be borne in mind that the field of metallurgy has historically been in the vanguard of experimentation and development of substitutes in the direction of the cheapest and most abundant raw materials. In short, the infrastructure for weathering a crisis at manageable cost within tolerable time is more sophisticated in this sector than in the energy sector. While, as recent events have shown, oil was grossly underpriced vis-à-vis substitutes, in the case of almost all non-fuel minerals the price increase at which either substitution or exploitation of lower-grade sources becomes feasible is a great deal less than it is for oil, and the process involves substantially shorter time lags.

Another consideration as to the feasibility of powerful producers' alliances in non-fuel minerals is the size and distribution of global resources and the degree to which these can be controlled by certain configurations of countries. *A priori,* scarcity of a resource is not essential for the establishment of a successful cartel; what is required is *control* over present and potential supply. But the scarcity factor is important in the sense that it strengthens the hand of producing countries in imposing their terms and shaping the ultimate course of supplies, or costs. For it is crucial to the successful operation of a cartel that supply outside the membership be inelastic, i.e., that other suppliers are higher-cost producers with relatively small reserves. There are few minerals that are in fact, or are perceived to be, as potentially scarce as petroleum; and with the possible exception of copper, none is truly indispensable.

Furthermore, the distribution of world reserves cuts across categories of economic or political interest. Developing countries are estimated to have roughly 40–45 percent of the world's major non-fuel mineral reserves, with 35 percent in developed countries and 25–30 percent in centrally planned countries.[6] Developed countries which produce and sell major non-fuel minerals in competition with developing countries include Canada, Australia, and South Africa. Consequently, in a number of minerals (copper, among others) a cartel confined to developing countries would be ineffective, since supply elasticity outside the cartel would be substantial at least in the medium term (three to four years).[7] In such situations, then, the feasibility of a cartel would depend heavily on whether individual developed countries—facing complex factors including their own broad interdependence with developed consumer countries—would participate fully in the producers' alliance.

---

[6] Among the minerals reviewed here, world reserves of phosphate, tin, and bauxite are concentrated in the developing countries, which also account for about half of the copper and nickel reserves, whereas the reserves of iron ore, manganese, zinc, lead and silver are concentrated in the developed and centrally planned countries. Higher mineral prices would not significantly alter the reserve situation in favor of the developing countries; for many minerals the opposite would be true. However, because of conceptual and measurement difficulties, reserve estimates and views such as the above must be regarded with caution.

[7] For a discussion of these factors related specifically to copper, see Kenji Takeuchi, "CIPEC and the Copper Export Earnings of Member Countries," *The Developing Economies,* Institute of Developing Economies, Tokyo, v. X, No. 1 (March 1972).

Theoretically, the number of countries involved in a cartel effort need not be small, since the operative variable is "community of interest." But in practice, limited necessary membership is a facilitating factor also. The relationship between the amount of control by a cartel and the degree of its success cannot be stated in terms of a general formula. What is clear in the light of the wide geographic distribution of many of the minerals in question is that potential producers' alliances will have to include a wide range of heterogenous interests among their membership. Lastly, since deposits vary in grade and in the economics of exploitation and processing, price increases would continuously recast the configuration of the membership necessary to bring control to bear. Iron ore provides perhaps the best illustration of this last point, with resources distributed over four continents and among varied economic groupings. It also brings home the difficulty of neatly categorizing the producers and consumers of non-fuel minerals as groups with identifiably contrasting interests.

In addition to the above general considerations, one must return to the specific projections of the future market for individual minerals. For most non-fuel minerals the demand outlook, as noted already, is not markedly different from past experience. If decelerated economic growth is now the general result of the high cost of energy, then the predictions earlier in this article would become even less buoyant.

Finally, there is what might be called the naked bargaining position of individual producing countries at a given time. In relation to their levels of development and dependence on exports of their mineral resources for achieving developmental goals—not to mention the actual financial reserves required to play a tough bargaining game—no group of potential cartel members for a non-fuel mineral seems likely to attain as strong a position as the OPEC countries have held since 1970. The latter were dealing from a unique position of strength—in that they had no major conflicting trade interests, either domestic or within the group, enjoyed a high degree of independence from developed countries, and came to hold large financial reserves. In contrast, a producers' group for any given non-fuel mineral would be likely to include one or more large countries with basic agricultural needs or heavily dependent on the continued expansion of its export markets for manufactured goods. Moreover, whereas the OPEC states had completed the development of their oil resource base at the time of their concerted action, many developing countries that produce non-fuel minerals remain dependent on foreign capital and technology to develop, expand, transport and increase the processing of their resources.

Conceivably, some of the OPEC countries could come to the aid of a cartel in non-fuel minerals to the extent of supplying the financial resources for this kind of resource development, or to make up possible temporary shortfalls in revenues, even the "revenue foregone" by curtailment or non-development of a resource. But only the developed countries now command the technology, the wider development resources, and the markets on which many producers depend.

v

In sum, there are strong factors which seem to mitigate the feasibility of proliferating producers' alliances modeled on OPEC. Nonetheless, the possibilities for such alliances do exist in a few minerals. Foremost among these is bauxite, where the alliance-inducing factors seem to outweigh the obstacles, as illustrated by the preliminary consultations among Jamaica, Surinam, Guinea and other bauxite-producing countries. Moreover, in one case, Morocco, a major supplier of phosphate rock to the West European market, unilaterally raised its prices by a factor of three last fall; although the full extent of this recent price increase may not be maintained in the long run since there are large unexploited resources of the product, prices are certain to lie on a new plateau hereafter. There *is* an improved climate for group pressure or price leadership, and where the trend is toward higher mineral prices—often to pay the larger oil bills of the producing countries themselves—the new aggressive stance of producers would seem to make it irreversible.

Whether concerted pressure for higher commodity prices will be accompanied by true cartel forms of action and by attempts at supply constraints is still another question. As the above discussion makes clear, the obstacles to this kind of stronger action are especially great for the non-fuel minerals considered. Yet in a basic situation where developing countries urgently need resources for development, the chances of their resorting to such drastic measures could depend, in the last analysis, on the overall state of relations between rich and poor countries.

WORLD FOOD: PRICES AND THE POOR

By Lyle P. Schertz

EVENTS of the past two years have made food an increasingly worrisome item in household budgets and in the budgets of nations. In early 1974, food prices to the American consumer were 25 percent greater than two years earlier. This reflected dramatic increases in farm beef prices, while farm corn prices were double and wheat prices triple those of early 1972. Clearly something new has happened to a food market which has historically fed Americans well and for a uniquely small proportion of their income.

A series of events was associated with these price adjustments. In August 1971 the U.S. dollar was floated and a major realignment of international currencies set underway. Then inadequate rain cut the 1972 Soviet grain crop, while drought in Argentina and Australia crippled grain production; the Soviets began to purchase 28 million tons of grain, 18 of them from the United States. India's monsoon dropped below normal, cutting the cereal crop and eroding hopes for near-term self-sufficiency in cereal production. Peru's fish catch was a disaster; drought and typhoons slashed rice and corn crops in the Philippines; and, in the United States, the corn and soybean harvest was stalled by wet weather in the fall of 1972. The following spring still more wet weather delayed U.S. plantings. In July 1973 the United States, to limit rocketing price increases, instituted export controls on soybeans and soybean products. Finally, Congress adopted legislation that drastically altered the framework of American agriculture in the direction of a free market, with sharply lowered price supports and incentives for stockpiling.

In the developing new market situation, U.S. agricultural exports in calendar 1973 reached $18 billion, up from $9.4 billion the previous year and an average of $6.7 billion over the past five years. Although world cereal production recovered and indeed reached record levels in 1973, American agricultural exports in the current year continue high, and remain a critical element in the reversing of serious balance-of-payments deficits. At the same time, quantities of cereals allocated to PL 480 food aid programs have dropped to the lowest levels since the start of the program in 1954.

To comprehend the close interdependence among countries and peoples of the world these events reflect, a good place to start is with the brutal facts of the world food market—how it has been dominated by the affluent, whether Communist or capitalist, and how the poor have been the first to suffer in times of restricted overall food supplies. Next, we must explore whether the tight food situation of the past two years is likely to continue. What is the medium-term outlook for the world food balance, and how confident can we be of the best available predictions, given the variability of weather, the unpredictability of government decisions, and the energy crisis?

Key policy issues emerge. While they are stated in terms primarily of U.S. policy, they are in fact worldwide in their implications. In view of the new U.S. farm legislation and programs which essentially pull out all production stops, what will be the impact of international markets on our domestic food markets? How can the United States and the world adjust to—or moderate—the prospect of widely fluctuating prices in the future? Under anticipated conditions, will the United States share food with low-income countries and on what terms? And if American PL 480 programs continue to wind down, what needs in the lower-income countries will go unmet; what can be done about them?

II

For as long as there has been trade among nations, developed nations have commanded the food they wanted, when they wanted it. Wealth and high incomes have been the instruments of command. In times of abundance, this purchasing power has been subtle and has displayed a low profile; its impact has not quite achieved a critical mass which would earn the enmity of the have-nots. Only in times of food shortage and high prices does this power, and its related imperialistic effects, become shocking to its victims. Then, whether they be nations or citizens within, those with money have preëmpted what food they wanted; those without money have tightened their belts.

Today, people in the developing nations, two-thirds of the world's population, eat only one-fourth of the world's protein, and most of that is in the form of cereals. In countries such as India people consume less than 400 pounds of cereals per capita each year. On the other hand, in the developed countries, where large quantities of cereals are converted to protein, per capita grain consumption is 1,435 pounds in the Soviet Union, about 1,800 pounds in West Germany and France, and 1,850 pounds in the United States. All told, the billion people in the rich nations, with Cadillac tastes for livestock products, use practically as much cereal as feed for livestock as the two billion people in the low-income nations use directly as food.

The conversion factor is by now well-known. Although forages and other products inedible for humans can usually make some contribution to livestock productions, substantial shifts in such production are heavily dependent on cereals. In the United States, even after advances in feeding technology, a little less than two pounds of cereals are now needed to produce one pound of poultry. For hogs the ratio is 3.5 to 1, for beef 6.5 to 1.

Nonetheless, high-quality protein, particularly from livestock products, is a consumer preference throughout the developed nations—and they can afford to indulge their tastes more and more. Americans have come to consume an average of 110 pounds or more of beef per person a year, in addition to substantial amounts of other meats and livestock products. Similar trends in Western Europe and Japan have been increasing rapidly in recent years,[1] and now the Soviet Union and the East European countries are showing the impact of policies and programs to upgrade the diet of their peoples.

Such consumption of livestock products is in large part a matter of taste, not nutritional requirements. While the protein quality of livestock products is higher than that of cereals, that of soybeans and other food legumes is also high. The fact is that the physical requirement for protein intake is considerably less than that now consumed by the majority of Americans and many in other developed countries. Yet its continued expansion—with the use through conversion of ever-larger amounts of cereals for this purpose—appears to be virtually a political imperative.

Thus, while population growth has obviously been a significant factor in increasing world food demand, an even more striking feature of the demand situation has been the sharp recent increase in cereal consumption per capita in developed countries where populations have *not* been growing rapidly. The figures are startling:

[1] To take a variety of recent examples, red meat consumption went up in the 1960s by 25 percent in the European Community, 50 percent in Taiwan and Spain, and 150 percent in Japan.

PER CAPITA CEREAL CONSUMPTION
(in pounds)

	1964–66 Average	1972–74 Average	Percent Increase
United States	1600	1850	16
U.S.S.R.	1105	1435	30
European Community	900[1]	1000[1]	11
Japan	530[1]	620[1]	17
China	420	430	2
Developing Countries (ex-China)	370[2]	395	7[2]

Source: Economic Research Service, U.S. Department of Agriculture

[1] Figures for the cereal consumption of the European Community, and to a lesser extent of Japan, are reduced somewhat by the extensive use of non-cereal grains for livestock feeding. Japan's figure is also reduced by the fact of extensive direct imports of meat, thus cutting the livestock consumption of cereals within Japan.

[2] The 1964–66 figure was depressed in the averages by India's two bad crop years in that period. The percent increase to 1972–74 thus exaggerates an increase that was in fact minimal.

The reader will note that in this eight-year period the *increases* in per capita consumption for the United States and U.S.S.R. (250 and 330 pounds respectively, although some of the latter may have gone into stockpiles) were more than half the *total* consumption per capita in the developing countries. The table helps to explain the Soviet grain purchases of 1972. Traditionally, when the Soviets came up short on production, they steeled themselves to wait out the shortage, sometimes to the point of accepting large-scale livestock slaughter. But not in 1972, when winter-kill and dry midsummer weather disrupted the Soviets' cereal harvest expectations. Instead of tightening their belts, they made massive grain purchases on the world market. With the aid of these imports, the pace of their livestock development efforts continued unabated.

The Soviet Union's decision to protect diets was felt worldwide by both rich and poor. When the Soviets purchased practically one-fifth of the total U.S. wheat supply—production and beginning-of-the-year stocks—in the 1972–73 crop year, supplies normally available to others dropped sharply. Nations and people reacted by bidding up the price of the remaining wheat, the more aggressively because Japan and several other commercial importers of U.S. foodstuffs found their currencies worth substantially more in terms of dollars as a result of successive devaluations.

In contrast, the low levels of wealth and income of the poor countries once again determined how well they could compete in the food-purchasing power game. So long as the overall production of cereals is relatively responsive to needs, effects on the poor are minimal, especially over time. But in times of severe dislocation of the balance of demand and supply through sharply increased demand or curtailed supplies, the impacts can be harsh —especially in those countries unable to insulate their poor from the market through concessional means such as the U.S. food stamp program. For example, the 1972–73 Indian food grain crop dropped from 105 million to 96 million tons. In the tug-of-war between maintaining diets and saving foreign exchange, diets lost and food prices were allowed to increase. In some areas, food grain rations were cut in half in fair-price food shops, which serve many of the lowest income Indians. Per capita calorie availability dropped toward the critical levels of the mid-1960s.

Thus, in a world having great wealth and affluence among only one-third of its population, the 2,300-year-old words of the Greek cynic Diogenes come back to haunt us. When asked for the proper time to eat, he responded, in his own practical manner: "If a rich man, when you will; if a poor man, when you can."

III

Only a person of great—but false—confidence would speak with assurance of future developments in international food markets. We are dealing with a multitude of fundamental uncertainties. But perspective can be gained through an examination of history and of major forces impinging upon food production and consumption.

On the production side, only in the last 25 years have figures from all over the world been systematically compiled, and even today the data for many developing countries are at best broad estimates. Nonetheless, one can assess certain trends.

Over the period since 1955, the Third World has generated agricultural increases almost in step with the developed world. In both developed and less-developed countries (excluding Communist Asia), food production in 1973 was more than 30 percent above levels of the early 1960s and more than 50 percent above the mid-1950s.

Unfortunately, the upward production trend in the developing nations has been almost totally eclipsed by population growth, so that food production per capita over the past two decades has increased slightly less than half of one percent per year.

(Africa has not shared in the increase and in fact has shown a downtrend since 1961.) By comparison, per capita food production in the developed regions of the world has increased at an annual rate of one and one-half percent, or three times as rapidly. Mr. Micawber would have recognized the problem depicted in the tables below.

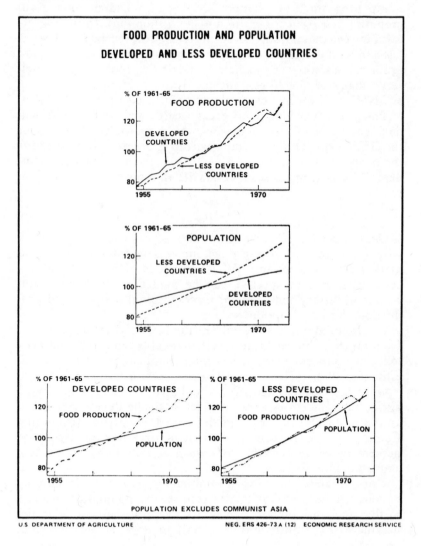

FOOD PRODUCTION AND POPULATION
DEVELOPED AND LESS DEVELOPED COUNTRIES

FOOD PRODUCTION
% OF 1961-65
DEVELOPED COUNTRIES
LESS DEVELOPED COUNTRIES

POPULATION
% OF 1961-65
LESS DEVELOPED COUNTRIES
DEVELOPED COUNTRIES

% OF 1961-65
DEVELOPED COUNTRIES
FOOD PRODUCTION
POPULATION

% OF 1961-65
LESS DEVELOPED COUNTRIES
FOOD PRODUCTION
POPULATION

POPULATION EXCLUDES COMMUNIST ASIA

U.S. DEPARTMENT OF AGRICULTURE   NEG. ERS 426-73A (12)   ECONOMIC RESEARCH SERVICE

In recent years the sharpest increases in per capita food production among the developed countries have occurred in Eastern Europe and Russia: 1973 per capita food production in both areas was more than 25 percent greater than in the early 1960s. Over the same period, increases in the United States and Canada were much more modest, at least partially due to programs restricting production; Western Europe's increases fell somewhere in between.

Africa's continuing decline in per capita production and accelerating dependence on food imports have now been further exacerbated by the devastating drought in the Sahelian Zone. South America's progress is spotty: Chile has had serious problems; Mexico has not lived up to forecasts of self-sufficiency; but Brazil and Colombia have made considerable gains. Asia's Green Revolution has improved that area's feeding ability, but even there, as well as in Africa and Latin America, weather variability remains a highly important factor accentuating crop declines and exaggerating production peaks.

All in all, worldwide trends have caused the United States to become more and more the major food supplier in international markets. American production has not only supported large and growing exports, but has also sustained domestic food consumption at the highest level of any people in the world. Outstanding land and water resources, along with a rapidly advancing technology based on heavy investments in research and large supplies of low-cost fossil fuels, have made it possible for American agriculture to move ahead while directly employing a steadily smaller work force.

When it comes to forecasting the future balance of food demand and supply, many factors must be taken into account: population and income changes, the availability and acceptability of substitutes for traditional foods, development and adoption of new technologies of production, potential changes in the use of water and land, prices of inputs such as fertilizers and fuels, and of course, weather. For most of these variables one can make assumptions for the future with fair confidence. Let us initially assume also that (1) fuel, fertilizers and pesticides will be available in adequate quantity and at prices consistent with trends up to October 1973, and (2) that weather will approximate the long-term average (normal weather).

Using the above approach, two points of overwhelming importance emerge in the projections of the U.S. Department of Agriculture. First, the role of the United States as the major supplier of food in international markets is expected to expand. Second, the dependence of the lower-income countries on food imports is expected, by 1985, to be nearly double the 1970 level. The two points add up to heavy dependence by the developing countries on the United States as a supplier of food.

The projections for the United States anticipate continued advancement of agricultural technology, as well as policy pressures to use exports of food to help pay for imports which underpin the American standard of living. Moreover, levels of production will depend substantially on returns to farmers and on government programs. If farm product profits remain at recent high levels, significant expansion of production is likely to occur as land not now in production is utilized to grow crops and forages, and new technologies are adopted more readily in order to capture these potential profits.

The expected expanding role for the United States also reflects anticipated developments in other countries. In Japan, for example, resource limitation coupled with a continuing drive to upgrade the diet as incomes increase should lead to a growing dependence on imports of food. On the other hand, the European Community has aggressively pursued policies promoting self-sufficiency in food production. These are expected to continue to be effective.

Developments in Canada would somewhat parallel those in the United States. For her size, Canada's role in world food is already extraordinary, and steadily growing. However, Canada's production is only one-sixth that of the United States, and heavily focused on wheat.

The prospective import level of the U.S.S.R. is one of the major uncertainties which will affect the world market, and especially the price and availability of food to the developing world. In the intermediate and long-run future, the Soviets' capacity to import large amounts of agricultural products will be determined largely by their ability to obtain credit from and sell goods to the West. To a large extent, this may involve the Soviet Union's natural resources, such as petroleum.

In the poor countries, statistical increases in food production will likely keep up with population and perhaps gain on it. Some areas, such as Brazil, will be able to expand the area de-

voted to crops; others will develop their cropping capacity
through irrigation, and one hopes most will have improved technology. However, nutritional improvement efforts and income
growth—above all, the use of cereals to produce livestock products—are expected to push demand ahead of local production
increases; hence the prospect that the poor countries will increase their dependence on imports of food, especially cereals
and especially from the United States.

It is important to remember that these prospective import
levels of the developing countries are in the context of only modest improvement of nutrition for the masses of people in these
countries. Under any conceivable combination of increases in
farm production, slowing of population growth, and increases
of income, an overwhelming number of poor people in these
countries will still be inadequately fed for decades to come. The
closing of the food gap between the rich and the poor is a long
way off.

In overall terms, the forecast for the decade would be a recovery of world food production: per capita supplies of food would
resume an upward trend. The crisis conditions of recent months
would not be expected to continue on and on, although farm
product prices would not be likely to fall to the relatively low
levels of early 1972.

IV

But what of the assumptions of normal weather and of adequate and historically priced energy components? Both, especially the latter, are open to serious question.

Unfortunately, man has not thus far been particularly successful in forecasting weather developments, or in modifying
them. Various modern developments, to be sure, mitigate the
effects of bad weather. Expansion of irrigation, improved drainage, soil and water conserving techniques such as ponds and ter-
races, shorter-growing, fertilizer-responsive plants, and mech-
anization—all soften the impact of weather.

Still, any farmer in India, Russia or America knows that if
you don't get rain, you don't get grain. But sometimes professional economists forget; there is a great tendency even for experts to assume that recent weather will continue or will change
to fit their image of the future. Such thinking generated much of
the famine talk in the mid-1960s, and subsequently the abun-

dance talk when the Green Revolution took hold. If the weather in 1970 had been poor instead of good, as it actually was, observers would not have been so confident about India's ability to feed her people, and forecasters of self-sufficiency would have been more cautious.

The cyclical assessments of Indian food needs are a special lesson for those of us attempting to guess at the prospective import requirements of the Soviet Union. Perhaps even more than in India, variations in Soviet cereal production are cut largely from the weather pattern. As former Soviet Agriculture Minister Matskevich has pointed out, only one-third of Soviet agricultural land lies south of the 49th parallel and only 1.1 percent of it lies in areas with an annual rainfall of as much as 28 inches. In contrast, almost all of the United States lies below the 48th parallel, and 60 percent of U.S. arable land receives at least 28 inches of rainfall annually. Little wonder, then, that there are frequent and wide changes in Soviet cereal production—such as the drop of 14 million tons in 1972, and then an increase of 40 million tons in 1973. A graph of the record since 1960 shows a marked upward trend, but it is like the teeth of a sharp saw, with the jags almost annual.

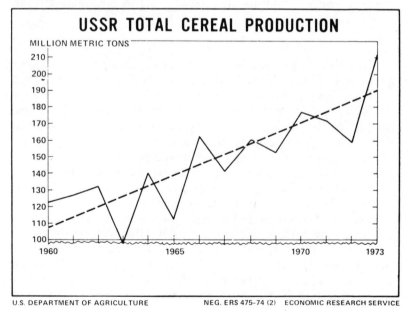

USSR TOTAL CEREAL PRODUCTION

MILLION METRIC TONS

U.S. DEPARTMENT OF AGRICULTURE   NEG. ERS 475-74 (2)   ECONOMIC RESEARCH SERVICE

Adversity in different regions of the world has differing implications for the rest of the world. For example, the tragedy of recent years and months in the African Sahelian Zone is a catastrophe for those people, but other parts of the world are not seriously affected. In contrast, in 1972 and 1973 much smaller proportionate changes in Russia set off worldwide reverberations. With the great dependence of the world on the cereal supplies of the United States, any substantial production changes in the United States can now have equally sharp effects on other countries.

And now, of course, we have the energy crisis. Fuel supplies are limited in many countries, and prices have increased severalfold. Fertilizer supplies (largely petroleum-based) are also limited, and the prices are sharply up, partly because productive capacity was already lagging behind increases in fertilizer consumption, and partly because of supply difficulties and higher prices associated with the crisis. Whatever the long-term course of the energy problem, in the near term farmers throughout the world—developed and developing—will be paying higher, possibly drastically higher, prices for both fuels and fertilizer. Further, in many cases these items will simply not be available in the amounts desired.

In the United States, the domestic supply situation for nitrogen fertilizers was eased considerably when price controls on domestic sales of fertilizers were removed in October 1973. Export prices had not been controlled, and U.S. manufacturers had found exporting more profitable than selling domestically. But, with the removal of domestic price controls, prices of domestic supplies moved up rapidly and much of the incentive for fertilizer exports was eliminated. Further, efforts have been directed toward giving higher priority for natural gas allocations to producers of ammonia, a basic ingredient of nitrogenous fertilizers. Electricity, diesel fuel, and gasoline used directly in farm production account for only about three percent of total U.S. fuel consumption, and steps have been taken to minimize difficulties for U.S. farmers in obtaining fertilizers and fuel. While shortages thus may not be severe, costs of these farm inputs will be sharply higher, probably more than 25 percent above those of last year.

In Japan and Western Europe, production costs may be at least as much affected. However, the effects of the energy crisis in these areas may be far more pronounced on the demand side. The rapid economic growth of Japan, for example, has been the fundamental factor leading to a richer diet, increased food consumption and ever-increasing imports of food from international markets. With the slowing of economic growth, this expansion of food consumption is likely also to slow down. Similar developments could easily occur in Western Europe. Thus, the prospective changes in food supply and demand among the developed countries are extremely uncertain, and may tend to balance out.

By contrast, the potential effect of the fertilizer and oil crises on the food balance of countries such as India and China is clearly negative, even ominous. Together these two nations import over one-third of the nitrogen in international trade. They and other low-income countries dependent on imports of fuels and fertilizers could be drastically hurt.

How severe will the impact be? A limited perspective can be gained from relevant numbers for India, which for the year 1974 has been planning to use 3.9 million tons of fertilizer—incidentally a very sharp increase reflecting improvement in agricultural practices and the use of fertilizer-intensive strains as part of the Green Revolution. Almost all of this supply is heavily dependent on imported petroleum and to a lesser extent on imported finished fertilizer. In the face of the present price increase for these products (nearly three-fold in the case of urea), it seems entirely possible that India's capacity to pay for and produce what she needs will fall short by as much as one million tons. Such a shortfall would translate into the loss of at least seven million tons of grain, which is equivalent to seven percent of India's current cereal consumption.

As for China, she is the third largest user of nitrogen fertilizer in the world and the largest importer.[2] Japan has been a primary

[2]Nitrogen Fertilizer Consumption and Trade
1971/72
(thousand nutrient tons)

	Consumption	Trade
United States	7,372	+ 946
U.S.S.R.	5,182	+ 873
China	3,346	−1,506
India	1,761	− 761
France	1,525	− 108
Germany	1,131	+ 190

+ Net exports
− Net imports
Source: FAO, *Production Yearbook,* 1972.

source of her supplies, and she has been a primary outlet for Japanese exports, taking over 80 percent. If Japan is forced to continue curtailing fertilizer production, the effect on China could be serious—and in any event the cost and the strain on China's limited foreign exchange capacity are bound to go up sharply. Similar effects will apply to virtually every developing country, hitting hardest those which have participated most actively in the Green Revolution.

In this potentially critical situation there is room for speculation about another set of government decisions. To what extent will the oil-rich countries take steps to ameliorate the impact of fuel and fertilizer availabilities and prices on the developing countries? Could the Arab nations become, in effect, an international Robin Hood, favoring the poor over the rich? Over a period of years, the resulting impacts could drastically alter traditional production and trading patterns. For the short term, however, the energy crisis hangs over any prediction of both levels of supply and price.

In sum, if one takes a measured view of all factors—and if the worst does not happen on weather and energy supplies—it is still possible to visualize an uneasy overall balance between supply and demand for food over the next decade. Yet both will fluctuate substantially from year to year and from area to area. Supply levels are bound to be affected both by weather variation and by the uncertain availability and price of fuel and fertilizer. The level of demand, especially for imports, is highly uncertain: the effect of the fuel crisis on the capacity of nations to pay, and especially the unpredictable decisions of countries such as Russia and China, are involved. Thus, one can now with confidence anticipate that under the circumstances that have now developed there will be wide fluctuations in prices in coming years.

V

Earlier we set out two major issues having significant international dimensions. What will be the linkages between our domestic food markets and international markets? Will the United States share food with the lower-income countries and on what terms? The first has special relevance to the rich countries, especially the United States. The second relates to poor nations. But the two issues are closely related, just as the futures of the poor and the rich nations are intertwined. The approach to either issue will set substantial restraints on the approaches that might be taken to the other.

By maintaining large stockpiles of grain, the United States has in past years been able to moderate price swings—nationally and internationally. As international "shortages" have developed—through increased demand, reduced supplies, or both together—the availability of U.S. stocks has dampened price changes in the international market while discouraging increases in domestic prices. In times of general surplus, the United States has in the past chosen to stockpile large portions of its domestic production, and it has also withheld land from production, rather than accept lower domestic prices or larger export subsidies in order to avoid a buildup of stocks.

In the past year—in a revolution experienced but perhaps not fully understood by Americans—this general situation of the past decade or two has completely changed. With bad weather in the U.S.S.R. and other countries, and continued expansion of domestic demand for livestock products in Europe and countries such as Japan and the Soviet Union, the jump in U.S. agricultural exports has virtually eliminated agricultural stocks held by the government.[3] Aside from an export limitation on soybeans/oilseeds and their products during the July–September 1973 period, importers—traders and countries—have continued to be free to buy any amounts of food commodities from private traders for export from the United States, and the usual shock absorbers of government stocks and export subsidies were not there to cushion the impact on U.S. domestic prices.

This direct contact between U.S. and international markets permits U.S. farm prices to be influenced by international markets and vice versa. For example, January 1974 Rotterdam import prices for U.S. hard winter wheat were over $6 per bushel—$3.30 above the levels of a year earlier. U.S. farm prices were up almost $3 per bushel. Comparable corn import prices were up $1.40 per bushel, and U.S. farm prices were up $1.20.

Not only have government stocks been depleted, but because of the expansion of foreign demand the United States has brought

[3] At the end of the 1974 crop year, U.S. stocks of wheat are expected to be four million tons, as compared with 38 million tons in the peak year of 1961. Feed grain stocks are estimated at 26 million tons in 1974, compared to 80 million tons in 1961. Very little of the total in 1974 will be owned outright by the government; in 1961, in contrast, practically all was government-owned.

land once held out of production back into production.[4] For 1974, there are no government programs designed to hold agricultural land from production. Thus, two of the important food reserves of the United States—government-held stocks of food and land held out of production by government programs—have been wiped out.

And in large part this is now a matter of law, not executive discretion. For the new farm legislation of 1973 means that, with economic forces as they are, government stocks of food will not be accumulated. In effect, the law allows U.S. market prices to reflect international and domestic market forces, without the high price support levels that formerly operated for key commodities.

True, there is in the legislation a mechanism—price support loans—similar to that utilized in the past for the accumulation of government stocks of agricultural products. But as a matter of legislative policy the "loan rate"—in effect, the price level at which it would be advantageous for a farmer to put his commodity into stocks rather than sell it on the market—was deliberately set low.[5] Now, with world price changes, the loan price of $1.37 for a bushel of wheat compares to the early 1974 price to farmers of $5.00! It was the policy aim of the new law to avoid the accumulation of large government stocks and their substantial budgetary costs; now events have not only eliminated previous stocks but produced a situation where any buildup of government stocks is unlikely.

In the absence of American stocks, and with the domestic American market and the international market moving together, it is a virtual certainty that food prices will be unstable—not necessarily fluctuating as sharply as they did in 1973 under the impact of a combination of extraordinary developments, but surely far more than in recent history prior to 1973. As surely as night follows day, local weather conditions around the world will change from year to year, producing changes in import needs

[4] In 1972, 60 million acres—almost one-sixth of U.S. crop land—was "set aside" and out of production. As a result of the complete removal of acreage controls, it looks now as if at least 47 million of these acres will be under cultivation in 1974.

[5] To be more precise, a system of "target prices" ($2.05 for a bushel of wheat, for example) was established to insulate farmers from excessive downward movement of prices; if farm prices fall below this level, the farmer still markets his crop but receives a cash payment for the difference between the actual and target prices. Loan levels were set well below these target prices, so that only under severely depressed or surplus conditions, especially in relation to current prices, would there be any incentive for the farmer to stockpile.

and export supplies. And the energy crisis will affect all, but some more than others.

Another major variable, particularly affecting grain markets, will be the behavior of the Soviet Union and other monopoly traders. When the United States had export payments and substantial stocks of wheat, international prices and shares of export markets among suppliers such as the United States, Canada and Australia reflected an awareness of both political and economic influences on the respective governments and on quasi-government organizations such as the Canadian and Australian Wheat Boards. In contrast, information about Soviet crop conditions, government budgets, political directions, consumer prices, and other relevant factors is extremely limited. The recent agricultural agreement between the U.S.S.R. and the United States calls for exchange of information on crop conditions. This is a step in the right direction, but much will still not be known.

Moreover, much the same factors apply to the People's Republic of China. In the current 1973–74 crop year, it has become a much larger buyer of grain in the world market, with purchases totaling probably more than nine million tons, a 50 percent increase over recent import levels. Moreover, China has switched heavily to the U.S. market, taking seven million tons of the total here and becoming the No. 1 U.S. wheat customer for this period. And this after a year when weather in China was generally good, with no sign of the catastrophes and internal conditions that produced the Chinese food crisis of the early 1960s. We simply do not know either the present guidelines for Chinese purchases (whether they too, for example, are now stressing protein enrichment) or the true state of Chinese stocks.

Inevitably, the question arises as to the rules by which the U.S.S.R. and other state-controlled economies should be expected to play. Basically, this is a worldwide question, for the impact reaches all. But it is particularly acute for the United States, in view of the increasing dominance of American supplies and the new vulnerability of the American price structure. Is it reasonable for the U.S. government to permit the U.S.S.R. and China to make purchases in the U.S. grain markets in any amount they decide? To do so subjects the U.S. market to possible wide fluctuations in purchases—amounting to possible manipulation—by political leaders of these countries, acting with full access to information on our crops and prices, as well as on their own crop conditions.

This matter is broader than just trade with the Soviet Union or the People's Republic of China. The Japanese government and Japanese importing interests work closely together. Just this last year Japanese concerns purchased relatively large amounts of cotton and shrimp, causing in both markets sharply higher prices as private U.S. traders attempted to buy their needs from remaining supplies.

Under such conditions there is an urgent need to develop understandings with large countries—especially those dealing as monopolies or near monopolies—as to the "rules of the game." At a minimum, the U.S. government and public must have information on developments within these countries. Weather, agricultural production, stock, and price information would appear to be essential if these countries are to have access to our markets.

Perhaps bilateral deals and understandings are not the long-term answer to this problem, but for the time being they are essential. In the Soviet case, for example, are we not entitled—in return for allowing free Soviet purchases in the future—to press for reasonable understandings on such matters as the access of other American commodities to the Soviet market, guaranteed minimum purchases year in and year out, and similar related matters?

VI

Important as it is—and dramatic to Americans—the issue of the state-controlled economies is only a part of the wider problem that all nations face, of adapting to the prospective variability of international food prices. In dealing with the problem, it is again the developed countries that have the mechanisms and the resources to insulate themselves from the adverse effects of quick changes. The European Community, for example, uses a system of variable levies on imports and through this and other mechanisms has managed to keep the level of internal agricultural prices remarkably stable even through the confusion of the past year. Even so, the prospective situation will force a rethinking of food and trade strategies by many countries. It seems likely that countries like Germany, Britain, Japan and Russia will press within the constraints of energy costs and supplies for increased agricultural production. Also, these countries, and even

countries like India and Turkey, will seriously consider carrying larger stocks than they have in the past.

Such stocks would presumably reduce the vulnerability of a
few countries to international price and supply changes. On the
other hand, steps in this direction will likely be intermittent.
Neither the governments nor the private traders of these countries have had substantial experience dealing in food markets
characterized by widely varying prices.

In addition, the state-trading nations, and some other developed countries, have ready mechanisms for controlling exports
and insulating their domestic price structure from shock price increases. Canada, for example, controls her exports of wheat by
decisions of the Wheat Board whether to offer wheat for sale and
at what price. Unlike the outcry caused by the U.S. soybean controls of last summer—where contracts actually underway were
in effect abrogated—the Canadian approach has caused no protest; contracts are not made unless supplies are estimated to be
clearly available, although of course the effect on the world
market of withholding supplies can be equally great.

In the case of the United States, any search in this direction
would lead us to examine similar export controls as well as export taxes and subsidies—and finally the renewed accumulation
of stockpiles. All of these could operate to mitigate price instability in the domestic market; some would help the world market
as well, though others would have the opposite effect. Each has
its difficulties, and these must be faced.

For example, although export taxes have been commonly employed by other countries to insulate domestic prices by reserv-
ing supplies for domestic consumption, Article I, Section IX of
the U.S. Constitution on its face seems to forbid such taxes. On
the other hand, for a brief period during the 1960s, techniques
were devised whereby wheat exporters on occasion paid the U.S.
government specified amounts, under a balancing arrangement
whereby on other occasions when U.S. prices were higher than
international prices they received a payment.

More practicable than either export taxes or subsidies might
be an arrangement to extend to commercial exports the controls
—in effect, a form of export licensing—that have applied for some
years to shipments of food under PL 480. Under this procedure,
the country desiring commodities approaches the U.S. government indicating the amount it would like to obtain. The govern-

ment, considering U.S. market conditions and the appraised needs of the applying country, decides on the amount to be financed by PL 480 funds. This agreement is made public, and the recipient government proceeds to deal with the private trade in making the purchase up to the agreed-upon amounts. For sales to the state-trading countries, since government financing would not be involved, the review process in the U.S. government could be focused primarily on supply availability.

Finally, there is the question of establishing food reserve stocks, on a national or conceivably an international basis. Since Biblical times when Joseph was called on to advise the leaders of Egypt, the deliberate building of stocks of food has been attractive to man as a means of stabilizing prices and assuring availability of supplies. What is obvious to leaders today has been obvious to leaders throughout history. Stocks of food can be used to supplement available supplies when production falls short of needs, and thereby mitigate price increases. Equally obvious is that the accumulation of stocks means less consumption and higher prices during the period of their accumulation.

Most agree that because of variability of production and unpredictability of other events, there is today a need for accumulating and utilizing stocks of food, in order that consumption is not forced to vary directly with changes in production. The mechanics and policy framework for establishing stocks of food and for managing these stocks are much less obvious, due to the multiple and sometimes conflicting objectives that stock programs can support. In practice such programs can operate in a host of ways: they can stabilize prices or, by withdrawing supplies, actually increase them; they can be used to stimulate production; they can be used primarily as a set-aside to meet acute shortages, which however means that their usefulness in stabilizing prices is reduced; their impact on private trade through commercial channels can be encouraging or discouraging; there is a question whether they can or should be earmarked especially for lower-income countries.

The choice among these objectives is by no means agreed upon among those who urge the creation of food stocks. There is, however, seeming agreement that such stocks need to be distributed throughout the world, and that there should not be overdependence on a small number of countries in times of shortage. Reconstitution of U.S. stocks alone is thus not an adequate answer

—and moreover would surely operate as it has done in the past, to lull others into believing that there was no need for them to act.

Costs of stocks also argue that all countries should be involved. Food stocks are expensive initially to purchase, and they are costly to store. Rough estimates of costs of storing grain stocks per month in the United States are $.60 per ton, exclusive of interest costs of money invested in the commodities or any allowance for deterioration of quality or physical losses. If one adds only the interest costs—at eight percent of a value based on grain prices 25 percent less than current U.S. market prices—one arrives at a figure of $21 for the annual carrying cost of one ton of wheat, or $14 for one ton of corn.

This, of course, leads to the question of how much needs to be carried. Any number of criteria or approaches might be developed. If price stabilization is the objective, the world might carry enough stocks to offset prospective declines of production in one, two, or more successive poor crop years. The prospective shortfall might be measured in terms of declines from previous years' production, from previous high production, or from trend; and the "required stocks" to meet shortfalls might be determined in terms of individual countries or the world, and in terms of individual commodities or in groups of commodities such as all cereals. For example, suppose it was decided that, internationally, cereal stocks should be equal to the largest amount in any one year of the past ten years by which world cereal production declined from the previous year. This would mean stocks of 38 million tons—involving an investment of $5 billion and annual carrying costs of over $600 million for years in which the whole amount was carried throughout the year. The U.S. share might be 20 percent (its proportion of world cereal production) or, it might be argued, 50 percent (its proportion of cereal exports)— meaning a capital commitment of $1–2.5 billion, and possible annual charges of $120–300 million. (There would also be an impact on the U.S. balance of payments through the loss of export sales for the amount contributed to the stocks.) Alternatively, if the U.S. share of world stocks was based on the largest amount in any one year of the past ten by which U.S. cereal production declined from the previous year, 18 million tons would be involved.

These calculations leave open, of course, what has become probably the most crucial question for the United States. Should the United States depend on private trade to carry the stocks or should they be held by the government? Evidence of the 1960s suggests strongly that the private trade will limit the stocks they carry if large stocks are carried by the U.S. government. How much they will accumulate and carry if the government does not have any stocks is not known. Serious consideration needs to be given to ways to enhance the carrying of stocks by private trade under both situations—with and without government stocks.

There are many other issues related to food stock programs. Questions as to timing and methods of building stocks are involved. For example, with food stocks low this past winter, prices high, and the prospective crop uncertain as discussed earlier, should stocks have been accumulated or should accumulation await lower prices? Similar questions arise with respect to disposal.

Another difficulty is the lack of public information on food stocks and on production, marketing and price developments. As already noted, the size of cereal stocks in Russia is not known; this type of secrecy would frustrate the effective planning and coördination of any international food reserve program. Statistics on production and marketing in many relatively advanced countries, much less the lower-income countries, are notoriously late, incomplete and inaccurate.

In sum, the cost and responsibility for any stockpiling plan present difficult problems. Any initial American act of leadership would involve short-term costs from withholding supplies in a ready market; and the creation of international stocks would require a new degree of constructive international action and one that would have to be made acceptable not only to the American Congress and public but to the complicated and different political constituencies of other countries.

For the United States, the issue comes down to the balance, or trade-off, among various factors. As long as the U.S. balance of payments is in doubt, the benefit from high export sales of agricultural products is bound to weigh heavily; on the other hand, it is possible that export averages would be enhanced if supplies to foreign customers could be assured from year to year at relatively stable prices. For dependability, an exporter of farm commodities may come to require not only supplies for which importers can bid but available supplies at relatively stable prices. Instability of food prices is already of priority concern to consumer organizations and labor unions. Farm interests, too, may become frustrated with the effects of instability. For the time being, the American farmer benefits from high prices; yet the day could come when U.S. farm producers would prefer, for example, cattle prices that stabilize at, say, $40, rather than $55 cattle one year and $30 cattle another.

Perhaps it is too early to say whether such a major international effort will be possible, and will commend itself to the nations that would have to take primary responsibilitiy. Eventually, U.S. interests may dovetail with an international food stocking program. But an active search for ways to stabilize prices, such as stocking programs, is not likely until the degree of instability is known and the effects of instability felt.

VII

We return to the special problem of the developing countries. They would benefit enormously from measures to limit the fluctuation in world food prices. But if such measures take some time in coming, and if they serve—as is likely—only to mitigate a general upward price trend, there remains the crucial question whether other nations, and specifically the United States, should take other steps to help developing countries obtain at least minimum essential levels of food.

In the past, the United States has clearly led the world in sharing its food with the poor. Since passage of the PL 480 food aid law in 1954, over $22 billion worth of U.S. farm commodities have been made available to other countries on concessional terms. In recent years, the cost of this program has been remarkably stable at a little more than $1 billion.

Under this program, food, and in some cases non-food products, have been made available to lower-income countries. The bulk of the commodities have moved under programs providing long-term dollar credit and, in earlier years, exchange for local currencies. Under recent dollar credit programs, recipient countries sold the commodities within their countries, invested the major portion of the proceeds in development projects, and assumed the obligation to repay the United States the dollar value on a long-term basis. Thus, PL 480 has been an important means for several countries to finance their economic development and to protect and in some cases enhance the food intake of their populations.

In addition, one-fourth to one-third of the commodities have moved under Title II donation programs, whereby the products were donated to the country and often to the individual recipients. School lunch programs and other food distribution programs have been involved. Voluntary U.S. agencies have played an important part in distributing the food in many of the recipient countries.

Against this record, what is the present outlook? While the United States is likely to continue to provide reduced but significant quantities of food under donation and emergency relief programs, the current prospect for long-term credit programs (Title I) is for sharp cutbacks. Admittedly these programs were extended by the 1973 Farm Bill, but quantities in the fiscal 1974 program will be only half of earlier levels—valued close to recent levels of $1 billion, but at prices that in some cases are more than double earlier prices. Moreover, partially at least in response to scarcer supplies and the related higher commodity prices, the United States during 1973 suspended procurement of commodities for even the Title II donation program for several weeks. Several individual country programs were terminated, and others sharply reduced. The smaller quantities of food available for long-term dollar credit programs were rationed among requesting countries, with priority given to countries such as Vietnam, Cambodia, Korea, and Pakistan which have been important for security reasons.

The reduction of international food sharing contrasts sharply with domestic food sharing. The FY-1975 Department of Agriculture food programs—child nutrition, special milk, and food stamp programs—were proposed in the January 1974 Budget Message of the President to be over $5 billion. This is a record level and represents almost two-thirds of the Department's budget. In contrast to domestic food programs, political support for PL 480 has been insufficient to offset higher commodity prices. Congress has paid scant attention to the decline of international food sharing.

In a larger sense, it can be reasoned that PL 480 has been a program for U.S. agriculture. At its start in 1954 and for several years, PL 480 programs were consistent with commercial objectives for agricultural exports. They permitted us to charge lower prices to poor countries without undercutting our prices to the richer countries. Through adjusting terms—use of the local currency and proceeds from sale of the commodities in the recipient countries, years of credit, interest rates, and commercial sales —effective prices were tailored to the customer's financial and security status.

With strong demand, negligible stocks, and high prices, it is not now advantageous to U.S. agriculture to move significant amounts of food under PL 480. The stark reality is that under present circumstances, it makes no more sense to U.S. economic interests to have a PL 480 food program than to have a PL 480 fertilizer or a PL 480 steel program. All of these commodities are needed desperately by the poor nations, but neither fertilizer nor steel has been in chronic oversupply with large stocks overhanging the market. We have not had concessional steel or fertilizer programs because supply situations were not conducive and because political power was not sufficient to generate them.

And so, as we do not have food surpluses and the related political pressure to move the surpluses, PL 480, as we have known it, may be passing away. I do not say that the United States should not or will not provide some and even significant amounts of food under the donation programs. But it is totally unrealistic to expect the quantity of food provided under long-term credits to be near the levels of recent years. The incentive for farm interests to push PL 480 has dropped sharply, and no major political force in the United States is embracing the food needs of most of the lower-income countries for whatever reason—charity, security, or economic self-interest.

To put it differently, neither we nor other rich countries are willing to forgo substantial foreign exchange earnings in the interest of feeding the poor, even though the developing countries have only limited resources to do it themselves. The experience of the International Wheat Agreement is instructive on how developed countries adjust to the economic realities of international markets. Provisions of the agreements specified obligations of member countries, but these obligations were changed successively in order to align them with the shifting commercial self-interests of the major members.

Thus, it is highly probable that commodity availability to the lower-income countries under PL 480 will be considerably less than it has been over the past five to ten years, leaving a significant gap to be filled by some other means.

One step in filling it is for the poor countries to give renewed emphasis to agricultural development. The cutback on PL 480 availabilities and high international prices should demonstrate conclusively the importance of giving priority to agricultural research and development. Surely finance ministers who have found it necessary to pay $200 per ton for wheat imports this year (instead of negotiating a PL 480 credit program) will be more sympathetic in the future to proposals for expenditures for agricultural programs, construction of fertilizer plants, and policies designed to increase domestic production. In these efforts they should give top priority to greater investment in agricultural research. The lower-income countries contain close to one-half of the world's agricultural lands (excluding China), yet have only 17 percent of the world's agricultural scientists and spend only 11 percent of the money devoted to agricultural research. Technology of the United States and other developed countries can help through technical assistance and training. Through effective linkages of national and international research centers, technology of the developed countries can be utilized in supporting the efforts of the lower-income countries to develop technology appropriate to their agriculture and societies. The challenge to the developed countries to support both academic and nonacademic training of lower-income-country scientists and agricultural program managers is of utmost importance. Trained human resources are an indispensable ingredient in an aggressive agricultural research and development program, and in improving the management and administration of programs aimed at assisting farmers in their production and marketing efforts.

But it is important that the input of the developed countries not be a substitute for investments by the developing countries themselves. We do service to ourselves and the lower-income countries when we recognize that, in the final analysis, improvement in the nutritional well-being of their people depends on how they organize and use their resources.

Finally, the world and the United States will need to evaluate trade-offs between food aid and other economic assistance. Most developed countries and international assistance agencies have limited but significant resources for assisting lower-income countries. Hitherto, they have never had to closely evaluate trade-offs between these programs and food aid programs, except occasionally on a recipient country basis. On a U.S. national level, such consideration could be avoided since the appropriations flowed from different congressional committees to different executive departments. PL 480 as a U.S. agricultural program preëmpted and relieved economic assistance agencies like the U.S. Agency for International Development and the International Bank for Reconstruction and Development. The international assistance agencies did not pick up food aid simply because it was in the U.S. self-interest to finance and implement a program of food assistance as a major adjunct to U.S. agricultural programs. It was mutually advantageous to have this division of labor. Resources for international assistance could be used for items other than food, and the Department of Agriculture could carry the cost of food aid.

Now, with the prospects dim for the Agriculture Department programs financing substantial food aid programs, assistance agencies and the lower-income countries themselves need to ask how the priorities for food aid and support of agricultural programs stack up with other development priorities. To a very significant extent, these agencies have increased the emphasis on improved agricultural production, but such emphasis should now be examined again. It is time for international agencies such as the World Bank to ask: "Shouldn't food aid be made an integral part of economic assistance programs?" And, more specifically, are the lower-income countries better off in times of food shortages using international aid availabilities to buy turbines, etc., or using the aid to buy grain to supplement their food supplies, with the proceeds from the domestic sale of this grain being invested in priority development activities in either the agricultural or nonagricultural sectors?

Indeed, poor countries face comparable questions with respect to use of their foreign exchange. The answers will vary. It is highly probable that the amount of food that seems wise under such programs will be much less than it has been under PL 480, but probably greater than it would be if the assistance agencies avoided the hard choice between food and non-food aid.

Admittedly, food programs under such an approach could not ignore U.S. agricultural interests in the case of our bilateral programs, nor agricultural interests of the developed countries in the case of international agencies such as the World Bank. However, these problems for food assistance should be no greater than they are for other items such as steel and fertilizer. Requiring purchases to be made in donor countries is a technique applied to other international assistance and would presumably be applicable to food assistance. The primary considerations would be the development and welfare of the lower-income countries, and food needs would be considered in the context of other needs.

As such choices are made, it is worth stressing that food assistance is not simply dissipated, but can be a form of investment. As with PL 480, the proceeds from the sale of food provided on a concessional basis can be used for investment in irrigation facilities, locally made machines, and production facilities—much as hard-currency loans can be used to provide foreign-made machines and perhaps with greater employment and productivity effects. Indeed the net effect of international assistance agencies embracing responsibility for food aid may lead to a very important synergistic relationship among priorities given to agricultural development, investments for agricultural production in lower-income countries, investments for nonagricultural production, and economic assistance. Integration of these concerns has not been addressed simply because, through PL 480, food was "priced" low, and the money once appropriated for food aid couldn't be switched to other assistance activities. Now the higher prices will make for more difficult and complex choices.

VIII

To sum up, the world food situation has changed drastically in the past two years and now promises to be seriously unstable for some years at least. To adjust to the new price situation is in itself a major challenge for the United States and other developed countries. Every aspect of our habits and policies must now be reëxamined. Americans must recognize that they have perhaps given themselves too much credit in the past for a generosity that in fact accorded with the market situation of American farm interests; so now they may appear to the world more to blame for hardships than a fair assessment would warrant.

But it is for the world as a whole to examine new approaches. The United States can play a major part, but better solutions to the food problem call for concerted action by many countries and by international organizations. Above all, the impact on the developing countries should be at the very top of our common concerns.

WORLD OIL COÖPERATION
OR INTERNATIONAL CHAOS

By Walter J. Levy

RARELY, if ever, in postwar history has the world been confronted with problems as serious as those caused by recent changes in the supply and price conditions of the world oil trade. To put these changes into proper perspective, they must be evaluated not only in economic and financial terms but also in the framework of their political and strategic implications.

I need not dwell here on the overwhelming importance of oil for the energy requirements of every country in the world; nor do I plan to elaborate on the fact that—except for the United States, the Soviet Union and a small number of countries that are, or will become, self-sufficient—most of the nations of the world will, at least for the foreseeable future, depend almost entirely on imports from a handful of oil-exporting countries, with an overwhelming concentration of oil production and reserves in the Persian Gulf area of the Middle East. Among those countries in the Gulf, Saudi Arabia is predominant in terms of reserves, production, and most important, in the potential to provide significant expansion of supplies. Inevitably, producing decisions by Middle East governments, especially Saudi Arabia, will play a pivotal role in future world oil availability and pricing.

Over the last three years or so, oil-producing countries have in fact taken over complete control of the oil industry in their countries. They have coördinated their efforts through the Organization of Petroleum Exporting Countries (OPEC) which was established in 1960. Since 1970, producing governments have imposed in rapid succession changes in previous agreements that had been negotiated and renegotiated with their concession-holding companies, predominantly affiliates of the Anglo-American international oil companies. These changes were arrived at under the threat that if the oil companies would not acquiesce, the producing countries would legislate such changes unilaterally or expropriate the concessions. In October 1973 the last vestige of negotiations was abandoned and producing governments unilaterally set posted prices on their oil.

In the exercise of this power, Middle East producing countries have raised their government oil revenues from taxes and royalties from about 90 cents per barrel in 1970 to about $3.00 per barrel by October 1973 and then to $7.00 per barrel by January 1974. In addition, as a result of the participation agreements between the producing countries and the oil companies, the governments earn additional income from the sale of their newly acquired oil. Its amount, of course, depends on the percent of government ownership and the price they charge for their oil. Agreements had been concluded, as recently as late 1972, under which producing countries acquired a 25 percent participation in the oil-producing operations and were also committed to sell most of their participation oil to the oil companies at agreed-upon prices; now producing countries are demanding that these arrangements be changed in their favor. Only a few arrangements have yet been concluded, but most of the producing countries will probably insist on at least the equivalent of 60 percent participation and a price for the sale of their oil corresponding to about 93 percent of the posted price—both changes most likely to be imposed with retroactive effect as of January 1, 1974. On such a basis, the government income from the total oil-producing operations in key countries would average about $9.25 per barrel.[1]

Meanwhile, the oil income of the Middle East producing countries has increased from $4 billion in 1970 to $9 billion in 1972, and to a presently estimated $60 billion in 1974. The oil revenues of all OPEC countries are increasing from $15 billion in 1972 to nearly $100 billion in 1974. Allowing for all their own foreign exchange requirements, OPEC producing countries will still have available surplus revenues on the order of $60 billion this year alone. And there remains a clear and present danger that under conditions as they exist now, the supply of oil from individual producing countries or a group of them to individual importing countries or a group of them might—as in October 1973—at a time unknown, again be curtailed or completely cut off for a variety of economic, political, strategic, or other reasons.

The quick pace at which the producing countries have effected

1 Incidentally, Saudi Arabia has implied that in its judgment the present high level of posted prices would have a disruptive effect on the international payments accounts and should, accordingly, be reduced somewhat. While it might be difficult to obtain the support of OPEC for a cutback of posted prices, Saudi Arabia could easily achieve a similar result by reducing the price at which it sells its own oil to a level equal to the tax-paid cost of the companies' equity crude plus a per-barrel profit comparable to what the producing governments have said the companies are entitled to earn. Such a price would be some $3.00 per barrel less than 93 percent of posted prices.

this radical shift in the balance of power is perhaps the most dangerous aspect of the current situation. Whatever the merits of their case (of which more later), the world faces frightening repercussions on account of the suddenness with which oil costs of importing countries and oil revenues of producing countries have been inflated. There just has been no time for mature consideration by the societies that have to deal with this new exercise of oil and financial power, be they recipients or dependents, producers or consumers.

The security of international oil supply operations is further affected by regional conflicts in the producing areas of the Middle East—in particular the still unresolved issues posed by the Israeli-Arab confrontation. There are other potentially dangerous and divisive possibilities, as reflected in Iran's policy of establishing herself as the major strategic power in the Persian Gulf and the Indian Ocean. This could, in due course, aggravate what is already a latent conflict between Iran and some of the Arab countries—not only Iraq, where the hostilities are acute, but perhaps even Saudi Arabia. There are also disputes between Iraq and Kuwait, unresolved boundary issues between Saudi Arabia and Abu Dhabi, and internal conflicts such as the Kurdish problem in Iraq. Further problems are posed by inherently unstable governments in many of these areas and by uncertain and unpredictable rules for the succession to power.

Moreover, within the Persian Gulf area there are varying economic and strategic relationships between some of the producing countries and Western powers on the one hand, and the Soviet Union and even Communist China—on the other. Moscow is deeply involved in Middle East affairs and with the strategic and national policies of some countries, particularly Iraq and Syria. As the producing countries increasingly assert their oil and money power, they are also likely to become increasingly involved as hostage or pawn in any major power struggle.

How can the nations of the world handle this new situation? What is the role of the international oil companies? Above all, how can the producing and importing nations avoid a confrontation or simply a series of reciprocal actions that must tend more and more toward economic chaos and grave political danger? Is there a way to reconcile the various national interests and to achieve constructive overall coöperation?

II

The first key fact that must now be recognized is that the position of the international oil companies has changed completely over the past few years. Up to about 1969 the major concession-holding companies still could determine levels of production, investments, exports and prices. Moreover, they still possessed substantial bargaining leverage in their negotiations with producing countries, largely by virtue of the surplus producing capacity that obtained in the Middle East, and even in the United States into the latter sixties.

All this has now gone. The producing countries have taken over from the companies the power to set production levels, to designate or embargo export destinations, to direct investments and to set prices. The oil-producing affiliates of the international oil companies have become completely subservient to the directives issued by the oil-producing countries. Nothing perhaps reflects the present state of affairs more dramatically than the fact that American- and Dutch-owned oil companies had no choice last fall but to become the instruments for carrying out the embargo on oil shipments to their own home countries.

Thus, the companies no longer possess any real leverage. About the only role that is, in effect, left to them in established producing areas is that of a contractor providing technical services, getting in return some privileged access to oil—at costs and prices determined by producing governments. The extent of even this "privilege" and the time over which it will be available are subject to unilateral cancellation at any moment, as were all preceding arrangements.

At the same time that they have been deprived of effective control over their producing operations, the role of the international oil companies in consuming countries has come under increasing fire, fueled also by the recent sudden increase in company profits. During the emergency, consuming governments largely abdicated any effective role; the companies thus had to make far-ranging decisions as to allocation of supplies, pricing, treatment of nonintegrated companies, and many other issues. It was the companies that kept sufficient supplies moving to all countries; now, after the event, some of their decisions are being challenged by consuming governments. It is extremely doubtful whether the companies still possess the necessary flexibility to cope with another similar crisis.

If the role of the major international oil companies in established producing areas is diminished, it is nonetheless important to understand what their remaining position is. The technical services they can provide are extensive, and vital to continuing development of the producing countries' resources as well as to efficient producing operations. Moreover, none of the producing countries is prepared to handle alone the disposition of the huge volumes of production they control: the downstream facilities of the majors provide assured outlets for the mainstream of their production, while remaining quantities of crude can be sold directly or used to support refining and petrochemical production in their own countries or in joint ventures abroad.

Because of their size, scope, technical competence and financial strength, coupled with their important positions in the production and development of oil, gas, coal, shale, tar sands, and atomic resources in areas politically secure, the international oil companies are bound to play a major—if not the major—role in expanding dependable additional sources of energy supplies. Even though their foreign crude oil resource base is subject to progressive erosion, the major internationals will accordingly continue to provide for the importing countries over the years ahead the most flexible sources of energy supply.

However, the international oil companies are no longer able to assure the continuity or price of regular supplies to oil-importing countries. And while they can hope to maintain continued preferred access to substantial production in support of their affiliates' crude requirements, even that is uncertain and contingent on the producing countries' self-interest in extending such offtake rights.

Downstream investment in refining, marketing, and transport thus tends to become extremely risky, because the viability of such investment is predicated on secure supplies. Meanwhile, as a logical part of their own development program, producing countries are using their control over crude availability to spur refining and petrochemical investment in their own countries and to acquire tanker fleets—all of which will in due course add to consuming countries' foreign exchange import costs and adversely affect the flexibility and security of their supplies.

In the circumstances, oil-importing countries can no longer expect the companies to fulfill their earlier most important role, as an effective intermediary between the interests of producing and consuming countries. Nor can the international oil companies function, as in the past, effectively to preclude direct dealings between importing and producing countries relating to oil supplies, prices, etc., which may easily lead to political confrontations. To the extent that the companies maintain their operations in producing countries, they in fact reflect the producing governments' economic, political, and strategic policies. To be able to hold on to whatever tenuous residual rights or preferences the producing countries might still be willing to extend, the companies will have no choice but to acquiesce in virtually any kind of conditions imposed or exacted.

All this points to a far greater involvement by consuming-country governments in oil industry operations than heretofore. One major objective will be greater "transparency" in oil company policies. Oil-importing countries cannot be in the dark with respect to negotiations in producing areas, when the decisions vitally affect the security and price of their essential oil supplies. They will want to know more about investment plans and policies in their own countries. And with transparency will inevitably come progressively more government interposition throughout internal oil economies.

But here, too, the international oil companies will have a continuing role to play. Producing countries will become increasingly involved downstream, as direct crude sellers and through investment. Consuming countries will become increasingly involved upstream, through various exploration and crude arrangements. Within this emerging fragmentation of world oil trade, the integrated facilities of the companies could provide an important, perhaps the major, core of efficient operations.

In sum, whatever arrangements on supply, financing, and pricing the oil companies may still be able to conclude formally with producing countries, in practice and underlying reality such arrangements cannot be ignored by the importing countries but are bound to be decisively affected by their policies. Moreover, with the vital concern the importing countries have not only for price but for availability of oil, it now appears inevitable that their governments will also in due course establish a comprehensive policy of surveillance and consultation—perhaps even some measure of control—with regard to oil company operations encompassing the whole range of oil activities vitally affecting their countries.

III

As the problems of oil have become matters that in many key respects can only be handled directly between governments, so their gravity has now become all too clear. Faced with the major "supply shock" of the October 1973 oil embargo and the overall cutback in Arab oil production, the immediate reaction of practically every importing country was to engage in a competitive scramble for oil supplies, coupled with offers to adapt its Middle East policy to Arab demands, and promises of all kinds of financial inducements. It was indeed a humiliating experience for historically independent and proud nations. What we were witnessing, in fact, was not only the fragmentation of the operations of the multinational oil companies, but also the polarization of the oil policies of the importing countries, with foreign petroleum ministers skillfully influencing individual importing countries through the device of handing out oil rewards and punishments.

Then, late in 1973, the advance in world oil prices dictated by OPEC countries was of such magnitude that practically every importing nation was suddenly confronted with major balance-of-trade problems of immediate and continuing effect. The cost of foreign oil supplies for all importing countries will exceed $100 billion in 1974, compared with some $20 billion in 1972. For developing countries alone, it will jump from $5 billion in 1973 to $15 billion in 1974—and the $10-billion increase will exceed all the foreign aid that these countries received in the previous year. Meanwhile, as noted, the OPEC producing countries will accumulate, during 1974 alone, surplus holdings of foreign exchange not needed for their own import requirements of some $60 billion—or nearly two-thirds of the net book value of total U.S. private foreign investment.

Obviously, this surplus accumulation of funds will somehow be recycled into the world's monetary system initially, probably mainly into the short-term Eurodollar market. But this process will not necessarily result in the availability of loans to the various importing countries in accordance with their individual foreign exchange needs. The creditworthiness of the borrower will decide whether or not Eurodollar loans will be available; many of the developing countries and some developed countries will not qualify under this criterion. Foreign grants and soft loans—some of them probably never to be repaid—will have to be made available, and the Monetary Fund and the World Bank are addressing themselves to this problem. I doubt that anything like adequate amounts can be made available.

But the financial oil drainage is *not* only a short-term and passing issue. It will be with us for many, many years—if oil prices remain at present levels (or rise as is now occasionally threatened), and if the oil-producing countries themselves are not prepared to make favorable loan arrangements to needy countries in addition to whatever the developed countries are able and willing to do. To the extent that oil imports are financed by a continued recycling of surplus oil revenues via investments or loans on commercial terms, oil-importing countries will face pyramiding interest or individual charges on top of mounting direct oil import costs.

Equally if not more disturbing is the question whether or not the producing countries owning already large surplus funds will be willing to continue to maintain or to expand their production and accumulate financial holdings that might result, in part at least, in nothing but paper claims that could not be repaid. If the producing countries make direct foreign investments, the bulk of such investments will obviously be placed in the advanced developed countries, where it would appear to be safest and most profitable. That will leave the less-preferred developed countries and the developing countries out in the cold. Moreover, the scope for such investments owned directly by foreign producing governments is likely to be limited. Accordingly, oil-exporting countries with surplus revenues might well decide to reduce production—to conserve their liquid gold in the ground rather than increase potential paper claims above ground. Oil revenue surpluses could thus well conduce to oil supply shortage.

There are thus valid reasons to fear that even where present policies of producing countries provide for expanding oil production, circumstances might arise where, in what they consider to be their own self-interest or even for any political whim, the governments involved abruptly cut their level of oil exports. Kuwait, Libya, Abu Dhabi, Ecuador, and Venezuela have already announced restrictions in their production. Iran has threatened to do so if the importers object to price levels.

The financial dilemma for oil-importing countries is clear. In order to finance oil import costs, they will have to look to progressively expanded foreign investment by, or indebtedness to, producing countries. Without any amelioration in the cartel prices and payments terms, the alternative for importing countries would be rather severe reductions in oil imports and oil consumption. To cut back imports drastically, to levels that could be financed out of current income, would hardly be a viable solution. The resulting shortfall in total energy, and the economic consequences of declines in production, employment and trade, would further undercut the oil-importing countries' ability to finance even sharply reduced levels of oil supplies. The contraction of energy consumption and economic activity would thus become a cumulative spiral.

In sum, the short- to medium-term implications of the present situation are simply not bearable, either for the oil-importing countries—especially the nations already needy—or for the world economy as a whole. In the wake of this topsy-turvy winter, with the Arab oil embargo against the United States now lifted, the temptation is momentarily strong to suppose that the oil crisis has now genuinely eased. The major industrialized countries of the world once again look forward to economic growth, though at lower rates, with worldwide balance-of-payments deficits, and with a terrible economic and political problem of inflation, to which oil prices have made a substantial contribution. But the oil balance-of-payments burden is just starting and the transfer of funds to oil-producing countries just beginning. In any case, no significant *lasting* relief at all is in sight for the needy oil-importing countries. The fact is that the world economy—for the sake of everyone—cannot survive in a healthy or remotely healthy condition if cartel pricing and actual or threatened supply restraints of oil continue on the trends marked out by the new situation.

IV

As a first step, the insecurity of oil supply and the financial problems that have arisen clearly call for a wide-ranging coordinated program among all importing countries. This was the main reason why the American government called for a conference of the major oil-importing countries in February of this year. This coöperative effort falls into two basic parts: first, what must be done internally by the importing countries; and second, what a coördinated policy should be vis-à-vis producing countries. With the oil-producing countries already coöperating closely through OPEC, coöperation among the oil-importing countries is a simple necessity; properly understood and handled, it can be the only way to achieve constructive overall adjustments.

Among themselves, the importing countries must first establish and coördinate their research and development programs with regard to existing and new energy resources. Unnecessary and time-consuming duplication must be avoided, and research and development efforts should be concentrated on those resources where optimum results can be expected. The skills available for research and the engineering resources that would have to be employed, if not pooled, should at least be utilized in accordance with a program for maximum overall efficiency.

The oil-importing countries must also establish a concurrent and consistent program of energy conservation which would provide for far greater efficiency in the use of energy resources. Here too the research effort and the measures to be taken should be coördinated on an international basis.

Whatever the course of foreign oil prices, policies to conserve consumption and to spur the development of alternative energy sources will remain relevant for the future. Moreover, a high degree of government involvement is essential to the success of such efforts—including the probable necessity of government guarantees putting a floor under the selling price of alternative energy sources. For if—as we shall see later—there is a chance that foreign oil prices will fall, then private interests working on projects for tar sands, shale, gasification of coal and the like, will not be willing or able to continue their efforts. If a major effort to develop alternative energy resources is to be sustained, particularly in North America, the criterion cannot be orthodox economic soundness weighing the price of alternative energy against the actual (or predicted) price of foreign oil. Rather, the decisive criterion must be the price to which foreign oil could and would *rise* if the alternative energy supplies were not forthcoming. The public interest in avoiding dependence on foreign oil dictates public support and a substantial measure of price guarantees by individual countries, notably the United States but perhaps others as well, again acting in coördination.

Thirdly, the major importing countries must be able to agree on a problem that has so far eluded their efforts—that of adequate stockpiling and burden-sharing. On stockpiling, no importing nation should now have on hand perhaps less than a supply equal to six months of its imports. And there must be clear contingency plans for restrained consumption and for sharing, if oil supplies are again cut off or curtailed—whether for political or economic reasons. Remaining oil imports must be parceled out according to some formula based not on the previous percentage of imports from the sources cut off, but on the basis largely of need—so that those fortunate enough to possess substantial national energy resources would have the smallest, if any, claim on the oil still flowing. Beyond that, I do not believe it would be politically feasible to establish rules that would require countries able domestically just to cover their minimum requirements to export some of their domestic energy supplies to a less fortunate country.

Moreover, oil-importing countries must abstain from trying to resolve their balance-of-trade problems by unduly pushing their general exports to other oil-importing countries or by restricting their imports from them. Such policies would only aggravate the problems of these other countries. Competitive devaluation of currencies or inflation of export prices would be self-defeating, since the oil-producing countries clearly intend to adjust the level of oil prices in accordance with an index of currency values as well as the cost of manufactured goods and other commodities in world trade. The oil-importing countries may have to act in many other ways in order to avoid such dangerous repercussions as severe deflation and unemployment. To deal with the situation will require an unprecedented degree of self-restraint, prudent economic management and political sophistication and wisdom. Past experience suggests extreme skepticism that the countries will in fact consistently follow such policies. But if they do not, the consequences for all of them could become very serious indeed.

Bilateral transactions between oil-importing and producing countries or their respective companies will inevitably be of growing importance. But in concluding such deals the importing countries must abstain from trying to obtain unilateral advantages—by making arrangements for oil imports that would tend to preëmpt sources of supply through discriminatory practices, or by transactions designed to tie up for themselves an excessive part of the import capacity of the oil-producing country. They must also resist the temptation to offset their oil deficits by the competitive rearming of the various Middle East countries, a practice bound in the end to produce a military disaster for all.

So much for the minimum initial requirements for coöperation among the major oil-importing countries. A measure of common appreciation does now exist for most of these "headings of coöperation" by at least a large majority of the relevant importing countries, although they have yet to be fleshed out by practical working arrangements or adequate guidelines for national behavior.

The hardest questions remain. Even if coöperation is achieved in all these respects, can it serve to do more than shorten the period of extreme vulnerability and cushion the impact of continued one-sided decisions by the OPEC countries? Is consumer coöperation truly adequate if it does not address itself to the key questions of price and supply?

I believe the answer to both questions is in the negative. When the brewing crisis came to a head last fall, the initial reaction of many importing countries was to try unilaterally to take care of themselves for both economic and strategic reasons—through barter arrangements, major investment offers to various producing countries, even in some cases extravagant arms supply deals. This tendency was an understandable reaction in the first phase of the new crisis, and indeed a continuing degree of individual national initiatives is not only inevitable, but can be healthy in some respects, in providing an infusion of economic and political alternatives into the changing relationships between oil-importing and oil-producing countries.

Already, however, the limits of the individual approach are obvious. Even for the most aggressive of the oil-importing nations, it has not worked effectively; they find themselves with very large obligations in return for very small increments of favorable treatment, or for nothing more concrete than a generalized promise for the future. Moreover, where there have been specific deals, these are as much subject to abrogation or revision as the basic arrangements themselves. "What have you done for me lately?" is not a question confined to the dialogue between politicians and voters.

Moreover, precipitate attempts by individual countries to go it alone can only obscure the nature of the problem, which is basically a common one that engages not only the interests of all the importing countries but the interests of the producers in a viable world economy and in their own regional and national political stability. The producers are bound not to see the problem in this light if one importing country after another posits this arrangement or that as its own selfish modus vivendi. And to defer attempts at resolution of the common payments problem while individual initiatives are being exhausted is bound to make eventual general agreement more difficult, because so many inconsistent cards will have been played.

Thus, it is my conviction that a constructive accommodation between the interests of producers and importers, enabling the latter to pay for and finance adequate oil imports, is possible only if the importing countries share a common appreciation of the need for a price adjustment as well as for the establishment of financial mechanisms to this end. Just as far-reaching coöperation among the producing countries has brought about the present situation, so a similar coöperation among the importing countries is now an essential prerequisite to a balanced solution. Only if the major importing nations act to coördinate their policy can they expect to be able to present the supply and financial problems they are facing in an effective manner—and to make clear the implications of these problems for the producers themselves. Moreover, only then could they impress upon at least the relevant producing countries what I believe are the two central elements in a satisfactory long-term arrangement—some downward adjustment in the level of foreign crude oil prices to all consumers, and specific relief, including long-term deferment of payments, for the neediest of the oil-importing countries.

V

If coöperation among oil-importing countries is essential to the development of constructive coöperation with producing countries, so too is a full and fair understanding by the importers of the case of the producing countries. Many of its key points were presented vividly in last July's issue of *Foreign Affairs* by Jahangir Amuzegar of Iran; these points and others have since been developed in a series of public statements by various leaders of producing countries. Nonetheless it helps to go over the main elements that enter into the attitudes of the producers, and to explore the validity of their arguments, seeking to arrive at a clear picture of what their long-term interests are.

A major goal of producing countries is rapid and consistent progress in their economic development so that they can become economically viable and secure by the time their oil reserves peter out. In the meantime, the pace of their industrial progress depends largely on the size of their oil revenues, and the level of oil prices is of decisive importance for their present and future prosperity.

The producing countries also cite additional reasons to justify the huge price increases that they imposed in the course of 1973. The large increase in oil prices, they say, is warranted by the alternative cost that would have to be incurred if oil had to be replaced by other energy sources such as shale oil, oil from tar sands, etc. Even though there is currently still a surplus of potential oil supplies, oil reserves may well be exhausted in perhaps 20 to 30 years. But in a free competitive market, prices would not, *at this time,* reflect *future* shortages of supply and would thus provide no encouragement for the development of substitutes. Accordingly, the oil-producing countries say that high oil prices are now necessary so that research and development programs for new energy sources will be promptly initiated. Otherwise, with the long lead time required, energy would be in short supply when world oil production begins to decline.

Also, so they argue, high oil prices now will result in oil conservation and encourage the use of oil for the most essential and valuable purposes where it cannot be so easily replaced, such as for petrochemical production. The highest-value use, they maintain, should in practice be the basis for oil pricing.

The producing countries also assert that the high current oil prices redress the injustice of too low a level of prices in the past, when oil prices had fallen behind those of manufactured goods and food which the oil-producing countries had to import. Relatively low oil prices in the past have, they maintain, unduly enriched the developed countries at their expense. (Whatever the degree of validity of this argument for past periods, it should be noted that the increase in oil prices between 1970 and January 1974 has, according to a United Nations analysis, amounted to 480 percent and was extraordinarily larger than that of practically any other commodity. The share of petroleum in world imports of about $316 billion during 1970—the last year for which detailed statistics are available—amounted to about 7.7 percent; at January 1974 commodity prices, the value of 1970 imports would have increased to \$618 billion, of which petroleum would have accounted for as much as 23 percent.)

Oil-producing countries are aware that high oil prices may harm the progress of other developing countries. But primary responsibility for economic assistance, so they postulate, rests on the rich developed countries. And even though oil-producing countries maintain that in development terms they are still poor, they have stated that they, too, will make a substantial contribution to support developing countries, and a number of them have indeed done so. In addition, they will endeavor to convince other raw-material-producing developing countries that they, too, could improve their economic position substantially if they would only follow the OPEC example.

The producing countries also complain that in the past they have been deprived of economic development based on their oil resources, such as refineries, petrochemical plants, tankers, and energy-intensive industries. Instead, enormous quantities of gas have been flared. Accordingly, it is a basic part of their development policy that investment in local petroleum-processing plants should be undertaken on a large scale within the oil-producing countries, and that they should participate far more in the whole operation of the transportation and exporting of oil.

Obviously, there is substantial merit in many of the points now so forcefully advanced by the oil-producing countries—and it is no effective answer to point out that Western initiative was largely responsible both for the discovery of oil and for the development of its manifold uses. The major oil-importing nations, in particular, must give heed to the legitimate grievances and aspirations of the oil producers.

On the other hand, the producing countries cannot continue to take the position that the economic situation of the major importing countries is no concern of theirs. It is one thing to adjust oil prices to the real or imagined wrongs of the past, another to carry that adjustment to the point of jeopardizing the future economic, political, and strategic viability of importing countries. For if this happens, the viability of the producing countries themselves must surely be affected over the years to come.

There is thus no alternative for the importing countries but to try to convince the producing countries that there must be responsible accommodation between the interests of importing and producing countries. In order to carry conviction, it is essential that there be basic unity among importing countries about the underlying assessments and their policy goals. In the light of the extremely sensitive relationship between consuming and producing countries, a contrary position of one or two major importing countries would tend to destroy the effectiveness of this approach. It would also further strengthen the producing countries in the sense of power that they believe they hold over importing countries, and would encourage them to conclude that they could effectively maintain their internal as well as external security in the face of evolving world chaos.

In actual fact, however, many producing countries, in spite of the extraordinary concentration of oil and money resources in their hands, are as yet quite fragile entities, without substantial strategic and military strength in world affairs. They have been able to assert themselves because of the disunity among, and unwillingness of, importing countries to take any firm position vis-à-vis the producing nations. Whatever the concern of producing countries and companies in the pivotal transition from surplus producing capacity to tightness of world oil supplies, the oil-importing countries were largely complaisant about the course of events. Now, unrestrained exercise of their oil and money power by producing countries presupposes that the importing countries will continue to acquiesce and remain passive, even if the world's economic and political stability is at stake. This cannot be a safe basis upon which the producing countries could proceed. If the worst is to be avoided, the producing countries must be made to recognize the danger of pursuing such a course.

There is also the danger that this concentration of oil and money resources would tempt the Soviet Union to make use of fundamentally weak and socially unstable producing countries—by proxy, so to speak—in order to undermine the economic and political stability of the non-Communist world. Soviet adventurism cannot be ignored, especially the application of Soviet power through controls over certain governments such as those of Iraq or Syria, as well as by internal threats through Soviet support of subversive opposition to governments. There exists, in practically every one of these countries, the potential for sudden revolutions by extreme elements.

All of these factors are clearly known to the various dynasties and national governments. Most of them must have inevitably

reached the conclusion that their hold on power, which is sometimes tenuous, depends in the final analysis on a satisfactory relationship with the non-Communist world. We are all interested
in the maintenance of a peaceful cohesion among Middle East
countries. But they must recognize that if this cohesion is mainly
used to enable them to enforce their will on the rest of the world
through the use of oil and money power, they would not only
undermine the position and strength of the importing countries
but would also expose their governments and nations to extreme
risks.

The oil-exporting countries must be aware that their own independence could not safely be assured if the United States and its
allies were to be fatally weakened vis-à-vis the Soviet Union. It
would not be in their self-interest to refuse to supply the vital
oil needs of the world or to insist on an unmanageable level of
prices, and risk the economic, political, and strategic consequences of such policies.

VI

So far I have been making the case for unprecedented coöperation among the oil-importing nations, and for much greater
understanding by both producing and importing countries of
each other's needs and of the common interests that affect both
groups. If reason alone controlled human affairs, one might conclude that a satisfactory solution was possible from greater understanding alone.

Unfortunately, that is not the case. One must in the end come
back to the harsh economics of the energy situation worldwide,
and of the rapidly rising trends in oil consumption that have
lain at the root of the present crisis. For it is these trends essentially—far outstripping the growth of indigenous energy sources
—that have made the oil of the OPEC countries, especially in
the Middle East, so vital to practically every nation of the world,
and have thus given the OPEC countries the bargaining leverage
to establish the present unilaterally controlled price and supply
situation. With all the understanding and sympathy in the world,
the producing countries cannot be expected not to use a bargaining position as strong as the present one of OPEC and its Middle
East members. In last July's *Foreign Affairs*, Carroll Wilson
argued that the United States would be placed in an intolerable
state of dependence on Middle East oil if it did not develop other

sources of energy to the maximum and at the same time curtail
the rate of growth of its energy consumption from 4.5 percent to
a suggested three percent. Essentially the same analysis must now
be applied to the oil-importing nations as a whole, not for the sake
of eliminating a critical degree of dependence on the Middle
East—for that is simply not in the cards at least for the rest of this
decade—but for the sake of containing thereafter the problems
of oil supply and finance and of establishing now an acceptable
degree of balance in the bargaining positions of producers and
consumers of oil.

The starting point should be the period from 1968 through
1972, when energy consumption in the non-Communist world
as a whole increased at 5.6 percent per year, and oil consumption
by 7.5 percent per year. The result was that Middle East oil production went up by an average of 12.5 percent per year.

Now the prospect for the period from now until 1980 is for a
substantial expansion in non-oil energy sources and in oil production within the major oil-consuming countries. Yet it remains
as clear as it was a year ago that no drastic technological breakthrough is in sight at least in this time frame. We are still talking
about natural gas, coal, hydroelectric power and nuclear fission
as the primary alternatives to oil—and one need hardly add that
even substantial increases in some of these are still fraught with
difficulty.

In response to the new situation, it is already reasonable to
postulate some conservation at the margin in response to higher
energy costs. Given the dynamic energy needs of Japan, the
developing countries, and to a lesser extent Western Europe,
however, it is difficult to see that "conservation at the margin"
will in itself produce a dramatic drop in the growth of energy
needs. Supposing, for example, energy consumption grew at
only 4.6 percent per year instead of the 5.6 percent of the 1968–
72 period, the picture might look something like this:

	1972	1975	1980	1972–1980
	(Millions of Barrels Daily Oil Equivalent)			(Average Annual Percentage Growth)
Primary Energy Demand	80	91	115	4.6
From Non-Oil Sources	35	38	48	4.0
Oil Consumption	45	53	67	5.1
Indigenous Oil Production	18	19	27	5.2
Oil Imports	27	34	40	5.0
Needed from the Middle East	18	23	29	6.3

Obviously, this is a broad-brush projection. But it is enough, I believe, to demonstrate two fundamental conclusions: (1) that even *at current prices* this rate of oil imports could not be sustained by the oil-importing countries on a current payments basis; (2) that with production increases fairly well spread among the producing countries, none would be under any pressure to lower prices or to increase production further. (This is a modest conclusion; actually the pressure would be greater for production cutbacks than for increases. The oil simply might not be forthcoming.) In short, mere "conservation at the margin" —itself more than many governments are now asking of their people—will neither avoid economic calamity nor provide a balanced situation vis-à-vis the producers.

To get these essential results I believe we shall have to go considerably further. Again for illustrative purposes, let us see what the situation would be if the oil-importing countries could manage genuine austerity in their use of energy, cutting their growth rate to, say, 3.3 percent. (The reduced U.S. growth rate would have to be less than this; with all U.S. energy waste, it would still involve a major change in habits and ways. For Japan and the developing countries, the impact on production growth would be far more severe. In short, this kind of reduced rate of increase does deserve to be called austerity.) In such a case, using the same assumptions for non-oil sources and indigenous oil production, a revised table would look like this:

	1972	*1975*	*1980*	*1972–1980*
	(Millions of Barrels Daily Oil Equivalent)			(Average Annual Percentage Growth)
Primary Energy Demand	80	87	104	3.3
Oil Consumption	45	49	56	2.7
Oil Imports	27	30	29	0.8
Needed from the Middle East	18	19	18	0.1

This level of austerity would, I believe, be just adequate to permit the major industrialized nations to maintain viable economic and industrial operations, including continued growth but at a lower rate than might have been projected on the basis of previous oil prices and supply availability. Even then, most of the oil-importing countries would, at least until the latter part of this decade, be exposed to a very substantial and—in the case of some countries—nearly unmanageable financial burden. In short, while the deliberate initiation of such austerity would require an act of political will far exceeding what is actually happening in most importing countries, the choice will in the end be compelled by financial pressures. The longer it is put off the worse it will get.

Once undertaken, this austerity policy could in time achieve some trade balance between the producing and consuming countries. In particular, the huge annual accumulation of surplus funds by Middle East producing countries would start to decline about 1978 and would reach manageable proportions shortly thereafter. Put differently, the importing countries would in aggregate terms be able to pay for their oil by a steadily increased flow of goods and services to the producers. At the same time, however, since the ability of the importing countries to supply goods and services is concentrated in only a handful of them, the financial burden of oil imports would vary greatly, remaining very substantial for the less-industrialized developed countries and especially for the developing countries which are net consumers of oil. Thus, it would remain essential to have financial mechanisms and arrangements that would cushion this differential impact and make it bearable.

Turn now to the situation of the oil exporters. The second table suggests that their total exports would level off and then start to decline slightly by the end of the decade, as the importing countries managed to increase their non-oil sources of energy and as indigenous oil sources were tapped more fully (principally the North Sea and the North Slope in Alaska). The table also assumes that oil producers outside the Middle East will increase their total capacity somewhat, and will be motivated to produce at maximum attainable levels—since practically all of these nations need their oil revenues for immediate development purposes. Thus, the total demand on the Middle East would tend to decline by the end of the decade.

This is not to suggest for a moment that the Middle East oil producers would then be in difficulty. They would still be supplying more than 60 percent of the oil moving in world trade, and Middle East oil would remain vital to Japan, Western Europe, and the developing nations—in an austerity situation, any further cuts would reach the bone more rapidly than in the present somewhat "soft" situation. In short, the Middle East producing countries as a group would remain in a strong position.

At the same time, the production levels of individual countries in the Middle East would be placed seriously in question. Kuwait (like Libya in North Africa) is already pursuing policies designed to conserve its oil reserves and thus to stabilize output below previously attained levels of production. On the other hand, Iran and Iraq look to increase their production very substantially from present totals of roughly eight million barrels a day to 12-13 million barrels per day. If these trends were to continue, and if the need for Middle East oil were to level off at 18 million or so barrels per day, it is evident that the remaining suppliers—especially Saudi Arabia and Abu Dhabi which had previously benefited from oil revenues far in excess of their development needs—would then have to accept a drastic reduction in their levels of production, or alternatively to seek to increase their output by reducing their prices (and thus giving consumers an incentive to ease up on their austerity).

It is an open question, which of course cannot be analytically resolved, whether in the light of these circumstances the various Middle East producing countries would decide to "fight it out" among themselves by competing for exports through price reductions. They might seek to go in the opposite direction, to enter into a production and export control agreement under which they would rearrange their respective production and export levels. At the same time, they might try to increase their prices and tax takes so as to provide for the needs of those Middle East countries that would have to reduce some of their previously anticipated production. On a rational basis, the latter course might be chosen, since any price and tax reductions would tend to force others downward as well, so that the Middle East as a whole would obtain lower revenues for the same or a higher level of production than before the initial price and tax reductions.

In trying to assess what under such conditions the producing countries might actually decide to do, we must think not only or even mainly in economic terms, nor draw only on past experience with regard to the cohesiveness of private cartels in similar circumstances. At most, the economic facts of supply and demand frame the problem; it will still be decided by national governments in the producing countries, and their policies are likely to be governed by an extraordinary combination of political and strategic as well as economic factors.

On the basis of such a broad assessment, the short-term argument for controlling production and maintaining or further raising prices and tax takes must encounter a growing awareness of wider relevant considerations. For such a course—in effect responding to consumer austerity by higher producer prices— would surely leave the importing countries with even worse financial problems than are now in prospect. Even more heavily than now, the burden of paying for restrained but more expensive oil imports would fall upon lagging economies suffering from extremely serious financial problems. Even more than now, the producing countries would have to ask themselves whether they could expect to remain islands of prosperity in a worldwide depression, or of political stability when the will and ability of strategically powerful nations to support them had been eroded.

VII

To sum up, four elements are essential to move to a reasonable adjustment: far-reaching coöperation among the oil-importing nations, an understanding by the importing nations of the interests and aspirations of the producing countries, a clear-cut (and painful) program of energy austerity by the oil-importing countries, and a recognition by the producing countries that even in an austerity situation any attempt to hold prices high must result in worldwide dangers to which they could not be immune. Only with far-reaching consumer coöperation can it be expected that the producing countries will come to this necessary conclusion; at the same time coöperation without austerity will not do the job. Both are needed, and a large new dose of political will, not yet in sight, will be required to achieve them.

The key to a reasonable solution is time: to make the financial burdens on all oil-importing countries tolerable and to bridge the gap until the day, not too far distant, when the producing countries, at least in the aggregate, will have reached the point where they can be paid in goods and services—and where they will have joined, for practical purposes, the ranks of the developed nations.

And the basis for such an adjustment, in turn, is the acceptance of a principle that, while the sovereignty and control of nations over their natural resources remains unquestioned, such control cannot and must not lead to the unrestrained exercise of power, but must be based on a mutual accommodation of interests or, as the United Nations Declaration on the Establishment of a New

International Economic Order puts it, on an appreciation of "the reality of interdependence of all the members of the world community." Otherwise it will be destructive to all.

Such a principle is not, of course, confined to the case of oil. The April meeting of the United Nations General Assembly, and the United Nations reports prepared for it, have underlined the degree to which the rise in food and fertilizer prices over the past two years—created in these cases by market forces in combination with national domestic agricultural policies—have damaged the interests of the needy developing countries in particular. The United States especially has it in its power to adopt measures that would ease the actual cost of food supplies to this group of countries; one suggestion would be that the United States provide grain and other crucial food to needy countries on concessionary terms or through the application of PL 480 funds. A similar move might be undertaken by the major countries that export fertilizer. Now, as preparations are underway for a World Food Conference in the fall, such moves would be even more in order, based on the continued operation of market forces for most consumers but with measures to cushion the impact on needy countries.

Oil remains the biggest and most difficult case. Since 1970 the price and availability of oil moving in world trade have been determined progressively by the OPEC countries unilaterally, to the point where the present situation effectively is one of price imposed by a cartel. Completely free market prices for traded oil are not a practical alternative; in a free market the existence of large reserves and the very low cost of developing and producing such oil would mean a market price that would be very low indeed. Such a price would not be acceptable to producing countries—since it would not provide them with the budgetary and foreign exchange revenue badly needed for their economic development. Nor would it in fact serve the interests of importing countries as a whole—since it would lead to wasteful consumption of oil on the one hand, and on the other would provide no inducement to the major countries to push forward in good time with research and development on new and more costly energy resources which will be needed even more once readily available supplies of oil begin to stagnate or decline.

Accordingly, the price of oil moving in world trade is bound to be a kind of administered price, not necessarily negotiated directly between producing and importing countries but at least established in a way that would attempt to accommodate and reconcile the economic and financial interests of both groups. In addition, the specific plight of the needy oil-importing countries should be provided for, if not through a two-tier pricing system, then at least by long-term deferral of payments and easy credit terms for loans.

In sum, I believe that the world situation would now call for solemn undertakings that would assure the essential oil requirements of all the importing countries on terms and conditions that are economically and financially sustainable. This should be accompanied by measures to deal along the lines proposed with the cognate cases of food and fertilizer. At the same time, it is imperative that all the necessary provisions be made to safeguard the essential economic interests of the producing countries into a future when their position will inevitably become less strong than it is at present. Such a combination of actions would be an act of statesmanship in which the oil-producing countries and the oil-importing countries could and should join not only for the common good, but perhaps even more so in their most cogent self-interest.

Today, governments are watching an erosion of the world's oil supply and financial systems, comparable in its potential for economic and political disaster to the Great Depression of the 1930s, as if they were hypnotized into inaction. The time is late, the need for action overwhelming.

BEYOND DETENTE: TOWARD
INTERNATIONAL ECONOMIC SECURITY

By Walter F. Mondale

ECONOMIC issues are now front and center for the world's
political leaders, topping the agenda of both domestic and
foreign policy concerns. While the major international
security issues of the last quarter-century are still with us—the
competition in strategic nuclear arms, the struggle of differing
political systems, the confrontation of massively armed alliances
in Europe, the menace of great-power involvement in local conflict—these are now being overshadowed by the risk that the
operation of the international economy may spin out of control.
For if this happens there will be no graver threat to international
stability, to the survival of Western democratic forms of government, and to national security itself.

Last June West German Chancellor Helmut Schmidt spoke
plainly at the NATO summit meeting. As he saw it, the most
serious risks facing NATO were not military. The growing economic difficulties of its members, he said, "include dangers that
cannot be exaggerated. Inflation and the necessarily following
recession pose the greatest threat to the foundations of Western
society."

Throughout the crisis of the Presidency, it was difficult for the
American public to focus on international issues. What serious
discussion there was dealt almost exclusively with the problems
of détente with the Soviet Union. It is on this issue that Secretary
Kissinger has called for a great debate, and Senator Fulbright
is responding by holding extensive hearings to air the views of
both critics and supporters of the Nixon Administration's dealings with the Soviet Union.

Certainly détente is important. The gains in East-West relations must be consolidated on a realistic basis; negotiations on strategic arms, the European Security Conference and the question of force levels in Europe must be pursued, and the attempt to progress toward a peace settlement in the Middle East (itself in part a test of the scope of détente) must command special and unremitting attention.

But just as inflation has now emerged as by far the most pressing domestic concern, so international economic policy is now our top external challenge. In terms of the scale of the problems and the imagination required for their solutions—and especially in light of the inadequate attention economic questions have received in recent years—this is the area which calls for our greatest efforts. The priority we have accorded for years to traditional political and security concerns must now be given to international economic issues. If we do not resolve them, the security problems that may ensue could dwarf those that now remain.

II

That economic problems have become critical in their own right should now be evident to us all. The first serious talk of major depression since World War II is gaining currency. Editors and economic analysts, from *The Journal of Commerce* to *The New Republic,* are pointing to the danger signs of economic collapse. By midyear, even though the shock of the Arab oil embargo and price rises had been largely absorbed in the United States, inflation was running above ten percent, real GNP was declining by 0.8 percent, while unemployment stayed high at 5.2 percent and was expected to rise.

In Europe and Japan the situation is, if anything, worse. By August the rate of inflation was roughly 18 percent in Great Britain, more than 20 percent in Italy, 15–16 percent in France, and about 25 percent in Japan. Real GNP was dropping in Britain and Italy, while even West Germany, with the healthiest economy in Europe, and Japan, with almost miraculous growth rates in the past, were both down to only two percent growth. High interest rates have choked off investment everywhere while unemployment has grown ominously in almost all major European countries. To these grim statistics must be added the oil bill, which this year will contribute to a European balance-of-payments deficit estimated at $20 billion, and growing concern, fed by the collapse of the Herstatt Bank in Cologne and the near collapse of the Franklin National Bank in New York, that the world's major financial institutions may be in jeopardy. Bankers in Europe and the United States are deeply worried that more banks may go under.

The outlook for the bulk of the poor nations is even more bleak. The additional aid required this year to meet the increased cost of food and energy is not materializing. This shortfall, and the lower North American harvest now projected for this fall, may be laying the groundwork for widespread famine and food shortages.

So far, however, the main dangers lie in the future, at least for the industrialized countries. At this writing, competitive devaluations have not taken place. Arab oil receipts are being recycled. The IMF has acted to help Italy and other countries meet their massive balance-of-payments problems stemming from the oil price rise. In early July, central bankers meeting in Basel agreed to try to help banks in financial trouble. The OECD is now predicting a lower inflation rate in the major industrialized countries for the last half of 1974.

Yet industrialized countries will remain under economic pressure. Even if oil prices soften somewhat, the energy bill will remain staggering. In the United States serious proposals have recently been advanced for at least two more years of stagnant growth to tame inflation, and the prospect of more than six percent unemployment has been greeted with equanimity by Administration officials.

Austerity measures in Italy, France and West Germany now appear to be slowing inflation, but before these countries can breathe a sigh of relief they are already gritting their teeth over the possibility of recession. Europeans and others must confront growing internal pressure to resort to unilateral beggar-thy-neighbor actions—export and import controls, exchange controls, devaluations and dumping. Arab oil revenues may grow into a massive and mercurial threat to international financial stability. Informal cooperation among economic authorities in the major countries, which has been instrumental in containing the crisis thus far, may not be able to stand up under persistent stress.

Ultimately, the intensity and duration of the current economic crisis will depend upon what governments do about it. While it is imperative to avoid self-fulfilling prophecies of economic doom, there is no automatic guarantee that things will come out all right. Therefore, responsible leaders of all political persuasions throughout the industrialized world must, as a matter of prudence, give serious consideration to the grimmer assessments.

As they look upon the international economic scene, moreover, apprehension is fueled by frustration, because the problems are beyond the span of control of individual nations. With the growth in economic interdependence, the problems are inextricably linked, and only a comprehensive and systematic international effort can deal with them.

III

There is nothing new in the idea of a comprehensive approach to dealing with the world's economic problems, nor in giving such concerns high priority in our foreign policy. Even as World War II raged, and with the consequences of the Great Depression still vivid, major efforts were made to build new economic institutions on a worldwide basis. The Soviet Union was represented at the Bretton Woods Conference in 1944, which established the International Monetary Fund and paved the way for the World Bank, and the Soviets also were invited to participate in the Marshall Plan.

Both Bretton Woods and the Marshall Plan stemmed from the recognition of interdependence—that the economic health of the major countries of the world affected the security and well-being of the others. It was clear that some kind of international economic system would rise from the ashes of World War II and the real task was to assure that it promoted recovery and did not go haywire as it had after World War I.

During this same period, the late 1940s, there was a parallel effort to build a comprehensive system of collective military security via the United Nations. This, too, was based on the conviction that security was interdependent, or as it was fashionable to say at the time, indivisible.

These first tentative structures for a reasonably universal economic and security system cracked apart in the intensity of the cold war. The industrialized market-economy countries ended up organizing the international economic system on their own while the Communist countries withdrew into autarky and set up their own more rudimentary arrangements. The Third World was so dependent on the industrialized world as to be only an appendage of it.

Over the next two decades, the 1950s and 1960s, the colonial nations of the Third World became independent, but wielded little economic or political power. Competition between East and West, along with traditional ties to the West, assured the Third World a certain amount of development assistance. Over time the Communist countries grew stronger and came to trade more with both the West and the Third World, while the latter began to participate to some degree in the management of the international economic system through the World Bank and IMF—in particular the Committee of 20 dealing with monetary affairs.

But at the beginning of this decade, we in the United States and the rest of the Western industrialized world, including Japan, clearly controlled our own economic security. Interdependence seemed only limited. For practical purposes the international economy *was* the economy of the Western world. We did not depend on the economic behavior of the Communist world in any significant way, and we were largely in control of what we needed from the Third World, despite the clamor of its representatives for greater equity.

The situation has changed markedly in the last four years. The West's international economic system is no longer insulated. Both the Third World and the Communist countries have dramatically demonstrated a capacity to disrupt it through cartel pricing of oil and massive grain purchases respectively.

In addition, just this year a "Fourth World" has precipitated out from the Third. Its members are those who lack major resources or economic power. The nations in this group are more dependent, more deprived and more aware of it than any large segment of the world's population in history. That some of the desperate nations of this Fourth World now may have access to nuclear weapons only adds to the prospects for tragedy.

There is a new distribution of economic power in the world and we must learn to deal with it. However, the sudden emergence of this changed economic equation is not just the result of Soviet grain purchases and the oil crisis. The impact of those developments has been directly proportional to the long-range changes already underway inside the Western international economic system.

By the early 1970s this system faced a visible breakdown in the way it managed its monetary affairs, and was already in the throes of an acute crisis of inflation—which spread from country to country in accordance with a sort of Gresham's Law toward the highest national rate. Inflation accompanied by stagnation was a new and bewildering phenomenon, undermining confidence in our ability to manage our industrial economies. Aid to developing countries had declined, generating increased desperation and resentment. In the last year, all these developments combined to form the essence of what may now be termed a total crisis: one that is both economic and political and involves the entire international system.

Fortunately this crisis coincides with a period in which political and military security issues are muted, and some of the major divisions in the world are being bridged and even healed. But we must seize the opportunities presented by détente and other improvements in the international picture to deal effectively with our economic problems, or the progress we have made toward a more secure world may be undone.

In the late 1920s there was also a version of détente, symbolized by the Treaty of Locarno, and at the same time an emerging depression. When the nations of the world failed to cooperate to deal with the depression, its consequences rapidly unraveled the elements of that détente, and in the end economic collapse contributed mightily both to the emergence of grave threats from Germany and Japan and to the paralysis of other nations, including the United States, in the face of those threats.

It is not alarmist to suggest that something of the same sort could happen today. If the economic crisis continues to deepen, détente, now stalled at several key points, could well go into reverse. Already the economic pressures on the members of NATO are undermining their defense postures and reducing Soviet incentives to negotiate. A more grave economic crisis in the West could generate dangerous temptations for the relatively less-affected Communist countries, possibly reviving their hope for the "demise of capitalism" and encouraging a more aggressive and interventionist foreign policy.

However, the dangers are not solely from the Communist world. New or dormant ambitions may be kindled in countries internally divided by economic disruption. Economic differences could precipitate a breakdown in our security relationships with Japan and Europe, leading perhaps to go-it-alone defense policies with profound consequences for regional stability. Other countries may become so self-absorbed as to completely with-draw from their responsibilities for international security: Great Britain may be nearing this point already, and some believe that Italy is past it.

The time has come to face the fact that the fundamental secur-ity objectives underlying the process of détente are now linked to the world economic situation. The economic cooperation that is required will involve us most deeply with our traditional postwar allies, Western Europe and Japan, but it must also embrace a new measure of comity with the developing countries, and in-clude the Soviet Union and other Communist nations in sig-nificant areas of international economic life. Only thus can the present precarious period of détente lead beyond uncertain balance-of-power arrangements to the worldwide sense of com-mon economic interest that is an essential underpinning of a rela-tively peaceful world.

IV

The economic and financial dislocations created by last year's fourfold increase in oil prices pose the most urgent set of issues with which we must deal. The size of the price increase and the abrupt manner in which it was imposed (not to mention the use of oil as a political weapon) smacked of economic aggression. The first task of a foreign policy aimed at enhancing economic security should be to try to get an oil price rollback. Because of overproduction and decreased consumption there is some pros-pect for lower oil prices. We should do all we can to encourage the trend (and ensure its being "passed through" to the con-sumer), but as a realistic matter we must also plan our economic strategy on the assumption that high oil prices will continue.

The oil price hike is like a huge tax levied on most of the world's economies. However, it is a form of taxation without representation, for the size and expenditure of this tax is beyond the control of those who pay it or of their governments. Most of the payments made to the oil producers are remaining in Geneva, London and New York, where they are recycled back into the world economy. Nonetheless important problems remain:

—the burden of recycling the oil receipts is threatening to un-dermine the stability of the international banking system;

—the recycling of oil "tax" receipts is not putting funds into the hands of those who need it most.

To these pressing issues must be added the longer-term problem of how to handle the continued acquisition of foreign exchange reserves by the oil-producing countries—an accumulation which could reach over a trillion dollars by 1980.

Today oil revenues are taking the form of short-term demand deposits in European, and increasingly American, banks, while the banks themselves must make longer-term loans for normal purposes such as capital investment, and now also to help governments meet the balance-of-payments cost of the oil price increases. The possibility of being caught in the squeeze (borrowing short and lending long) is real, particularly since no one knows how volatile the oil funds will prove to be.

Banks are also being pressed to hedge against potential exchange rate fluctuations stemming at least in part from the balance-of-payments drain of higher oil prices. This can involve extensive foreign exchange dealings of the kind that drove Franklin National and Herstatt to the wall.

The private international banking system must not be asked to take on alone this task of recycling oil receipts. Not only is it too great a burden on the system, but it also means that the recycling, the loans that are made, will be on the basis of commercial criteria when larger political and security objectives often should be controlling. Thus we find bankers understandably concerned about the credit-worthiness of countries such as Italy, when unfortunately the overriding issue is whether democracy will survive or be replaced with a far Left or rightist revolutionary regime—with profound effects on NATO and stability in the Mediterranean.

To ensure that such political and strategic requirements are met, and to calm the anxieties of the international banking community, governments must now take on the task of reapportioning credit and financial resources. Acting together with the central banks and the IMF, governments must in some fashion assume the responsibility of lender of last resort. Clearly, certain safeguards must be built-in so that private banks do not have a blank check that they can cash to save themselves from the consequences of imprudence and mismanagement. But this risk is far less significant than the risk of collapse of major financial institutions and even of governments.

Such support for the international banking system, hopefully, will be sufficient to meet the reallocation problems of the industrialized countries without the need to resort to large-scale direct government aid, although such a possibility has been the object of lively debate among policy planners in Washington throughout the summer. For the have-not nations of the Fourth World, however, a substantial governmental aid effort is required.

The poorest countries—primarily on the Indian subcontinent, in Africa, and in parts of Latin America—are suffering severely from the oil price hike. It has been estimated that the increase in the oil bill for the developing countries this year more than cancels out the aid they are receiving. The skyrocketing costs of food and fertilizer are equally large. As a result, the developing countries face a total increase in import costs this year of $15 billion, which is twice the amount of all the aid they receive.

While some of the developing countries will get by, for others —notably India, Pakistan and Bangladesh—it is not an exaggeration to characterize the situation as desperate. Just to get through this year will require an estimated $3 to $4 billion in additional aid, if the lives of nearly one billion people are not to be threatened by economic collapse and ultimately starvation. The special $3 billion oil loan facility set up last June by the IMF will be of some help, but because of the IMF's formula for lending to its 126 members, the poorest countries cannot get sufficient assistance from this source.

Additional help is needed; it can take many forms, from financial assistance to concessional sales of food, fertilizer and energy. The U.N. Secretary-General's effort to develop a special emergency fund or the IMF's Committee of 20 proposal for an IMF-World Bank joint Ministerial Committee on aid to the less-developed countries could become means to work out a package of emergency help. Moreover, the joint Ministerial Committee in particular, to be set up in October with its membership from both the developed and developing countries and strong representation by finance ministers, holds out the possibility of becoming a much needed vehicle for more long-term planning and greater support for international economic development.

Whatever the means of international cooperative action, the main need now is for the United States, the other industrialized countries, and the oil-producing countries to make a firm commitment. We have to stop waiting for the other fellow to act, and as a practical matter this means the United States must take the lead in proposing a specific commitment for itself. Once that decision is made, the logjam should break on other countries' contributions, and we can turn to the resolution of technical issues such as whether assistance will be in the form of debt rescheduling, food assistance, etc.

Even though American leadership is essential, the United States cannot, and should not, become the primary source of increased development assistance—which by 1980 should amount to an estimated $12 to $13 billion annually according to a World Bank study. Along with Western Europe and Japan, the oil-producing countries and the Soviet Union need to pick up their share of this responsibility. The oil-producing Arab countries in particular will soon have massive reserves and liquidity. By the end of this decade it is estimated that Saudi Arabia, Kuwait, Qatar, the United Arab Emirates and Libya may accumulate up to $966 billion in reserves. A significant part of this should somehow be brought to bear on the plight of the Fourth World.

The vast projected increase in Arab financial reserves underscores the fact that the oil price crisis is not a one-shot affair. Even if oil prices soften, the balance-of-payments drain will go on and on. Loans and interest will pile up. The burden will be great not only in the developing countries but also on the industrialized countries which are the oil producers' largest customers. There will be a continuing challenge to handle the stresses of recycling on the banking system and the industrialized economies.

Over time there is hope that the oil producers will put their excess funds into longer-term securities and equity investments. We should welcome such investment. However, there may be real limits, political and economic, to the amount of Arab equity investment that can be absorbed in the Western industrialized countries, including the United States.

The problem is not just economic nationalism, although there is already popular concern in the United States about Arab and Japanese purchases of American industry and real estate—and it is not hard to imagine the reactions to a Saudi Arabian purchase of 25 percent of U.S. Steel along the lines of the recent Iranian investment in Krupp. There are serious policy questions, too. For example, we regard equity investment as an essentially long-term proposition, but it is not clear the Arabs view it the same way. If Arab countries bought large holdings and then pulled out from companies like General Motors or General Electric, this could have a major impact not only on the companies, but on the stock market and the U.S. economy. We and others will want some measure of control to provide safeguards against these and other possible actions inimical to our overall national interest.

On the other hand, Arab governments will be concerned about the hospitality their investments are to receive. Although they are now in the process of taking over the holdings of the international oil companies in the Middle East, they clearly do not want the same thing to happen to their foreign investments. Given the benefits and potential risks for both sides, there appears to be a reasonable incentive to work out reciprocal assurances on how Arab equity investments will be handled in the industrialized world.

Thus the outline of a new pattern of cooperative effort can be envisioned. The oil-producing countries should be granted a larger role in the IMF and the World Bank, where today they have almost no executive positions. The developed countries could make commitments to protect the equity investments of the oil-producing states in their countries in return for appropriate assurances about the stability of such investments. In addition, the oil producers should put some of their reserves into the international lending institutions and engage in long-term aid to the less-developed countries (and possibly provide some short-term balance-of-payments assistance to troubled developed countries). Such a broader distribution of oil producers' revenues would also serve to reduce somewhat the volume of short-term bank deposits, ease the pressure on the banking system, and limit the size of equity investments in the developed countries.

The difficulty in arriving at such a new pattern of relationships and responsibilities cannot be overstated. There is an impressive lack of enthusiasm on the part of the oil producers toward helping their former brethren of the Third World, apart from Arab nations and a few others with whom they seek special ties. But there are a few encouraging signs, too. The World Bank is apparently finding it possible to borrow from Saudi Arabia, Kuwait and even Venezuela, and if the rate is not exactly concessional (reportedly eight percent), it is a step in the right direction.

If some such pattern of greater cooperation is to come about, American leadership is again essential. The United States has the largest single voice in the World Bank and the IMF. It is our overall support that reduces the risks to the oil producers who are channeling funds to the less-developed countries through loans to the World Bank. The United States is the greatest potential market for Arab equity investment, and the response of the American government in providing assurances and establishing rules for such investment is likely to set the standard for the rest of the world.

V

We must also give priority attention to the international dimensions of inflation and the threat of recession. Inflation is the most politically regressive force at work in the world today. It has been said that no country has ever had an inflation rate of more than 20 percent and continued with a democratic government. There may be no magic in this figure, just as there is little precedent for our current situation. But it is sobering to recognize that the United States is about halfway to this rate of inflation, Britain and France are approaching it, and Italy and Japan have been beyond it. Elsewhere, among semi-industrialized and developing countries, rates are usually far higher. No other phenomenon provides as firm a common denominator for all the weak and minority governments now prevalent in the non-Communist world.

Even factoring out the impact of the oil price hike, the present economic situation is essentially unprecedented. The international economy, characterized for decades, if not centuries, by boom-and-bust cycles, was brought under reasonable control after World War II. The objective of full employment was for a time achieved in most developed countries through Keynesian management. However, "stagflation"—high inflation and low growth—began to appear in the 1960s in Great Britain and elsewhere. Now we have what *The Economist* has called "slumpflation," in which there is recession or zero growth while inflation is soaring.

Unfortunately, our comprehension of the problems involved in this phenomenon has not kept up with our vocabulary in describing it. There is grave concern that no one really understands the present economic conundrum, nor knows how to deal with it.

This concern is exaggerated. The monetary and fiscal tools of economic management *can* be adequate to deal effectively with the present situation. What is needed are new, more selective measures for the domestic application of these tools and a new appreciation of the need to take into account the international aspects of our economic difficulties.

It is an obvious but important fact that we are in the grip of two quite contradictory pressures. On the one hand, even the most economically powerful nations, the United States included, are now highly vulnerable to international economic developments. On the other hand, national governments are expected to deal effectively with all aspects of domestic economic conditions from unemployment to the supply of beef. The choice for governments is between trying to reduce problems to proportions they alone can manage, by seeking to insulate the domestic economy through a return to trade and monetary controls, or going on to a new and deeper level of international coordination of domestic economic policies.

One of the hopes in adopting a more flexible exchange rate system has been that it would make it possible for countries to pursue different national policies in their struggle with inflation and recession. While the system has worked well in many areas, it appears that the increased flexibility of countries to follow their own monetary and fiscal policies under the floating rate system may be seriously overrated. For example, if the policies of individual countries stray from the international norm, they may import too much inflation or suffer too much competition. Hence countries are likely to coordinate their monetary policy at least as closely with their major trading partners as they did under the fixed rate system—witness Giscard d'Estaing's recent and unprecedented pledge to conform France's policies and inflation targets to those of West Germany. This sense of interdependence significantly constrains most countries' abilities to fight inflation unilaterally, since monetary policy has become a central if not the exclusive weapon in this struggle.

Thus, although controlling inflation is preeminently a national responsibility, there is now a requirement for closer international coordination to ensure that the major countries are not working at cross purposes with one another. Several cooperative efforts can be envisioned. Adequate international funding for oil-generated balance-of-payments deficits will help avoid devaluations and the consequent boost to inflation. The balance-of-payments objectives of the major trading countries should be brought into line. Efforts to coordinate monetary policy, an elusive objective in the past, deserve renewed emphasis. Each country snould try to assure that its domestic policies are not really exporting inflation or unemployment; all must avoid beggar-thy-neighbor reactions.

In effect, industrialized countries must coordinate their overall economic programs concerning growth, inflation and employment. The United States cannot, for example, consider unilaterally embarking on a policy of controlling inflation by two or more years of stagnant growth, oblivious to the fact that this could lead to a major recession in Europe (not to mention its impact on the American people).

We are fortunate that the American economy of all the market economies is least sensitive to international economic pressures. But we are not invulnerable, and ill-considered policies which look good in the short run can have an important adverse impact on our economy through the effects they have on others.

The United States therefore has an important stake in better international economic coordination, whether through existing institutions or through the creation of some new, more efficient international mechanisms. But even the existing institutions such as the OECD can be much more effective if we are prepared to exercise leadership, use our influence on behalf of increased international coordination, and, of course, accept the constraints that may well go with it.

VI

The handling of trade policy will have a major impact on whether we are effective in fighting inflation and holding the line against recession. In the short run, the most urgent task is to head off increasing pressures for trade restrictions. In the long run, we need to find ways to assure fair access to commodities and raw materials at prices which are stable and reasonable.

The liberal international trading system that exists today, and which has been one of the key elements in the growth of the international economy over the last two decades, is now under serious political and economic pressure. Increasing unemployment and sluggish growth in sectors of national economies are tempting governments to control imports and to subsidize exports in selected cases. At the same time, inflation or shortages in still other economic sectors encourage export controls.

With interest rates as high as they are, the utility of monetary policy alone as a tool to manage economies is approaching its limit, and the use of fiscal policy is constrained in many countries by the dictates of internal social and political cohesion. There is therefore a real prospect of increasing reliance by governments on a patchwork of import and export controls to manage their national economies. The likelihood of turning to trade restrictions is, of course, increased in many countries by the balance-of-payments drain resulting from high oil prices.

An encouraging sign came from the OECD in July when the members pledged not to resort to such controls. However, without more concrete action on the underlying economic issues, the pledge may count for little. Italy slapped on import restrictions in the teeth of major Common Market obligations. While she faced a clear emergency and the import control measures are supposedly temporary, other countries may face similar emergencies. Moreover, there is doubt about how temporary these controls are, since the consequences of the oil price rise will continue indefinitely.

To contain such pressures, it is imperative to start up the long-immobilized trade negotiations. The Europeans and Japanese, once reluctant participants, are now eager to move ahead before protectionist pressures in their countries intensify to the point that negotiations become impossible. The Europeans want to begin serious bargaining this fall and fear that further delay, even to December, could entail serious risks.

This requires prompt action on the trade bill which is before the Senate. The reasons for the delay on the trade bill illustrate the pull between the issues of the past and those of the future on our response to the international economic crisis.

From the outset, the Nixon Administration pursued the strategy of linking most-favored-nation treatment for the Soviet Union, a matter more political than economic, to the broader economic purposes of the trade bill. Confronted with the issue of the right of Jews in the Soviet Union to emigrate free of harassment, President Nixon stalled, apparently hoping the problem would either go away or that the need for the other parts of the bill, combined with the threat of a veto if an emigration amendment were included, would be sufficient to get the bill he wanted. In other words, his Administration viewed the trade bill primarily as a vehicle to advance its détente objectives rather than as an essential means for dealing with the grave international economic issues that confront us. Understandably, a vast majority of U.S. Senators also found it appropriate to pursue what they considered valid political objectives vis-à-vis the Soviet Union by tying MFN to freer emigration.

At this writing there are encouraging signs of progress on the emigration issue, as the Executive has come to realize that the only approach is to work out a firm agreement on this subject with the Soviet Union. Such a solution would pave the way for prompt passage and an early start to the next round of trade negotiations.

A major long-term issue, which should be given priority attention at the trade negotiations, is the issue of access to commodities and raw materials. The rules of the General Agreement on Tariffs and Trade (GATT) focus on the problem of access to markets. What is also needed are rules and other arrangements providing for fair access to sources of supply at reasonable and stable prices.

The impulse to assure access to supplies is not a new form of colonialism. First, while the oil price increases are one obvious example of the kind of irresponsible price-fixing that should be brought under control, it is important to recognize that this is not solely, or even primarily, an issue between the less-developed and industrialized countries. The U.S. embargo on soybeans, the Japanese embargo on fertilizer, and widespread controls on scrap iron are all examples of steps by industrialized countries inimical to international economic stability.

Second, complicated equities are involved. Supplier countries which are also underdeveloped have an economic and moral case for an increased return on their products. Cartel pricing of oil and the efforts to build producer cartels in bauxite and copper are in part aimed at redressing what developing countries have always considered unfair terms of trade. Rightly or wrongly, they have felt that the industrialized countries set the price of their commodity exports as well as the price of their imports, and did so to the developing countries' disadvantage.

The problems the copper- and bauxite-producing countries have encountered in developing a cartel arrangement lend weight to the view that commodity cartels are difficult to achieve. However, efforts to construct such cartels have a destructive impact even if they fail; and continued inflation in the price of imported industrial goods will further stimulate efforts to raise commodity prices—if not by cartels then possibly by unilateral tax increases such as those imposed on bauxite by Jamaica.

The desire on the part of producers of raw materials to revalue their output is also based on concern over the exhaustibility of their resources. The developing countries now have a clearer appreciation of the enormity of the development task as well as little reason to believe that they can depend on anyone but themselves for the resources required. Those with finite resources are therefore particularly anxious to squeeze all they can out of them and are not likely to be very responsive to lectures on economic morality by the developed world.

Third, there may be justifiable reasons for individual countries to impose export controls in legitimate short-supply situations. However, the objective of such controls should be to allocate the short supplies equitably between the domestic economy and foreign purchasers and not solely to export inflation. Otherwise export controls can lead to retaliation, disruption in trade, and further disorder in the international economic system.

Stability in the price and supply of commodities is important if we are to deal with inflation over the long term. In comparison with other goods, most commodities were, until recently, low priced and there was thus a low rate of investment in producing them. With the surge in demand in 1972–73, production could not respond, causing shortages and large price increases. New investment in commodity production will bring the cycle down again, but this wide up-and-down swing in commodity supplies and prices is both wasteful and inflationary. It operates to the disadvantage of suppliers and consumers of commodities alike. To deal with this issue, as well as head off pressures for further cartels, means must be found for stabilizing individual commodity prices and supplies to the extent possible.

The United States bears a special responsibility and burden in this regard. We are now the major source of foodstuffs traded in world markets. Since 1971 U.S. farm exports have more than doubled and in 1973 amounted to $18 billion. The United States and Canada control a larger share of grain exports than the Middle East does of oil. The world has literally come to depend on U.S. agriculture for its well-being. At the same time, the surge in world food demand has also directly affected inflation in the United States. The temptation to resort to export controls, as we did briefly for soybeans last year, could well recur.

On the other hand, the United States also has a big stake in unfettered access to raw materials. For example, we import 100 percent of our chromium and tin and more than 90 percent of such important commodities as platinum and nickel. The United States thus has a particular interest in developing reasonable rules governing export controls, along with arrangements for assuring access to supplies at reasonable and stable prices. These rules must protect the domestic economy of countries from world inflation, and yet provide a responsible source of supply.

In addition to the clear need for new GATT rules on access to resources, and the urgent need to explore stabilization arrangements for specific commodities, there is the question of commodity reserves. At present the United States has large strategic reserves of several key raw materials, which might be used to help stabilize world prices more than has been the case to this point. However, if we move in this direction it should be in concert with others, and under arrangements through which other countries would share in the cost.

The creation of a world food reserve is urgent. This is a complex problem, made more difficult and pressing because American and Canadian reserves have been drawn down to perilously low levels in recent years. They should now be reconstituted, but if they are to form the bulk of a world food reserve (designed both for price stability and to meet famine situations) then others must act in parallel and the direct and indirect costs must be fairly apportioned.

Moreover, it is inconceivable that the United States could take on the task of world food supplier through a reserve system, while markets for American food exports are restricted and denied by trade barriers. The forthcoming World Food Conference can be a major forum for addressing proposals for world food reserves. At the same time the trade negotiations should give priority attention to reducing trade barriers to American foodstuffs.

VII

The task of working out suitable forms of economic cooperation on the foregoing issues will fall mainly to the industrialized market-economy countries and to a lesser extent, the developing countries. However, the actions of the Communist world can either help or hinder these efforts.

Today the Soviet Union and the other Communist countries, including China, are at least superficially insulated from the economic tides sweeping the rest of the world. But, as we saw in the 1972 Soviet grain purchases, their erratic actions in world markets can have profound effects on international economic stability and, in particular, inflation.

The problem is how to integrate the growing volume of economic transactions with the Communist countries into the world economy. Its solution will take patience and a long-term effort. We need to find ways to deal with the issue of unfair pricing and dumping on the one hand, and massive unpredictable interventions in short-supply situations on the other. The former will be difficult because the Communists' concept of price, and of its function in their economies, is totally different from our own. The latter also will be hard, not least because the Soviet Union and other Communist countries do not perceive a problem. But a start can be made by pressing the Soviet Union to play a constructive role in alleviating the world food situation—at least to the extent of agreeing to provide the U.N. Food and Agricultural Organization (FAO) with all relevant agricultural information and not to jump into the market for large quantities of food without warning. And the Soviet Union should participate directly in whatever can be worked out for fertilizer supply and for a world food reserve.

The Soviet Union is also potentially a much greater source of economic development assistance than it is today. Total economic aid by the Soviet Union last year was only $622 million, while its military assistance was estimated at $1.7 billion. With the less-developed nations in such desperate condition, the Soviet Union should be persuaded to reorder its aid priorities.

Finally, the Soviet Union must be brought to realize that the need to exercise restraint in East-West political competition has an economic dimension as well. Soviet efforts to get the Arabs to maintain their oil cutback and embargo were just as menacing to Western security interests as Soviet military support (and apparent encouragement) for the October War. Certainly progress toward a reasonable and viable Arab-Israeli settlement is fundamental to a lasting arrangement on oil supplies and prices, and this in turn is a major economic security interest of the United States and its allies. This is an additional reason why, if the Soviet Union imposes obstacles to peace in the Middle East, it will be running grave risks of jeopardizing improved East-West relations.

We must, of course, have no illusions about the difficulty of moving the Soviet Union to recognize the long-run interest it has in cooperating in these areas. Soviet officials often regard the raising of legitimate trade problems as being "anti-détente." Economic aid to the less-developed world has always been regarded as a political weapon. The notion of exercising restraint is novel and controversial to Soviet leaders in regard to political issues, let alone economic interests.

Yet, the Soviet Union's hopes for basic internal improvement —hopes central to the power position of the Soviet leadership— hinge on the development of much greater economic ties with, and in effect economic assistance from, the industrialized world. Moreover, it was the Soviet Union that became in World War II the greatest victim of the chain of political and security consequences stemming from the Great Depression. If there is another worldwide depression, the Soviet Union too will suffer.[1]

Hence it should be in the Soviet interest to involve itself more responsibly in world economic cooperation. Indeed, the West is now justified in making such cooperation a central test and touchstone of détente. Western credits and peaceful non-strategic trade should be related to commitments on the part of the Communist countries to work out a reasonable code of economic behavior with the Western market-economy countries, and to participate in the new aid effort required for the developing countries.

Today, the fact that major aspects of détente—SALT, MBFR and the European Security Conference—are bogged down is raising serious questions about ultimate Soviet intentions and the durability of détente. However, we need not, indeed cannot, remain fixated on issues that divide East and West. By taking advantage of the measure of détente we now have, and by moving forward to systematically engage the Soviet Union in some of the economic problems besetting us, we can test the strength of détente and the broad intentions of the East. This also may be the only way to establish the kind of relationship that will enable us to resolve the East-West issues we still face.

---

[1] In a recent column, Victor Zorza comments on the Soviet attitude: "While some Soviet leaders appear to welcome the opportunity for gain with which the instability of the West may present them, others are not so sure. 'We are well aware,' says Georgi Arbatov, head of the Soviet Institute of U.S. Studies, 'that the crisis of bourgeois society may have various political results, that the crisis of the 1930s produced Roosevelt and the New Deal in the United States, and Hitler, Fascism and war in Germany.'" *The Washington Post,* July 30, 1974.

VIII

From this examination of the specific immediate and long-term actions now required, it is possible to envision the general outlines of a system of international economic security:

—A deeper measure of coordination of national and international economic policies among the industrialized nations in Europe, North America, and Japan.

—A new role for the oil-producing countries in the management of the international economy and new responsibilities for aiding stability, growth, and in the poorest countries, economic development.

—A new relationship between the industrialized and raw material producing countries assuring more stable prices and supplies.

—A more constructive involvement of the Communist countries, particularly the Soviet Union, in world trade and the task of economic development.

Not all of these broad objectives should be pursued at the same time or with equal vigor. Some of the specific issues in the present crisis are clearly more urgent than others, and for a few problems there may not be ready answers. But the important thing is that U.S. policies be informed by a comprehensive vision of the kind of world economic system we hope to achieve.

And we must begin at once. With each passing week the economic problems we face become less susceptible to wise solutions. Progress on the urgent issues will facilitate tackling the longer range questions.

Initiatives and cooperation must come from many quarters if such a vision of worldwide economic relationships is to be realized. In particular, American leadership is indispensable. We are still the largest single economy and have the greatest impact on international trade and finance. Only if the United States plays its full part can the current trend toward economic fragmentation and disorder be turned around in the direction of a comprehensive and global effort of economic cooperation.

At present our government is poorly equipped in terms of talent and organization to handle such a role. Compared to the credentials of the Secretary of State and Secretary of Defense in the field of international security, those charged with international economic affairs are by no means the kind of strong group the United States put together in 1947 on a bipartisan basis and could surely assemble again.

Organizational remedies are no substitute for political commitment and capable people. But one clear need is to coordinate the diverse governmental organizations that affect international economic policy: State, Treasury, Commerce, Agriculture, the Council of Economic Advisers, the Federal Reserve, etc. The present Council on International Economic Policy has never been able to perform the task of developing coherent policies and strategies. Perhaps what is needed is something more akin to the National Security Council, with a statutory base and a strong substantive staff that can cut through the welter of conflicting interests and views to develop clear policy alternatives.

But there should be at least one major difference from the NSC system: the director of such a staff on international economic policy must be accessible to the Congress and to the public. The issues involved are too closely related to domestic policy to be shrouded from public view by the trappings of diplomatic or even presidential confidentiality. And the Congress must, as it did in 1947 and 1948, play a crucial affirmative role. For this it will need to exert greater efforts to coordinate the work of the many committees and subcommittees that have an impact on our economy. The new Budget Committee and the congressional Office of the Budget can make an important contribution in this regard by exerting more responsive and responsible control over fiscal policy.

IX

Finally, an effective international economic policy must be grounded on a sound and equitable domestic economic program. Help for the international banking system or emergency aid for the have-not nations cannot possibly command the necessary support if the new Administration turns a blind eye to six percent unemployment. President Ford has an opportunity now to explain the facts of our current economic crisis to the American people and to take and propose decisive action. There may be strong differences over the right combination of policies and how the cost of meeting our present difficulties should be apportioned, but there is also a tremendous desire in Congress and the public for firm and bold leadership.

Because international economic issues bear so directly on our domestic concerns, moving toward a new system of international economic security and making it our first priority in world affairs could provide a basis for rebuilding the consensus among the American people in support of our foreign policy. The source of increasing isolationist sentiment in the United States is not some atavistic streak in the American character, but rather the fact that the ordinary American no longer sees his primary interests as being served by the current definition of American foreign policy.

If we can redefine our foreign policy and our national security to include not only the concern over strategic position and political influence but also the basic issues of inflation, economic stability, jobs and growth, and in fact make these a key concern, we will find that once again a broad consensus on our world role is possible. If such domestic needs gain a prominent place in our diplomacy, the American people will not only support efforts of international leadership, but will be willing as they have been in the past to accept short-term sacrifices in order to achieve long-range success. To meet the threat we now face to our economic security, foreign policy must truly become the extension of domestic policy by other means.